# PINKY

## Poverty to Prosperity

## Frank Browning Clark

### Edited by Kristen Clark, Ed.D.

*Kathy, you have been
a great friend!
Frank*

Tellwell Talent
www.tellwell.ca

ISBN
978-1-77302-558-2 (Hardcover)
978-1-77302-556-8 (Paperback)
978-1-77302-557-5 (eBook)

# DEDICATION

I dedicate this book with love from the very bottom of my heart to my wife Marilyn; I do not think we ever had more than two serious arguments in our married life. She is one very special person, caring, understanding, patient, and can be described with every positive attribute one could think of. She has always been there for me and the rest of the family. She is my sweetheart. I know it was not easy for her and my family dealing with my work at the Modesto Police Department, Vietnam, all those long hours at Gallo, golfing, backpacking, and fishing. She is a very special person. She was my mother's shining star; the two had a mutual love that could not be measured. I think back about my mother, and I am truly amazed. How did she ever do it, raise all of us kids, feed and clothe us, provide shelter and a million other things? She was truly the angel of all angels. How very fortunate I have been to have had such a special family, our boys, grandkids, great grand kids, brothers and sisters. I'm the luckiest guy in the world.

# TABLE OF CONTENTS

# PREFACE

Several members of my family have been after me for some time to sit down and write an autobiography. When you get to be 80 years old, I think maybe you forgot more than you remember. But you can be selective, you can improvise, you can make things up. Who can challenge me, just two people: my dear Aunt Alleene, who is 90 years old and my brother Marvin who will soon also be 90. I have had a pretty darn good life, been very fortunate financially, married for 56 years to a wonderful woman, have the best kids, grandkids, and great grandkids as you could ever pray for. I have been fortunate to have lived and grown up in Oakdale, California. There is no finer community in the world, and it is inhabited by the warmest, kindest, and most compassionate people you could ever expect to find.

Had you been a betting person I don't think you would have given any of us kids a chance of amounting to much, but with the exception of one younger brother, we all turned out to be hard working, respectable members of our communities. I could not be prouder of my family, but I cannot take much credit for that; it all, and rightfully so, goes to my mother Gladys. She gave birth to 12 children, raised nine, and six of those were raised by herself after turning 45 years of age. My wife, Marilyn, has many of the same traits as my mom, fastidious, hardworking, loving, and a wonderful mother.

In 1949, when my dad suddenly left mom and six kids in Richmond, California with no warning whatsoever, and not a penny to our names, Mom must have been beyond despair. I know she took a deep breath, buckled up, and with determination decided she would get us through this. We moved back to Oakdale into an old two room shack. There were no bathrooms, no heat, but better than most times, there was running water and electricity. Mom applied and was accepted to receive county welfare. On the side, mom was cleaning houses, taking in ironing, making a go of it. Keep in mind from 1949 until 1954 we had no car, and mom walked everywhere she went. If she had to go to Modesto, she took the bus and then walked. Gradually, we began to live a better life: food on the table, clothes for school, lunch money, and a roof over our heads.

A monetary gift from a total stranger allowed mom to purchase a vacant lot in Oakdale, and with the help of various community members who provided us with a little building, we finally had a place we could call home. With mom as an example, I became a hard worker with a determination to be successful and independent. My brother Freddie used to say how lucky I was to have done so well, to which I always replied, "Yes, Freddie, the harder I work the luckier I seem to get."

Mom: The Angel of All Angles

# THE FAMILY: 1923-1938

This chapter was prepared by my oldest brother Samuel Marvin Clark in August 2015. It is his recollection of his earliest memories up to 1938 when the family moved in with Grandma Eva, whom everyone called Evvie, and Grandpa Marvin in Colorado Springs, Colorado.

\* \* \*

David Wesley Clark, age 22 and Gladys Easter, age 18, our mom and dad, were married in Crosbyton, Texas on April 9, 1923. Dave had been living at home with his folks and working on the farm. Having no place else to go, the newlyweds moved into the Clark family farm house which was already crowded as one of his brothers was married and had moved into the old homestead with his bride. Imagine the stress of living in a small house with ten adults. Even though Grandma Eva had five grown sons there, she also had a two-year old daughter running around the place. This toddler was named Myrtie.

She was not the last child grandma had. Almost 3 years later, Grandma had her final child, a daughter named Alleene.

On December 15, 1923, still living with the Clark's, Gladys gave birth to the couple's first child, a daughter named Hazel Inez. Sadly, this child only lived to be 15 months old when she was taken away by typhoid fever. A little more than two years had passed when a baby boy named Wesley was born, but he only survived a couple of days. In 1927, still without a home of her own, Gladys was now living in the home of her family, the Easters, who were sharecroppers in Crosby County, Texas, near Ralls. Dave was away working on a dairy farm in some other county, the only job he could find during those tough times. Still, conditions were just as crowded as they had been at the Clarks. There were several younger brothers and sisters still at home, and those who were big enough to work helped their father, Bob Easter, try to make a living from dry land farming.

Gladys was pregnant again and gave birth to a boy on July 29, 1927. Probably to everyone's surprise, the baby boy had red hair even though both parents had dark hair. Someone remembered that there had been redheads in the Easter family which would explain the first little carrot top in the Clark family. No one would have suspected that this mysterious hair color would appear four more times in future years. The baby was named after his grandfather Samuel Marvin Clark and would be called by his middle name as was his grandfather.

Mom's family, the Easter's, circa 1920 on the farm in Crosbyton, TX

Come 1929, Dave, Gladys, and little Marvin were living in Canyon, Texas where Dave worked as an auto mechanic. He worked in a small shop owned by Billy Smits where he was probably serving an informal apprenticeship while learning his trade. Sometime later, Dave opened his own shop and was joined by his brother Fred who was eager to leave the farm for an opportunity to learn the mechanics trade under his brother. A few months later, Dave and Gladys became the parents of baby girl in May 1929 and named her Eunice Claudine. Her nickname was *Pooger*. In the fall of 1930, there was an auto accident involving the entire family. Everyone was injured, but poor little Claudine was killed. She was only 18 months old. Even as her third child was taken from her, Gladys learned that she was pregnant again, and on August 20, 1931, another boy was born. Not a red head this time, but a blonde-haired baby, the only boy in the family not to have the flaming red hair. They named him David William Clark, after his father and his maternal grandfather William Thomas "Bob" Easter. He became the first little brother in the family. He was soon given the nickname of *Dode* by a small cousin who couldn't pronounce David.

\* \* \*

The Great Depression had made its appearance in Texas, as well as all across the nation. Tough times affected everyone, but Dave had a trade and there were always automobiles that needed to be fixed. People just did not have any money; so, Dave collected whatever he could for his labors. Dave made a down payment on a small house in Canyon. Unfortunately, not long after the family of four moved in, the house caught fire one night and burned to the ground. Luckily, the family was spending the night at Grandma and Grandpa Clark's place out at the edge of town, so no one was harmed by the house fire; however, they did lose all of their possessions in the fire, and had to remain living at the place until a check was received from the insurance company. A check in the amount of $500.00 was issued to Dave. How thoughtful of him to think of taking out an insurance policy on that little house. Hmm... Now $500.00 was a small fortune in 1932, and it allowed the family to buy some new clothes and rent a small house.

By 1933, Dave's third brother, Ernest, had left the farm and gone to work for the Santa Fe Railroad as a section hand.

Working for the railroad in the depression years was considered a good job because it was steady work. The railroad transferred Ernest to Colorado Springs, Colorado and provided housing in what was called a railroad bunkhouse. It was a small, simple apartment in a row of four apartments. It had one or two bedrooms and a living room/kitchen combination. Ernest's family consisted of his wife Anna and three children. During the hottest part of the Texas summer, Gladys gave birth to another red-headed son named Leroy Phillip Clark on August 12, 1933. Dad named the baby after the doctor who delivered him, Dr. Leroy Sidoris. The mother of the child had no say in the matter.

About the time new baby Leroy had his first diaper pinned on, Dave took off for Colorado to check things out. Surely conditions there must be better than they were in Texas. His brother Ernest put in a good word for him to his section crew foreman, and he went to work for the Santa Fe Railroad. Two to three weeks later, he returned to Canyon driving Ernest's 1929 Chevrolet sedan. He hastily loaded his family and a few belongings into the car and pointed it toward Colorado, all the while telling his frightened family of the horrors of crossing the mountains by way of the dreaded Raton Pass in New Mexico. The fear was real because these Texans had never seen a mountain. As the Chevy pulled up to the bunkhouse, there were hugs and kisses and all the kids were excited to see cousins they barely knew, and the new baby was passed for all to see. Dave soon left the railroad and went to work for a finance company repairing autos that had been repossessed, so they could be sold again.

In early 1934 Dave was seriously injured in an auto accident. The vehicle rolled over three times, and Dave's back was fractured in four places. After being released from the hospital, a long period of recovery was needed before he could resume normal activities. With Dave unable to work and no income, the family moved from the small rented house back to the railroad bunkhouse. Thankfully, Mr. Murphy, the supervisor for the Santa Fe Railroad, let the family move back in at no charge for rent until the breadwinner of the family was able to return to work. By late summer of that year, the Clark family had moved to Pueblo, Colorado, about 45 miles south of Colorado Springs. Dave soon secured a job with the local Chevrolet dealer, Jackson Chevrolet Co. It should be noted that as soon the Clarks in Texas learned of Dave's injury, they immediately loaded up and moved to Colorado Springs. The group included Dave's parents, two young sisters, Dave's brother Fred and his family. Shortly after Dave's move to Pueblo, his brother Fred also went to work for Jackson Chevrolet.

In the spring of 1935, Gladys received a heart-breaking telegram from Texas that both of her parents had been killed by a tornado that completely destroyed their house. Her sister Thelma was seriously injured but survived the storm. Gladys traveled by train back to Texas to attend her parent's funeral. While she was away, Dave's sister Myrtie came to Pueblo from Colorado Springs to take care of the kids. Myrtie was probably about 15 years old at the time. It was not long after this event that the family was uprooted again. This time the move would take them to Monte Vista, Colorado, a small railroad town southwest of Pueblo, about 125 miles away. The reason for the sudden move was not known by anyone in the family except Dave. The new residence was a two-room cabin in a tourist court, what would be called a motel today. Dave immediately went to work for Wilson Chevrolet Co., the local car dealer.

Once again, the dust had hardly settled when Dave's brother Fred and family arrived in Monte Vista. Fred also found a job with Mr. Wilson at his dealership. Before long, Dave was promoted to the job of service manager at the garage, but settling down was not in the cards for the Clark family. Soon they were on the road again and relocated in Salida, Colorado, a town less than 100 miles north of Monte Vista. Once again, a tourist cabin became their new home. This group of cabins was owned by an Italian family named Spino. Marvin and Junior Spino were the same age and soon became friends. The friendship, however, was short lived because the Clark family only stayed in Salida for a short time. This time they moved to Grand Junction, Colorado, not far from Utah. The year was 1935.

In Grand Junction, the family took up residence in an unpainted structure consisting of four apartments in a row. They moved into a one-bedroom apartment with a combination kitchen and living room making up the rest of the dwelling. The three boys slept on the floor on what was called a pallet which was a folded quilt on the bottom and another quilt on top. They were living out on the edge of town which meant there was nothing beyond except for sagebrush and desert. Dave, once again, went to work for the local Chevrolet dealer, Central Chevrolet in downtown Grand Junction. Great Depression or not, Dave could always get a job and seemed to prefer working on Chevrolets. School had already started when Marvin enrolled in the third grade. The others were still too young for school. By the time school was out, Dave was once again overcome by wanderlust, which for our family was an unexplained malady. All of the Clark's belongings were thrown in and on top of the old Chrysler, and they were heading down the road again, destination unknown. They crossed the Utah state border and did not stop until they reached Ogden. They arrived flat broke without enough money to rent even a tourist cabin.

It was the summer of 1936, and camping out under the trees seemed perfectly reasonable to Dave. Camp was set up in an unkempt area that was adjacent to Ogden's city park with a small creek separating the two areas. There was a footbridge crossing the creek and leading directly into the park. Other campers were already occupying some of the camp sites. Some had small tents, and others had no more than an automobile parked under a tree. There were some old battered picnic tables in some of the camps. The Clarks were among those that had nothing but an old 20's something Chrysler with a mattress on top and all other belongings crammed into the back seat area with the three boys. The mattress was put on the bare ground at night where the parents slept, and the boys slept in the car as best they could. True to form, the next morning Dave drove to downtown Ogden, and before noon, returned to the campgrounds and announced that he had a gotten a job with the Hinkley Plymouth and Dodge dealership. The Clark family continued to live under the stars until late summer. With fall approaching, Dave knew he would have to rent a house in a neighborhood near a school that Marvin could attend. When the school year started, Marvin enrolled as a fourth-grade student in Pingree Elementary School. The house Dave rented was within a reasonable walking distance for a nine-year old. It was not long before yet another move was made, and this time to an old house which was even closer to school.

As fall turned into winter, it became apparent even to a nine-year old that his mother was pregnant. On New Year's Day 1937, a baby boy was added to the Clark family, and of course, he was a red head. At this time, Dave was working for the Chevrolet dealership that was owned by a man named Franklin Browning. For reasons known only to himself, Dave named the new baby boy Franklin Browning Clark. By late spring, before school was out, Dave moved the family to an area called North Ogden, 5 or 6 miles out of the city. It was a farming community, and the new home was an old farm house owned by the Hull family who just lived up the road a ways. It was a tough summer, as Dave was no longer working for Mr. Browning, and he didn't come home much. The family really did not know what he was doing or why he left the Chevrolet agency. When he did come home, he was usually intoxicated, arriving with very little, if any, money in his pockets. Sometimes he would stay for a few days and then leave again.

* * *

Marvin turned 10 years old that summer and sometimes would work for a farmer named Jones who lived next door. Farmer Jones paid him $0.50 a day to pull weeds in his carrot field or to help him pitch hay into his barn to feed his livestock. Also, he would pick cherries and apricots for other farmers in the area. He would make $0.75 to $0.80 a day for these jobs. Down the road about a mile, there was a small country store where some grocery items were purchased with the meager amount Marvin was bringing home. Gladys had planted a garden, so that also provided some vegetables. They had no money to pay the light bill, so the power company turned off the power. Kerosene lamps were put into use as in the days before electricity. The end of summer was coming, and the situation for the Clark family had not improved.

It was almost time for the kids to start school again when Dave returned home one evening in an old 1926 Durant. He threw a mattress on top of the car and filled back seat with whatever belongings he could fit, along with the four boys. Everything else was just left in the house. The old Durant was a two-door sedan, and it was crammed so full there was no room for the boys to sit upright, so they traveled lying on their sides, backs, or bellies. The departure was so sudden, it seemed like Dave felt something or someone was chasing him. After driving all night, Dave steered the old car through Pocatello, Idaho. He continued across a bridge over the Snake River, turned down a dirt road, and set up camp on the banks of the Snake River. The stay in Pocatello was not very long, maybe a week or two. Dave pawned everything that had any value to raise gas money to keep on going down the road to somewhere. Somewhere turned out to be Filer, Idaho and a 100-acre apple orchard. Dave parked the old Durant and set up camp at the edge of the orchard. He now had an old patched up 8x10 tent that a man had given him in payment for some auto work he had done for him.

\* \* \*

Both Dave and Gladys went to work picking apples in the huge orchard. Marvin was left in the camp to care for his younger brothers, including 9-month old Frank. What a lot of responsibility for a 10-year-old boy. Young Dode was no trouble for his older brother, but Leroy was another matter. He would not stay in the camp; he would take off to go find his parents. He was only four years old, but he always found his mom and dad in that giant forest of apple trees. It was as if he had the unerring nose of a bloodhound. He would be with them when they came home for lunch.

By early October, the apples were picked, and it was time for the pickers to move on. Someone must have told Dave that Arizona was nice in the winter, so he was soon headed in that direction. The old Durant was stuffed to the brim along with the addition of five crates of Idaho apples that Dave managed to squeeze into the back of the car. They crossed the dry desert country of Nevada at the top speed of about 35 mph. It was a big thrill for the kids to see Boulder Dam (now Hoover Dam) and drive across its top into Arizona.

The cotton was ready for picking near Chandler, Arizona. The Clarks purchased cotton sacks and were soon at work in the fields. They moved into an old shack of a house that had seen better days. The routine was the same as in Idaho; Dave and Gladys would go to the cotton fields and leave Marvin to look after his brothers. As usual, Leroy would leave to go find his parents, and again he always found them. They would return to the house at mid-day for lunch and then return to the fields. The Clarks picked cotton for various growers in the Phoenix area, Buckeye, Litchfield, Chandler, Glendale, etc. When the cotton was all picked, work became scarce, so they worked in the carrot fields and grapefruit orchards. By mid-summer a lot of people were stranded and broke. An offer was made by the County to give families enough gas money to go back where they came from. Most of them needed to return to Arkansas, Oklahoma or Texas. The Clark's were issued a check in the amount of $50.00 which they used to head north back to Colorado. It was late summer 1938 when Dave, Gladys, and their four boys arrived in Colorado Springs, and once again, at Grandma and Grandpa Clark's front door.

# FRANK BROWNING CLARK:
# BORN 1-1-1937

I came into this world on January 1, 1937 at Dee Hospital in Ogden, Utah. Mom thought we might win a prize of some sort, being the first child born that year, but it was not to be. I was like number eight or thereabouts. Not even a close second. The winter of 1937 in Ogden, Utah was particularly harsh with nighttime temperatures down around minus zero. Mom was in the hospital waiting for my birth, and my dad was nowhere to be found. At home in the little dingy two-room shack that we were renting were my three brothers, Marvin (Sam), 9 years old; Dave (Dode), 7 years old; and Leroy, 3 years old, all alone. The electricity, gas, and water had been turned off by the utility companies for nonpayment of bills. My big brother Marvin, who apparently was quite industrious, had some kind of trivial job delivering coal and working on local farms, but was making $0.50 a day for his labor. So at least he was feeding the family at that tender young age. He managed to sneak enough coal in his coat and pants pockets to come home and keep the old iron stove going, so they did not freeze to death. Just imagine in today's world, two little boys, three and five years old, staying home alone for 11 or 12 days with a nine-year old babysitting them, keeping in mind he was away working most of the time. Incredible indeed.

As luck would have it, my dad's brother, Hershel, who worked for the Santa Fe Railroad, happened to be coming through Ogden about that time. He managed to wire around the gas, water, and electricity, so we were back in business. Mom was in the hospital for eleven days, and during that time, my dad came by just long enough to name me: Franklin Browning Clark, after the owner of Browning Chevrolet in Ogden where dad worked. Well, again dad eventually came home, packed up everything he could get into the car, and away we went. This was the pattern of his life for as long as I can remember. It seems like only yesterday, 1938 or 1939, that our family was in Arizona picking cotton, and I was riding on the top of a "tow sack" being pulled by my mother. Cotton pickers pulled a long cloth bag, about eight feet long, behind them. They made their way through the rows of cotton, stuffing the cotton bolls they picked into the bag as they went along. On a good day, you might make a dollar for 10 hours of work.

Times were tough, there were no support systems like we have today, no welfare, no unemployment benefits; you just did the best you could and that meant going hungry much of the time. When we did have groceries, it was something mom or dad picked up at the company store which was owned by the same people who owned the cotton fields. They would charge outrageous prices and then deduct it from your meager wages. Many times, you owed them more than you had coming. This was exactly what they wanted, as it kept the field workers from moving on until the crops were all in. When mom went to pick cotton, she did not take me along. She left me with my brothers. She would leave a baby's bottle of milk to be fed to me sometime around noon each day. Unbeknownst to anyone, Leroy was drinking my milk. Mom would come in at the end of a long day, and little Frankie was throwing fits and crying incessantly. The doctor at the little itinerant medical clinic could find no cause for my malady. It was finally my brother Marvin, who owned up to the fact that Leroy was drinking the milk intended for me. After that, mom always took me with her on the tow sack. My family says I could not possibly remember, but I do as though it were only yesterday, floating on my back down a small canal in the cotton field. My family says the incident did in fact occur while my brothers were babysitting, and I was left unattended for a short time, but all suggest it was impossible that I could remember that occurrence. In later years, I excelled in the backstroke. That was my very earliest remembrance of life on this earth.

When the cotton and grapefruit picking ran out, we were left totally destitute, without a penny nor any food or a place to stay. What to do? Seeing a potentially disastrous situation developing, the county and state came up with a plan to give all of these stranded families enough money to go back to where they came from. Our family received $50.00, and we were soon on our way back to Colorado.

We headed for Colorado to stay with my dad's parents, Eva and Samuel Clark. My grandpa was very stern, never saw him smile, joke, laugh, or even take a drink. He was kind of an old sour puss. My grandmother on the other hand was the "rock", loving, kind, sweet, hardworking, thrifty, and cunning, she could do it all. My earliest recollection of her was when I was about two or three years old, and I had taken on the propensity to swear. Not really bad words but things like *dam*, *hell*, and when I really wanted to be nasty, *shit*. Well, once it just slipped out. "Hell." Grandma looked at me, and I stared back. She then slipped her false teeth out and clicked them at me. It literally scared the shit out of me. "Frankie, are you ever going to say that word again," she yelled. "God dammed, no grandma," I replied. It was the one and only time she ever gave me a whippin'

# COLORADO TO CALIFORNIA:
# 1938-1942

While I cannot remember many specific details of what went on when we lived in Colorado, I know we moved around a lot, as that was dad's pattern. We lived in Grand Junction, Pueblo, back to Grand Junction, and then back to Colorado Springs. My brother Marvin says that our dad and his dad, (my grandfather) got a hair up their ass sometime in 1939 and just announced that they were leaving, hitting the road to sell plaster deer and other small animals. They had come into possession of several plaster molds and began making these animals. Once taken out of the mold, they were cleaned up and painted, and then sold to be displayed on one's front porch or living room. They were gone several months with no one hearing a word from them. Poor mom and grandma were left with six kids to feed, clothe, and care for with absolutely no source of income. Grandma began making trips to the local mattress factory picking up the cloth coverings that were

17

ripped from the old mattresses before they were remanufactured. These she hand-sewed together to make rags that she peddled to local garages and service stations. Mom managed to find a couple of jobs cleaning houses for $0.25 an hour, and Aunt Myrtie, who was 16 years old, found employment as a maid and babysitter. The family also got some government assistance in the form of a commodity truck that came around once a week, dropping off food items such as flour, beans, rice, etc. Somehow they managed to get by. When dad did return, he was driving a 1926 Buick. He almost immediately announced that we were moving to Carlsbad, New Mexico. As usual, everything that would fit into the car was crammed in, mattress on top, and kids in the back seat laying on top of everything. That only lasted a few weeks, and we were back in Colorado with Grandma and Grandpa Clark.

Within just a very short time, another hair grew up dad's ass, and he announced that we were moving to Oregon, where ever the hell that was. Again, throw everything into the car, put the mattress on top, kids into the back seat, except this time there was an addition. Aunt Myrtie had gotten married, so she and her new husband Bob would accompany us. How did we all fit in that little car? We ended up living in an old, rundown wooden shack on 82nd Avenue, just outside of Portland. Dad and Bob set up a sales stand and displayed the plaster animals, only rarely selling anything. Bob and Myrtie got tired of the whole thing. Bob's dad sent them money to get tickets on the Greyhound bus, and they were headed back to Colorado. Dad, of course, was drinking off and on per usual. I don't

18

mean just drinking, but being drunk a large portion of the time. Mom was picking strawberries all day long to make just enough money to feed us. Even at the young age of three, I can remember mom crying, crying, and crying because of all the back pain she was suffering. But every morning she got up, fixed our breakfast, and off to the strawberry patch she went, and pregnant to boot. My sister Eva Sue was born on November 3rd, 1940.

Just after a few months on 82nd Avenue, dad was ready to move again. Somehow he found a job as a mechanic over on the coast at a little town called Ocean Lake. We stayed there a few months, and dad was off again, this time to Oregon City, just south of Portland. He landed a job at the Yellow Cab Company servicing and repairing taxi cabs. That lasted a few weeks, then on to the Pontiac dealership in Oregon City. We managed to hang on there for the several months. It seemed like maybe we had found a home at last. Dad's drinking had tapered off, and things were good. My brother Freddie Eugene was born at home on June 11, 1942.

\* \* \*

A letter came in September 1942 from my dad's brother, Hershel, was still working for the railroad, and was now living in Richmond, California. With World War II in full swing and the defense industry flourishing in the Bay Area, jobs were abundant. Now Grandma and Grandpa, Myrtie and Bob, and my Aunt Alleene and her husband Alvie had all moved to Richmond. "Come to Richmond," Uncle Hershel pleaded.

"Things are good!" We had no car, so Myrtie and Bob drove up to Oregon and picked us up, and as customary, stuffed everything, including six children now, into the back seat with the mattress on top. California, here we come!

On our way to California from Oregon

It has been said that Dad did not like the weather in Richmond and was fearful that our sister Sue, who had some medical problems, would not fare well there. Grandpa had a sister, Aunt Missoura, (not sure on the spelling) who lived in Central California in a little town called Oakdale. So after only a week in Richmond, we were on our way to Oakdale. This simple move was perhaps the most significant and important event in my life. We found a house to rent right away. For $25.00 a month, it had two bedrooms, kitchen, living room, dining room and a nice little room off the kitchen for big brother Marvin to sleep in. He immediately padlocked it to keep the other boys out. Good decision. It was the nicest house we had ever occupied, downtown, 603 Third and E. It was situated right behind today's Bliss Café where a parking lot is now located. The house was later moved out near-what is now known as Shively's a bar and grill, but on the south side of the highway at the Old Richina Ranch. The landlord, Harvey Hubble, came to the house in his 1918 Chevrolet touring car on the first of the month, 8:00 a.m. sharp to collect the rent. He'd have coffee with Mom, maybe a bite to eat, and was on his way.

Dad immediately got a job at Haslam Brothers Chevrolet-Buick Garage. Life was looking pretty good for me and my four brothers and one sister. Dad immediately put a chicken wire fence around the property, and soon we had red leghorns running all over downtown Oakdale. Oakdale had its first Oakies. Dad shortly clipped their wings, so that problem was solved. Mom would occasionally go out to the back yard, grab a chicken, put its head on the chopping block and whack it off, throwing the chicken onto the ground to "bleed out" and go to chicken heaven. People driving or walking by were amused, (dammed Oakies). Well true to tradition, it was not long before dad left his job, moving down the street to Clark's Ford Garage (no relation to us) and starting over. He also procured a job there for $0.50 an hour for my 15year-old brother Marvin, who had decided to drop out of high school. It should be noted that later on he went into the service, came back, and graduated from high school in 1947. From there he went on to graduate from the California School of Arts and Crafts, later becoming the art and publicity director for Boise Cascade. Not bad for an Oakie. My grandpa and grandma decided to join us in Oakdale and moved down here settling down at an old gas station called Pumpkin Center on Highway 120 and Orange Blossom Road. They lived there a few weeks, then eventually found a house on G Street behind the East Side School. They lived out the rest of their lives in that house.

\* \* \*

Dad wanted to be on his own and he had abstained from drinking. Life had never been so good for our family and especially Mom. I think she really believed that she was to finally be rewarded for all of her hard work and suffering and putting up with my dad. Dad left Clark Ford and opened his own auto repair shop adjacent to Hinky Dinks Bar on East F Street, today's H-B Saloon. He had an excellent business, and life was good; however, there was one little flaw. In the wall between the shop and Hinky Dinks was a window, much like you would find at a drive up window today. The temptation was too great; soon dad was ordering drinks through the window. The devil was back. Dad lost that business. Somehow, and I am not sure where he got the financing, but he came up with enough money to build an auto repair shop right behind the house at Third and E. He stopped drinking, took uncle Bob in as a partner, and business boomed. Again, life could not have been better, but not long after that, the devil returned. Dad started drinking again, and the court locked up the business with several court filings.

According to a story recently passed down to me by my brother Marvin, Dad had a man, Martin O'Donnell, working for him as a mechanic when the court locked up the business. Apparently, he was owed some back wages by my dad, or at least that is what he claimed. My brother Marvin was walking along Third Street across from the Moss Rose Bakery when a car pulled up to the curb. The car was driven by O'Donnell, who was a rather big guy, six-foot-two, 200 lbs. or so, and a black patch over his blind left eye that was frightening and intimidating to a 16-year-old kid who was half the man's size. He stopped my brother and approached him, and he asked my brother to unlock Dad's garage, so he could take something of value to match wages he was owed. My brother told O'Donnell that he knew nothing of his dad's business and did not have a key, as the lock belonged to the police. Marvin told him he would just have to wait for my dad to return home to deal with him. Marvin started to continue on to high school and the man grabbed him and threaten to give him a licking if he did not cooperate. Marvin jerked away and went on to school. A couple of days later, Marvin was at Grandma and Grandpa's house, and he relayed to them the incident with O'Donnell. Marvin left the house and said he was going to the movie theatre downtown, only a block from our house, and then walk home. Our grandpa had been a U.S. Marshall in the Oklahoma Indian Territory many years back and still had his .44 caliber service revolver in a drawer in the bedroom.

For some reason, call it intuition, after dark about the time the movie was letting out, grandpa put on his coat, slipped the revolver into his waist band, and told Grandma he was going over to our house to check on Marvin. He parked on Third Street, 100 feet or so south of our house and got out of the car. There was an alley near by that ran between K & L Body Shop and Zaro & Cisi's grocery store. The story goes that Grandpa heard a commotion of some sort in the alley, and upon looking into the dimly lit passage, saw that a man had Marvin pinned against the building and was choking him with his forearm. Grandpa pulled the .44 caliber from his waist band, walked up to the man's blind side, and wacked him over the head with the gun. The man, O'Donnell, went down with a thud and began to bleed profusely from the wound across his forehead. Grandpa was a very quiet 65-year-old man who would not hurt a fly. He also was six-foot-five inches tall and weighed about 230 lbs. He picked O'Donnell up and pressed him against the wall with a stern warning, "Don't you ever bother this boy again or you will have hell to pay." Grandpa took my brother home, visited with mom for a while, and left. We never saw or heard from O'Donnell again.

\* \* \*

Dad was down and out when Kenneth Kaufman, who owned the Pacific Pea Packing cannery (later Hunt Wesson) along with his brother Roy, cosigned a note at the bank with my dad for $1,500 to obtain the Plymouth-Desoto franchise for the Oakdale area. I am sure my dad had never seen that much money (later, when I worked at First Western Bank, I dug up the note that Mr. Kaufman had cosigned for the money). Almost immediately, my dad disappeared for several weeks, and when he returned, the money was gone, as well as any possibilities for an automobile dealership. Our family was on the move again.

\* \* \*

It was 1946. My brother Marvin had joined the Navy in 1945, just before the end of WWII at age 17; my brother Dode at age 14 joined the army a few months after the war ended; and then my brother Leroy joined the Navy at the unbelievable age of 13. Once again, we packed up, stuffing everything into a borrowed car, putting the mattress on top and all five the kids into the back seat and pulling a trailer headed for Stockton.

# GROWING UP IN OAKDALE: 1942-1952

I have complete clarity on pulling up at 603 Third and E Streets in Oakdale in mid-October 1942. I thought "wow" what a nice house. Next door, on the corner of Third and Yosemite Avenue, was an old two story brick building, now housing a gift and hobby shop that had at some time in the recent past burned to the ground. Some of the walls were still standing with large 4x6 foot windows facing our place. They were burned out of course. Over the next couple of years, the basement of that old building became my personal playground, lots of crushed junk, pots and pans, glassware, tools that I dug up from the rubble. Then one day while digging in a pile of burned debris, Bonanza! I had struck the mother lode! It must have been the cash register, a vending machine, or some other kind of apparatus that collected money. Six years old, I had no idea what to do. Tell mom whom I trusted, or keep it a secret and take out a few coins at a time? Any bills that had been inside had burned. I could retire at only six years of age. Well, it was not long before mom got wise, tootsie rolls, bubble gum, and on occasion, a maple bar from Moss Rose Bakery across the street. I had to confess. Mom and I dug up the area and came up with about $15.00. At her suggestion and accompaniment, I went to the post office, also across the street, and made an investment that proved very financially sound. Remember, this was 1942 and just the beginning of the biggest war the world had ever seen. There was a big scramble by the government to raise as much money as possible to support the war effort. I am not 100% clear on this, but as my memory dictates, it went something like this. The post office made available defense stamp books to the citizenry. They came in a variety of denominations. $25.00, $50.00, $75.00, and $100.00. So, for example, you got a $25.00 book and began buying stamps (like postage stamps) and glued them in. When the book was full, it had a cash value of $25.00, or you could convert it to a "war bond" valued at $27.50 after five years. Not a bad return for those times, and it was patriotic. Well, even at six years of age, I saw a golden opportunity here to take my investment portfolio and get into the stamp business. I bought $15.00 worth of stamps and stuck them into my stamp book. When I got to within 2 stamps of having it full, I walked the neighborhood stopping every prospective and patriotic-looking citizen I came into contact with. My pitch was simple. "Hey, I only need two more stamps to fill this book and turn it in for a war bond." Who could turn down a cute little red headed six-year-old? I know my mom had nothing to do with it, but the books disappeared, along with my portfolio. Who knows, if I had not been sidetracked, I might have helped win the war a lot sooner.

The future looked bleak. Here I was, now seven years old, no source of income, no bubble gum or tootsie rolls, and no prospects in sight, but I had the run of downtown Oakdale, coming and going as I pleased. I started every Saturday pretty much with the same routine, going clockwise out our back yard and making a right turn onto Yosemite Boulevard. Across the street to the east was Wilson Salyer's Oakdale Feed. Next door was the Union Ice and Coal business, and then the Standard Gas station on the corner of Yosemite and F Street. Clay Dorrah worked or ran the ice and coal plant, but we will talk more about him later. So, as I headed out in the morning, my first stop was the Western Auto store, owned and operated by Jim Pollard. It is hard to believe, but at the age of seven, I owned my very own single shot .22 caliber rifle. I cannot remember where or how in the world I came to possess it, but I did. The shell extractor did not function, so after each shot I would have to take out a little pin knife and remove the expended shell casing. All I knew about gun safety was that you never pointed the gun at anything you were not going to shoot, and that bullets went a really long way. So, one day I waltz into the Western Auto store to purchase a box of ammunition. Not wanting to shoot anyone, as I walked down the street and into the store, I carried the gun with the barrel facing up into my arm pit. When Mr. Pollard saw this, he was somewhat dismayed and let out a gasp in concern, "Pinky, (a name bestowed upon me by the local postmaster) what are you doing carrying that gun like that? You will shoot your arm off (unlike the Xmas story and shooting out your eye)." I was trying to be very safety conscious. If the gun went off, it would only hurt me, not some innocent soul standing nearby. Safety minded, I thought I was over the top. "Pinky, we are going to make a deal with each other, okay?" asked Mr. Pollard. Well, I was not sure about a deal, but I asked, "What's a deal?" He explained it this way, "I am going to confiscate your .22 caliber rifle (no idea what that meant), and for the next few weeks, you are going to come into the store on Saturday at, say 9:00 a.m., and I will give you lessons in firearm safety. When I am done, I will give you an examination." I had been to the doctor for examinations, so I was not sure about that one. Continuing the conversation, he explained, "If you pass the examination, I will return your rifle and give you two boxes of .22 caliber shells." Well, that was a no brainer even to a seven-year old. Shells cost about .25 cents a box. What a deal! Mr. Pollard put me through the safety course, and the things I learned about firearms and safety have stuck with me all my life. Thanks Mr. Pollard. Oh yes, when he returned the rifle, he had fixed the shell extractor.

I continued my adventures along the Stanislaus River, never going down stream but heading up the river all the way to Orange Blossom, which was almost five miles from our home. I was a loner and enjoyed my time exploring the wilderness. I became a crack shot. I swear I could light the head of a match at 50 yards, (maybe that's a little bit of an exaggeration), but I did bring home salmon, pheasants, quail, dove, and cotton tails. Mom was a great cook of wild game, so we all enjoyed those feeds. My ability to hunt and kill wild game became a great asset when we were without any food whatsoever. I could help provide a little food for our meager meals.

I seem to have digressed from telling you my Saturday routine. Let's get back to that. Then it was next door to Mr. Milt Seeber's drug store. Man, he had a lot of neat things in there. He would take me into the back room and explain what he was doing, how and why people ordered and needed medicine. His daughter, Nancy, was in my first-grade class, and to this day, over 70 years later, we remain friends. One day while wandering around the store, I spotted what I thought was a dollar bill laying between some products on the display rack. It had to be a dollar bill because I had no idea anything larger existed. I picked it up, and to my amazement it was a $20.00 bill. I knew 20 was much larger than one because I could by now count. What to do, what to do? I rushed home and immediately explained my new wealth to mom. She said, "Well, Frankie, this is remarkable and very fortunate." Then she used the word unfortunately. "Unfortunately, this is not your money but belongs to some poor soul who lost it. I tell you what Frankie, turn around and take this money right back to Mr. Seeber." Well, my mother had instilled in me to always be honest, so I went straight to Mr. Seeber and informed him of my newfound wealth. There was no question in my little seven-year-old brain that this $20.00 bill now belonged to me, despite what my mother had said. You know "finders keepers, losers weepers" made sense to me, especially when I had the $20.00. Well, Mr. Seeber did not particularly agree with my juvenile logic. He explained to me that my newfound treasure might just belong some "poor old lady" who had nothing, or someone very ill who needed the money more so than I did. After patiently listening to him, he had me convinced. I, but somewhat reluctantly, gave the money to Mr. Seeber. He looked very sternly into my eyes and said, "Now Pinky, being honest sometimes has its rewards. I want you to remember this as long as you live, and honesty is always the best policy, perhaps not always monetarily, but just making you feel better in your heart. Here is $2.00 for you doing the right thing and returning the money to me. I promise you I will make every effort to locate the rightful owner." I have never forgotten Mr. Seeber's words and advice. On to the next business place, the Live Oak Hotel and next door, the Stage Depot.

When you walked past the Live Oak Hotel there were always a bunch of old people sitting in the lobby, looking out at the passing cars and people. I think it was an early answer to today's residential care facility or rest home. I would stop by and visit the old people, and they seemed to enjoy talking with and kidding me. Clay Dorrah, who was now Oakdale's police chief, would come in and set me on his lap and start questioning me about my brothers or what I might have seen on my journeys around town. If I was lucky, he would give me a coin "hickey", good at the bus depot for a $0.10 purchase. These guys were fun, but boy to a seven-year-old kid, they seemed awfully old. God bless them. The bus depot was an exciting place, big Greyhound busses pulling up, people coming and going, hugs and kisses, tears and laughter. Inside the depot, operated by Ira DeLong, was Oakdale's very first frosty machine. I never before or since have tasted anything as good as those frosties. There was a lot of card playing going on in the backrooms of the depot. Some people left with big smiles on their faces, others looked pretty sad. Well, if you stood there long enough by the frosty machine, one of those smiling (lucky) faces would notice you and spring for a frosty. Was I a little beggar? Well, I guess so, but those frosties were mighty good to a seven-year-old with no source of income.

Next door to the bus depot was a very small enclave in the wall, maybe about six feet deep and six feet wide. That was the proprietorship of Shorty the Shoe Shine Man. As far as I can determine, he was Oakdale's first, and at that time, only black man. Well, Shorty always seemed busy shining shoes, and it appeared to me that the money must be rolling in. Years later, when I worked at First Western Bank, Shorty came in and gave me $10,000 wrapped in old newspapers and opened a savings account. Guess I was correct. Anyway, I decided to get into the shoe shining business. With $2.00 from Mr. Seeber, I purchased some shoe polish, a couple of brushes, and some black and brown shoe dye. I told my dad what I was planning to do, and he made me this neat little shoe box for customers to put their foot on while I shined away. This was one of the few times I ever remember having any interaction with my dad. Thanks, Dad! I had no idea whatever happened to that shoe box until last year, 2015. I was visiting my brother Jim in Oregon, and he said, "Hey, want to see something?" Out came the old shoe shinning box. I was in tears (and a couple of bottles of Willamette Valley pinot). I brought it home and still have it.

With that new shoe box and all of the required paraphernalia, I was back in business after the failure of my war bond venture. Financial success never looked better. Soon I had some regular customers, and at $0.10 a shine, I was knocking down $1.00 to $2.00 a week. Life was good. The bubble gum and tootsie rolls were back. I am sure that Shorty was aware of what was going on, as Oakdale was a small town. One day with my shoe shine box in tow, I stopped by to talk with Shorty, after all, we were in the same business and had mutual concerns about the increase in shoe polish prices, imports of inferior Italian shoe brushes, etc. Shorty called me *Pinky*, as did most of the local downtown merchants. He said, "Pinky, we need to talk. Sit down here." He invited me to the very highest seat on his shoe shine stand. "Pinky," he said, "you know I used to be just as white as you are, white as a peeled potato. Then I got into this shoe shine business, day after day putting that black shoe polish on my hands and rubbing it onto those shoes. Well, do you know that before long — well, just look at me. I turned as black as that coal across the street at the ice and coal store. Honest to God that is what happened as sure as I am standing here." Well, by now I had forgotten my grandmother's false teeth, and I yelled out, "Holy shit!" "Now Pinky, I would hate to see that happen to you," said Shorty. "Tell you what I am going to do, I will give you $0.50 cents for your box and polish." Man, I was between a rock and a hard place. I had $2.00 invested and a good business going. "Tell you what Mr. Shorty, $3.00, and I keep the shoe box." "Deal", says Shorty, and he stuck out his hand to seal the deal. At the time, it was one of the biggest corporate buyouts in Oakdale's history.

Three dollars and out of business, what to do, what to do? Well, across the street from our house there was a hardware store ran by Al Sipe. Anyway, in my wanderings around Oakdale, I stopped in at the hardware store just to look around. I spotted a used push lawnmower for sale. The gears began to turn in my head. There is money to be made mowing lawns and no fear of shoe polish. It was marked for sale, $4.00. I only had $3.00, so I offered Mr. Sipe $0.50 cents. He chuckled and said he was not in business to lose money. "Well, what if I gave you a dollar now and another dollar in a couple of weeks." He just laughed and said, "Well, okay." I paid him the dollar and kept the other two bucks for future expenses.

I rolled the new piece of equipment across the street to the house, and mom, who had just given birth to my sister Patrician Ann (Patty) on August 4, 1943, helped me sharpen the blades with an old file. I was now in the landscaping maintenance business. Now, I am eight years old and have my own business. I even hand printed up little business cards on small pieces of paper and posted them on a bulletin board at the post office. Pretty soon, I had more business than I could handle. Only solution, raise my prices. Well, I lost some business, but the price increase offset that. Pretty soon, I was giving my mom money to save for me.

I still managed to find time to do my wanderings around town along with my best friend "Shorty" the dog. He was a terrier/corgi mix about, 35 lbs., and no connection to the shoeshine man. I will discuss Shorty in a later chapter. One of my favorite stops was the Safeway grocery store located where Bank of America is now. The manager was Norman Ardis, a devout Jehovah's Witness who continually attempted to get me to his place of worship. When I did go to church, it was across the street from our house at the United Brethren, and the pastor was Reverend Mahoney. At that time, I always carried a set of red dice in my pocket and was ready to roll for a nickel or a dime at the drop of a hat. I often asked the good reverend to roll, but he would say no, chastise me for indulging in such an evil practice, and give a little laugh. He was a wonderful man, but back to Norman. He could take a dime between his fingers and make it spin on the counter by the cash register. Try as I might, I couldn't do that, but there was a standing offer that if I did, I could keep the dime. Finally, I figured it out. I put the dime on edge and put the finger of my left hand on top of the dime then flipped it with my finger of my right hand. It spun like crazy. After a brief argument about my technique, Norman conceded and gave me the dime.

A few days later, Shorty the dog and I were back at Safeway, and Norman made me another offer I could not turn down. He picked out a huge watermelon from the bin and set it on the counter. "Tell you what Pinky, if you can carry this watermelon to your house (one block away) without dropping it, it is yours." It was huge, and in reflection, I think it weighed more than I did. But I loved watermelon, and it was a challenge. If I failed to make it home, Norman said I had to go to his church the next four Sundays. Now it's me against God and Norman, pretty stiff odds for an eight-year-old. Well, I staggered out the door, made it to the curb, and started to cross the street. That watermelon was slipping out of my grasp, and there was no way I was going to even get across the street much less a block to home. Norman stood in the doorway watching with anticipation and a smile on his face. A car pulled up and blocked my way from crossing the street. The watermelon was clear down past my waist and getting away from me. "Pinky!" the man in the car shouted out, "What have you got there? Looks like you could use some help." The car was the Oakdale Police car and driven by Clay Dorrah, the Chief. He got out of the car, holding up traffic and walked around to my side and removed the watermelon placing it in the police car, along with Shorty. "Get in," he said, "and I will give you a ride home." Shorty, the watermelon, and I did in fact make it home. It was delicious. But how was I going to face Norman, and worse yet, how was I going to get out of going to church with him?

Now comes the little white lie. A few days later, I was confronted by Norman at the store, and excitedly he said that he and his wife would pick me up at 9:00 a.m. on Sunday, and we would all go to church together. "Not so fast," I replied.

"When Chief Dorrah saw me with that watermelon, he thought I was stealing it, and he arrested me, and took me home to my parents." Well, after I explained it to the Chief, he started laughing so hard, he just told me to take my watermelon and get into the house. "So, Mr. Ardis (Norman), you see the situation was completely out of my control, and I certainly could not bring that big old watermelon back to the store." He just shook his head and walked off laughing. Pinky had won again!

When I made my rounds in the downtown area, I was always sure to check the coin returns at the phone booths, paper racks, the ice house, and any other vending machines I was aware of. Most of the time I drew a blank, but every once in a while, a dime here a nickel there, it all helped. While checking the phone booth at the post office, I discovered a wallet. Lo and behold it contained $23.00! I rushed home to mom, and she checked it out. The wallet belonged to Mrs. Richard Benedix who lived in Valley Home, five miles north of Oakdale. Well, we had no phone, so mom and I walked over to Hope's Meat Market next door (now Medlen's House of Beef), and used their phone to contact Mrs. Benedix. She drove right into town and soon knocked on our door. She thanked me profusely and asked why I had not just kept the money and thrown the wallet away. I explained that mom had raised me to always be honest and do to others like I wanted done to me. She smiled and handed me $3.00 from the wallet. I gave it to mom and she put it away somewhere. Not long after this incident, mom gave birth to my sister Terry Lynne on February 2, 1946.

Previously, I mentioned that my dad had an auto repair shop for a short period of time that was located on F Street next to Hinky Dinks. Being curious one day, I wandered into Hinky Dinks just to see what was there. I knew what a bar was, as mom had sent me many times across the street from our house to Dukes Bar to get dad. This nice Old Italian man (he looked old to an eight-year-old kid) approached me inside and asked if he could help me. I said, "No, I'm just looking around." He was sweeping the floor and tiding up the place. "What is your name kid?" he asked. "Frankie Clark, but people call me 'Pinky'. I don't like that name, but I guess I am stuck with it. What's your name sir?" I asked. "Well what a coincidence." Coincidence? I did not know what that meant. "My name is also Frank, Frank Deliberto, and I own this place." I explained that my dad had the place next door, and he said he had never met my dad but had spoken to him, as he periodically handed a drink through the window in the wall between businesses. Being a little brash for an eight-year-old I said, "Mr. Deliberto why don't you give me a job sweeping up, and you can do something else more important." He smiled and asked, "What do you charge?" I thought about that for a minute and replied to him, "$0.25." Was this to be every day, twice a week, what were the conditions? "This place is the dirtiest and needs cleaning the most on Sunday morning," he said. "Could you come on Sunday mornings say about 9:00 a.m. and sweep up? Also, you'll have to clean and polish the spittoons." "I don't know what a spittoon is, but I can learn," I replied. "How about the pay?" "No pay," he said, "You can keep the money you find on the floor." "Hmm, I am not sure this is a good deal for me, but I will try it." I showed up the next Sunday at 9:00 a.m. as promised and began sweeping. Wow, I found $0.35! This was going to turn out better than I had anticipated. I was ready to leave and said so long to Mr. Deliberto when he reminded me about the spittoons. He had them all lined up by the sink, seven of them, ready to be washed and polished. "What's in there?" I asked. He explained the contents. I gasped and suddenly, what only a few minutes ago had looked like a great deal for me had turned to disgust. Well, a deal is a deal, and two hours later, I was on the way home. Somehow, that $0.35 did not seem like a lot of money. Well, true to my word, the next Sunday I was back. I swept the floors and found $0.75 this time, and somehow those spittoons did not seem so bad second time around. This went on all summer, and I had plenty of spending money, and even a little to give mom to save for me. It was only years later when Mr. Deliberto confessed to me that every Sunday morning before my arrival he would throw a few coins on the floor for me to sweep up. He was a good man, and I loved him.

Hinky Dinks also sponsored the local hardball team. The players met every Sunday morning during baseball season at 9:00 a.m. at the bar before they headed out for Sunday's game. Some would have a nip or two, others just coffee. One day, I was approached and asked if I wanted to be the bat boy. Having no idea what that meant or entailed, I asked the man who approached me to explain it. Well, that guy was Bill Dickerson, a local sheep rancher, gentleman, and great baseball pitcher. "There is no pay, but you get to go with us to Modesto, Patterson, Sonora, Stockton, Escalon, and a couple of other towns. You watch the games, have a little bit to eat, maybe a soda or ice cream bar. When the batter gets through batting you pick up the bat at home plate, and put it back into the bat rack. Each team provides their own baseballs, and when there is a foul ball, you run it down, and return it to Mr. Deliberto," explained Orville Guenther, one of the players. "He will give you $0.10 for each ball returned." Well, before each game there would be other kids there to watch the games. I was not always the first one to a foul ball, some of the kids knew about the $0.10. Most did not. At the start of each game, I made sure all of the kids knew that if they returned the foul ball to me, I would give them $0.05. In the end, I made a little more money, and did not have to run quite as fast. Baseball season came to an end, winter was approaching, and I was tired of cleaning spittoons; so, I informed Mr. Deliberto that I was terminating our business relationship and taking a job at the new bowling alley behind our house as a pin setter. We shook hands, he thanked me, and out the door I went. Pin setting was a much harder job than I had envisioned. Hot, sweaty, noisy, now I know why they legislated child labor laws. Three hours a night, two nights a week, and all for $0.10 a line, $0.30 an hour or thereabouts. I was getting pretty tired of my new job and about ready to quit when I was approached by the bowling alley owner, Mr. Ernest Orr. "How's your math Frankie?" he inquired. "Straight As," I replied. "How would you like to be a score keeper during league nights?" I took the job, two nights a week at $1.00 a night, plus all the Cokes and ice cream I wanted. I loved keeping score, and it did help me with my math. The real bonus was people quit calling me Pinky; it was Frankie or an occasional *Red* which to this date I hate.

\* \* \*

My life of happiness and security virtually ended. Dad came home after three months of total obscurity. I am sure he felt disgraced and embarrassed for his actions, but I think no remorse. He had blown the $1,500 Mr. Kaufman helped him secure in the form of a loan from the bank in order to get the Desoto/Plymouth franchise from the Chrysler Corporation. Dad borrowed a car from somewhere, hooked up a small trailer to it, and we loaded everything we could from the house at Third and E Streets into the car and trailer with two mattresses on top of the car. Mom's beloved handcrafted oak table and chairs were left behind, as well as many other beloved pieces of furniture, china, etc. We were off to parts unknown, and at the last moment here came Shorty, and he jumped into the back of the trailer. We kids, Sue, Freddie, Patty, Terry and I yelled for joy as he scrambled onto the back of the trailer. We were off to Stockton, California. What exactly awaited us? No one knew, including my mom and dad.

Just about in the middle of downtown Stockton Shorty fell or jumped out of the trailer. We yelled at dad to stop, but he just kept driving. I know he must have heard us, but it made no difference. Shorty ran as fast as his short little legs would carry him but to no avail, he just faded in the distance. I screamed and screamed, but dad just sped up, totally oblivious to Shorty's predicament, or he was totally ignoring it. I just don't think he cared. Shorty was my best friend, my only friend at the time. I was going to be very lonely. I cried for several days. I hated my dad.

Shorty

We traveled down Country Club Boulevard for several miles and then finally turned north until we came to the Calaveras River. There in front of us, located right next to the river, was an old army-type barracks, about 200 feet long. On the west end lived a man and a woman, names unknown. The east end had no partitions or anything, just a door that opened from the outside in, exposing the entire building interior. No electricity, no gas, no water, no toilet facilities. Keep in mind my mother was five or six months pregnant at the time. I have little recollection of seeing my dad very often at this new location, except one time when we went to check out my throw lines that I had laid out in the river in an attempt to catch fish at night. Mom managed to salvage wood from other parts of the building, and then divided it off from the main hall. She then cut wood and sawed, pulled nails out of the building, until she put a partition between a sleeping quarters and the kitchen. My mom, five kids and my dad (when he was there) slept in a little bedroom, 10x10. To cook, we had a little two burner coal oil stove. At one end, you inverted a one-gallon jug filled with the coal oil (kerosene) and it flowed to two cotton wicks that you lit with a match. For water, there was a faucet several feet from the house that we carried water from to the house in a five-gallon bucket. Restrooms? We just went out in the weeds and brush. WATCH YOUR STEP. Mom washed the few clothes we had on a rubboard in a 10-gallon galvanized wash tub, and hung them on a clothes line next to the building to dry. She had no way to heat an iron, so we just went around in wrinkles.

I had been attending Magnolia school in the 4th grade when we left Oakdale late winter, I think 1946, and I was nine years old when we moved to Stockton. After missing school for two or three weeks, mom somehow got me registered at a school in downtown Stockton. Problem, we lived five miles out of town on Country Club Boulevard, and then two miles north on a dirt road, surrounded by corn fields with no transportation. There was a school bus that came out to Country Club Boulevard, but the problem was it cost $0.10 a day roundtrip to ride it. I have no idea where she got the money, but every morning mom gave me the $0.10, and I went to school. In later years, I was always suspicious that she had secreted some of the money I had given her from my earnings and findings in Oakdale. She had to have kept it a secret from my dad. I guess I was fortunate to have anything for lunch, but potted meat between two pieces of flour biscuits got pretty boring, but better than going hungry.

I only remember two events that occurred at the school. One of my classmates, I think his name was Tommy Quinn, invited me to a birthday party at his house. His dad, as I recall, was the District Attorney for San Joaquin County. I really wanted to go to that party, but again no transportation, and to my embarrassment the sole had come off of one of my shoes. My mom wired it back on with baling wire so at least it did not flap on the ground when I walked. Running was out of the question. Needless to say, I did not make the party. The only other significant event was when one day I was acting up in class and the teacher, as punishment, shut me up in the broom closet in the classroom. That should not seem like a significant occurrence except when class ended she had forgotten me. About 6:00 p.m. I was getting hungry and about to wet my pants when the door opened and there was the janitor. I think initially he thought I had broken into the school, but we sorted that out, and he called the principal who came down, picked me up, fed me, and took me home. Best meal I could remember having in a long time. But the event turned out to be somewhat of a blessing. When she took me home and saw our living conditions she was appalled. With some organization on her part she got the local PTA to bring us food staples every Friday night; so, that whole incident turned into a positive situation. We only lived in Stockton for three or four months, but they proved to be some of my most memorable times. Every day I was not in school, it was a Huck Finn adventure. I had the whole run of the south bank of the Calaveras River from the Stockton Country Club, west and east to College of the Pacific, (now named University of the Pacific, or UOP), fishing, exploring, mooching food from fishermen, finding soda bottles that could be returned for $0.02 a bottle (when I could get to the store). Fishing, I loved fishing. I also loved hunting, but somewhere along the way my .22 caliber rifle had gotten lost. Hmm...

We had now been living along the river for about six weeks and were getting along pretty well, thanks to my mom. I still wandered out along the river every day. There was not a day I did not think of Shorty, nor a day I did not say a little prayer for him, wondering what lucky little boy had him by his side. Deep down inside, I figured he had been run over or ended up in the pound. One particular day while making my way through the 8 to 10 feet high brush, I stumbled onto something that really energized my imagination. Before me in the brush there was a little dug out area with some boards that formed a small enclosure. Looking inside I saw the remnants of what appeared to be a demolished two-way radio. It was much larger than a table radio and had a lot more dials, tubes and wires. I was quite familiar with our recently ended war with Japan, only a few months past. I also knew there were lots of Japanese living in the area of Stockton, and I had seen POWs housed at the Stockton Fair grounds as we drove by during the war years. I fantasized that this had indeed been a secret location for Japanese sympathizers to radio the comings and goings of our ships plying the Stockton deep water channel. Man, I was excited! Suddenly there was a rustling in the brush about 6 or 7 feet away. Was it the Japanese returning? Didn't they know the war was over? My instinct was to run like hell, but at nine years of age, I was afraid to move. As I lay there trying to hide behind a bush, shivering and scared to death, I saw an object moving just ahead of me. Suddenly it emerged. Holy shit (sorry grandma), it was Shorty! Oh my God, I cried, I laughed, I cried, I laughed. My prayers had been answered. After six weeks of separation, twenty-miles distance apart, I had my best friend back. A miracle you only read about. He looked pretty tattered, under nourished, skinny, but he was still my buddy Shorty. I will never forget nor duplicate the joy and happiness that glorious reunion brought to me. Thank you, God for showing Shorty the way home. Meanwhile back at home, I showed up with Shorty, everyone was extremely excited, including my dad, who had suddenly reappeared. "Well I'll be dammed. That beats anything I ever saw!" he exclaimed. He never repented for going off and leaving him in the first place.

* * *

I had mentioned my brother Marvin (Sam) earlier in my story and that he had dropped out of school and joined the navy at the age of 17. Marvin was sworn in the day before hostilities ended and Japan's surrender. That made him eligible for any benefits that servicemen received in those days. After he completed boot camp, he ended up stationed at a navy base in the Philippines. Without getting into a lot of detail, a few months later he came home and soon was diagnosed with a severe lung disease that required surgery, resulting in the removal of one lung. While he was still in the hospital, my grandma Eva contacted the Veterans Administration to determine if my brother had any entitlements coming. The VA sent a representative to Oak Knoll Hospital in Oakland, California to interview my brother. Marvin was adamant that he had not been shot, injured in any way, or was entitled to anything from the government. The VA representative insisted on filling out the paperwork anyway. He had my brother sign it, and he submitted a claim for compensation. Time dragged on, and my brother and grandma Eva had long forgotten the application. About May of 1947, my brother went to the post office in Oakdale, P.O. Box 835. Our family had used that mail box since 1942, and the whole family got their mail there. In the mail box was a neat compact little brown envelope addressed to my brother. He opened it, and inside he found a government check in the amount of $525.00, a lot of money then. My brother had fully recovered from his lung surgery and had not yet married. At 5:00 a.m. the next day, he jumped into his little 1934 Dodge coupe and headed for Stockton and the Calaveras River. He awakened dad and lit a match so he could see the check. "Son, it's so good to see you, by golly let me get up and fix you some breakfast." My brother later said that he could literally hear the gears going around in dad's head.

In a few short days, Marvin and dad were in Oakdale, looking for real estate. Dad found two acres at the corner of Highway 108 and Mondo Lane that was for sale. $2,000, 10% down. Dad borrowed $200.00 from his son and bought the property. Payments of $25.00 a month for six years at 4% interest. Dad borrowed another $100.00, and he and Marvin headed to Oakland to an army surplus establishment and purchased a large army tent. I guess it was about 50 feet long and 30 feet wide. They loaded it into that little Dodge of my brother's and headed to Oakdale where they worked for two days setting it up on the newly purchased property on Mondo Lane. Back to Stockton, and dad announced we were moving back to Oakdale. I jumped for joy! My eyes lit up, and I envisioned the good life returning to our family. I immediately announced that Shorty and I were riding in the car with my brother, no matter what, or I was not going. I had no idea the misery and disappointment that lay ahead for our family. Had I known, I think I might have run away from home. The next day we loaded what we could into that little

Dodge coupe, threw the mattress on top as was customary, put what would fit into a little 6x8 foot trailer and left everything else in the building for some treasure hunter to rummage through. We were on our way "home".

\* \* \*

It was spring 1947. Thank goodness the school in Stockton mailed my mom a report card c/o P. O. Box 835, Oakdale. I was ready for the 5<sup>th</sup> grade in Oakdale come fall. I was 10 years old when we pulled up in front of the Mondo Lane property. "Wow," I thought, "my own circus tent!" The tent seemed huge to me. The flaps at both ends could be opened which allowed for a cool breeze to blow through, better than air conditioning; although, I had never seen or heard of an air conditioner. I was only there a few days, and I hated the place. Dirt floor, no water, no electricity, no heat, nor toilet facilities. I walked a short distance to the neighbor's house, once in the morning and once in the evening with a five-gallon bucket and got water from an old hand pump fed by a windmill. At least in Stockton you could use the great outdoors for a toilet and not be seen. Here the whole two acres were as flat as a pancake, no cover what so ever. The standard procedure was to only go to the bathroom at night or use a big bucket inside the tent. Within a week, one of the neighbors irrigated and our whole two acres were inundated with water, including the tent's dirt floors; now we had mud floors.

At night, the mosquitoes ate us alive. Dad's solution was for me to gather dried up cow chips and put them in five gallon buckets that were distributed at various locations inside the tent. At night, they were set on fire. His theory was that the smoke would drive off the mosquitoes and the heat from the fire would keep us warm. The mosquitoes loved the smoke and the heat, and we were still eaten alive if we left any part of our bodies exposed. With no bathing facilities, you ran around all the time smelling like cow shit smoke. After almost two weeks, mom borrowed a shovel from our neighbor *Old Charlie*, and she and I dug a hole about 5 feet deep and 3 feet by 3 feet on top. Old Charlie let us tear down a shed on his property and use the lumber to build a *shit house*. My mom was incredible; this outhouse was truly, in every respect, a work of art. The outhouse of all outhouses. She even went so far as to cut a crescent in the door. You could both see and feel her smile as she admired her work. It was first class, a two seater, one hole for grownups and a smaller one for the kids. There was even a holder on the wall for the Sears & Roebuck catalog. Keep in mind that mom was 8 ½ months pregnant with what was to be her 12th child, while doing all this work.

Dad had found a job at a garage up the road on the corner of Crane Road and Highway 108. There was also a small grocery store which made it handy for me to walk there and purchase essential food items (when we had money). Dad started drinking again, and even at 10 years old I could see what was coming. I got up in the morning, did my chores, and got the hell out of there. Hitchhiking or walking, I went back to my old haunts and wandered around Oakdale until the Plunge, our city swimming pool, opened. I know I was ragged and looked like crap, but the pool offered me the only opportunity to wash off that horrid cow manure smell. The pool was owned and operated by the City of Oakdale and supervised by Deana Giovannoni. She, in my eyes, was one of the most wonderful ladies I've ever known. Well, of course I had no money, and despite my previous successes at earning a few cents here and there, I was flat busted and no prospects of earning a penny. It cost $0.10 to get into the pool. I would just stand around at the entrance and hope someone would pay my way in. After an hour or two Deana would eventually feel sorry for me and say "Come on in, but don't you tell anyone I let you in for free." That went on all summer until the pool closed for the winter. She would also, on occasion, provide me with a free hot dog or give me something special she brought from home.

\* \* \*

I think it was about June 25th when I returned to the tent from my wanderings, no mom only my little brother and three sisters, and some lady I had never seen before. "Where is my mom?" I asked. The lady informed me that my dad had taken her to the hospital in town to have a baby. In my mind I mulled the question, "What in the world did we need with another baby when we could not take care of the kids we had?" Well in a couple of days, Mom was back with my new brother and her last child, James Alan Clark, DOB 6-26-1947. Within just a few days she was back working just as hard as in the past. There were a lot of farms around our neighborhood, so

Mom would glean fruit and vegetables where she could find them and not get in trouble for helping herself. Old Charlie had a nice vegetable garden, and he knew our situation, so he would bring us fresh vegetables and sometimes home canned items. We got by, but barely. Late one afternoon in July, I came home after my wanderings in Oakdale and from swimming at the Plunge, and Mom informed me to stay home the next day. "Why," I asked, "are we going to have company?" "No," she replied, "we are moving." "Awe Mom, you have to be kidding." My stomach just turned into a knot. "But why?" I pleaded. She said the Sheriff had come by with some papers and said we had two days to move. Apparently, Dad had not made a single $25.00 payment on the purchase of the property, so we were being evicted. The next day my brother Marvin was there in his little 34 Dodge and a small pull trailer. We loaded everything into the car and trailer, although there was not much to load. Mattress on top of the car, tie it down, same old routine I had witnessed for what seemed like the hundredth time. I told Mom I was not going. She had previously told me where we were moving to. It was on the corner of Old Stockton Road and A Street in Oakdale, where the Senior Center is currently located. I knew exactly where it was because I had used that route to the river many times when I went hunting along the river with Shorty and my trusty .22 caliber rifle. I called Shorty, and he and I just wandered off toward town. There was no one there at the time to stop me. When we got to Crane Road, about half a mile from home, we took a left and headed north to the river, a place I loved and was familiar with. I spent the day crying, feeling sorry for myself when I should have been feeling sorry for Mom and my brothers and sisters. Throwing rocks into the river, eating wild grapes, early peaches, and cherries off my secret tree, Shorty and I worked our way upstream about 4 miles and it was about six o'clock when we came to the remains of the old bridge that used to cross the river at Old Stockton Road. About a half mile up the road, that's where our new home was. I took a deep breath and headed for "home". I was starving so Mom fixed me a potted meat sandwich and a couple of apricots.

The place was not much of a home, but better than I had expected. A little shack, 20 feet by 20 feet, divided into two rooms. It did have electricity and running water, but no toilet. I wondered how dad was going to pay the rent, and how long before we were on the move again. The shack sat at the edge of a large olive orchard that ran almost to the river. There were trees to hide behind while you relieved yourself. I knew it would not be long before Mom and I would be digging a place for the new toilet. Mom would not be as helpful, having just had a baby, nor would she be as cheerful or have as much fun as when we built the toilet together on Mondo Lane. She was tired, both physically and emotionally. She worried about us kids more than anything else.

We scrounged up a bunch of wood from down the street at Lee Jones's pipe yard where they manufactured irrigation pipe. In a couple of days, and with Mom's help, we had a new toilet. A few days later, here came dad pulling the most god awful looking trailer house anyone had ever seen. Somewhere he came up with a 20-foot implement trailer flat bed. He had framed it with 2x4s, cut the tent into pieces, and used them to cover the framing. It had one little canvas door and no windows. He put this monstrosity in the orchard about 20 feet from the shack and facing A Street. I thought, "What a piece of shit. Who in this world would ever want something that ugly on their property, much less want to live in it." Dad put his hand on my shoulder, big smile on his face, proud as a peacock and announced to me, "Frankie, this is going to be your very own room." "Holy shit (excuse me grandma)," I told my dad. "You have to be kidding." He got very red faced and said, "After all my hard work to make this for you, and you don't even appreciate it?" "Appreciate it? Dad, I hate it!" I called Shorty, and it was off to the river for the day. Dad did not come around for a week, but when he did, I got the surprise of my life. He presented me with a brand-new Daisy air rifle BB gun. How do you rationalize that? We were dead broke, little or no food, no job, no public assistance. I mean things had never been leaner, and he showed up with a new BB gun, go figure!

\* \* \*

Dad was now gone more than he was ever at home. It was the middle of summer, and I was sleeping in that dammed trailer. Scared to death of monsters under the trailer and in the orchard, I was indeed frightened. I kept the door locked, although, that would not keep someone out. The scariest thing was having to walk out into the night to go to the bathroom. I was hot, sweaty, and stunk. Oh, for a shower or bathtub. Deana was gone from the pool, so I could not use my old tricks. Thank God I had the river, but it could be extremely dangerous that time of the year. Still along with Shorty, I went down by the bridge as often as possible, jumped in, and washed off some of the grime. Fortunately, I was an excellent swimmer. Shorty swam beside me to ward off the giant sturgeons.

* * *

It had been a long summer, Dad came and went, and I had no idea if he was working or not, but I knew he was still drinking. Mom was doing her best to care for all of us kids. Thank God for that BB gun. I must have killed a thousand robins out in the olive orchard. Mom very meticulously picked them, separating the legs and breasts. She would then mix the meat with rice and that was our supper on many occasions. I still frequented the river, but you cannot kill much with the BB gun. I would long for my .22 caliber rifle. I still caught a fish occasionally, and would bring that home to cook. Thank goodness for beans and cornbread, or we would have starved to death. The straw that broke the camel's back was one night, mom fried potatoes for dinner and that was all. The next night she fried the peelings from the potatoes of the previous night. She was so apologetic and in tears that she could not do more. I honestly cannot remember what the little kids were eating, especially little baby Jimmy. That night, as I lay in my bed in that damned trailer, I decided I would run away the next day. I was feeling sorrier for myself than I was for Mom or the other kids. I left the house with my BB gun the next morning and headed for the highway. When I came to the river bridge, I decided to walk across the railroad trestle rather than the bridge. I stopped midway across the trestle sat down and began crying. The thought entered my mind to just jump and go to heaven. After all, that was supposed to be a pretty good place. Sitting there, meditating (thank goodness no trains came), I came to the realization that things could not get any worse. Well, if that was in fact the case, that meant that they had to get better. Pretty good thinking process for a 10-year-old. Who could I turn to?

When we lived on Third Street, I did in fact have a special friend. His name was Larry Macken, my age, and he lived down the street at First and Poplar Streets. When our family moved to Stockton, we kind of lost track of each other. His father was a real estate broker, and his mom stayed at home, but was very active in the community. I left the trestle and wandered over to the Macken home to see Larry, but he was at a Boy Scout meeting. His mom, Myra, was home, and she invited me in with a big hug and such an enthusiastic greeting as anyone ever got. She was a former Olympic track star, a school teacher, and a very educated woman. She took the time to offer me something to eat. I am sure she had never seen anyone gulp food down so fast. She patiently began to draw out where I had been for so long, how my mom and dad were, where we were living, and so on. After hearing my story and watching me cry, she could not believe anyone in Oakdale had to live that way. She called some other lady on the phone who soon arrived at the house. I am sorry, but I cannot recall her name. Larry arrived home shortly, and he genuinely seemed very happy to see me. His mom and the lady put us in the car, and she said, "Frankie, I want you to show us where you live." I was so embarrassed I wanted to die, but we drove over to *the shack* and *my room*. Mrs. Macken and the lady were appalled when they saw where we lived. They insisted on stopping and talking to my mom while we boys stayed in the car. When they came out, Mrs. Macken was shaking her head in disbelief. She drove off leaving me there. It was about two hours later when Mrs. Macken returned. I had never seen so much food except at the grocery store. Box after box of groceries, keep in mind we had no refrigeration so everything had to be nonperishable. Throughout that fall, someone, thanks to Mrs. Macken and her friends, was always dropping off something in the way of food. If there was any food left over from a Lions Club or Odd Fellows event, it ended up at our house. That's why you have to love Oakdale.

* * *

In the summer, all of us kids went barefooted and usually got new shoes at the start of school. Well, school was starting, and I had no shoes. How my mom did it? How she sometimes would come up with money was beyond me. She gave me $4.00 and sent me to town to buy school shoes. There was a new clothing store that had just opened up next to the bowling alley. The man seemed so nice. He showed me some nice shoes, but they were out of my price range. He put his hand on my head and said, "Son, I can see you do not have a lot of money, so I am going to give you a special deal" (there's that word again I thought to myself). He said, "I am going to sell you two pairs of shoes for the price of one. Give me the $4.00, and they are yours." "Now that is a deal!" I thought to myself. When I got home, I was ecstatic. I knew mom must have been so proud of me. Everything was going better than it had in a long time. School started, and I was off to the sixth grade.

Unfortunately, the first rains came early that year. I looked in total disbelief. As I took off my "new" shoes that first rainy day, I noticed the soles were coming apart. That dirty son of a bitch had sold me cardboard shoes! Mom and I walked down to the store to complain and hopefully get our money back. The store was empty, and there was a *Closed* sign in the front window. Mrs. Macken came to the rescue again; Larry and I wore the same sized shoes. Revenge can be sweet sometimes, and you never know when you are going to get it. I never forgot that guy. Years later after I had become a police officer in Modesto, I stopped a car and the driver was intoxicated. Well, guess who? I had never forgotten! "Are you still selling shoes?" I asked the bastard. "What are you talking about?" he replied. "Oh nothing," as I drove off with him in route to the county jail. And while we were gone, someone let the air out of all four of his shoes, oh, I mean tires…I do not know who did that, but I did smile.

* * *

It was October and about 3:00 p.m. I was walking home from school which was about 1 ½ miles from home. Walking past the Odd Fellows cemetery, I saw a strange car in front of our house with a small trailer attached. There were two mattresses on top of the car and several boxes in the trailer along with some chairs. My first thought was, "Who in the heck is moving in with us, and where are they going to sleep." When I got into the house, there was Dad, and Mom was crying. Then it hit me like a bolt out of the blue. It could not be; we were moving! I was back in school, had rejoined my friends, and even had a girlfriend. Things were pretty good, and I thought I saw light at the end of the tunnel. I was just short of 11 years old and maturing fast. I was far ahead of most kids my age when it came to being street smart and capable of analyzing human situations. The landlord had not been receiving his rent, so once again we were facing eviction. I was storming around the house, inside and out, trying to determine what the hell was going on. I was not getting answers; I was frustrated. Dad was finished loading, and we were ready to leave. "Where is Shorty?" I asked. My dad said not to worry, Shorty was taken care of. "What the hell (I had not lost my vocabulary of swear words despite Grandma's admonishment) does that mean dad? Did you shoot him, take him to the pound? Where is he?!" I demanded. Dad finally said that a friend of his was going to take care of Shorty until we could come back and get him. "Bullshit!" I exclaimed, "Just like Stockton. You are going to go off and

leave him." Dad raised his voice and said, "Get in the car."
"No," I replied, "I am not going anywhere without my dog.
You have no business stealing my dog." Dad moved toward
me in an aggressive manner, and crying I got into the car.
Soon we were headed north, and I thought, "Oh God, please
not Stockton again."

Dad explained that we were headed for Richmond where
his brother Hershel, and my oldest brother Marvin lived. We
were moving into the Richmond Housing Authority. What
was the "Authority"? During WW II, the government built
hundreds of barrack-like buildings to house workers employed
in the shipyards and other federal facilities. They were two-
story, five units on the top and five on the bottom. Some were
one bedrooms, others two. Based on our previous housing,
they were pretty neat. Two bedrooms, an indoor toilet, heating,
running water, and electricity. While not happy being there, I
was so very pleased with accommodations. Dad found a job,
was not drinking, and came home on a regular basis. Other
than missing Shorty, I was temporarily pretty happy.

The housing was segregated, Blacks on the west side
and Whites on the east side. I enrolled in the sixth grade and
immediately made some really good friends. There were
no organized sports like we have today. No little league or
anything close. We kids went around the business areas in
Point Richmond and asked the merchants to support our
little baseball team. Shock Electric came along and agreed
to provide us with bats and balls, our team name: Shock's
Shockers. Soon the word got out, and we were playing other

teams that had been formed much in the same manner, no adult coaches, no adult umpires, just us kids: Joel Spinola, Don Washburn, and Don Love, just to mention a few players I can remember. We had a lot of fun and comradery. Don Washburn lived right on "the point" at Point Richmond. His father was an executive with Standard Oil. Their house was a palace. Three levels, a walkway that went out to a gazebo overlooking the bay, a maid. I could not even begin to fathom the luxury I was being exposed to. I know I liked it and was determined from that point on to someday be wealthy, healthy, and prosperous. Thank you, Don. The Washburn's also had a very nice little house at Stenson Beach, on the coast, right on the beach. I had the privilege of being invited there on three occasions. Crabbing, swimming, fishing, lots and lots of good stuff to eat. I had no idea that anything as opulent as this even existed. It really opened my eyes to the world. Then I would come back to their house on the point and walk back to the project. What a different world!

* * *

Where was Shorty? I dreamed of him often.
Was he even alive? God, I missed him.

* * *

You could walk through the "tunnel" in Point Richmond, and then the landscape spread out along the north side of the bay. I had applied for, and received permission, to sell vegetable and flower seeds for the American Seed Company. They sent me the seeds, and I went door to door selling them. I got no money but could pick out rewards depending on how many packages of seeds I sold. Anyway, one of my most precious rewards was a professional rod and reel from Berkeley. It was probably worth $25.00 to $35.00, and it was my most prized possession. I would wander out to the bay every weekend and fish. I got a lot of free lunches from other fishermen, who sat and fished from the shore, and a great education about people. Once I caught my biggest fish ever, a 25lb. sting ray, only to learn they were not edible and I had to turn it loose.

Near where we lived was a moth ball fleet of navy transport ships. They were huge and anchored where I liked to fish. Once, I managed to climb over the fence and actually get on board. It was scary, but to go into the control room and think about this ship and where it might have been and what action it might have been through was stimulating. I was usually pretty apprehensive and could not wait to get back to dry land. I caught a lot of fish, and mom was the very best fish fryer you could ever find.

* * *

Well, it was not long until the devil was back. Dad was on the bottle again. Everything went to hell. Pretty soon, no food, no money, no nothing. Then a little miracle happened. At the end of our complex was the only pay phone in the neighborhood. One day while checking the coin slot, I saw a loose wire behind the phone. This was not easily spotted but I saw it. I took the phone off of the receiver and hoped maybe a dime would drop into the coin return. Nothing, as usual. Then, phone in hand, I dialed operator and shorted the mysterious wire against the phone housing. Jing-a-ling!!! It was like a Las Vegas slot machine; the coins just poured out. I scooped up all $6.50 and rushed home to mom. She started giving me that old lecture about honesty. "Mom," I said, "there are ten million pay phones out there, and they are not going to miss this little handful of coins." This went on for several weeks before the phone company got wise and repaired the phone. We may not have gotten through without it.

* * *

Standing by the Key bus stop one afternoon, this very large Black lady stepped from the bus. She had four bags of groceries and had to make a return trip inside the bus to get all the bags. Obviously she could not carry this many bags. "Did you see any little colored boys around here?" she asked. "No ma'am," I replied, "but I will help you carry these bags if you want." "Why bless your heart young man. I would appreciate it." I had never ventured into that part of the neighborhood. As a matter of fact, I had never seen a Black person besides old Shorty at the shoe shine stand until I moved to Richmond. Well, I walked her home carrying two bags of groceries. When we got there, all these Black kids came out, and I mean she lit into them. "Where were your little Black asses at the bus stop? This little White boy came along and helped me.

Guess what? I am giving him your allowances, and you can go without for a week." Well, I had seen these kids, all about my age, at the school I attended. I thought that potentially I could be in trouble come the next day. Sure enough at recess they cornered me behind the cafeteria and I was scared shitless. "White boy, we are going to give you a whippin' you won't forget. Don't be fuckin' around with our folks or in our neighborhood." I had never been so frightened. Around the corner came this big Black guy. Anyway, he was bigger than any of us by a good margin. "What's going on brothers?" he asked. "We are about to whip this Whitey's ass and teach him to mind his own business." He spoke to the Black kids, "Come here, come her, and gather around..." This guy was Nu Nu Jackson. He was 15 years old, been in the sixth grade three years. "...You guys fucked up yesterday when you failed to meet my mom at the bus stop, right? he asked. They nodded their heads in agreement. "Now let me tell you, if anyone of you black-assed little bastards even say a nasty word to this little White boy, you will answer to me. Come on Whitey let's get out of here." I never, ever had a bit of trouble after that. Years later, I read where Nu Nu had become a fairly prominent middle weight boxer in the Bay Area.

\* \* \*

I loved baseball more than anything besides mom. The Shock's Shockers became quite a team, even mentioned a couple of times in the newspaper. The City of Richmond started a league for kids that spring and we were part of that.

I really looked forward to playing in a league. There was a man and his wife who lived several "barracks" away. He had a real interest in baseball and in some way we connected. I was 11 years old when he came up with a catcher's glove and invited me to play catch with him. Well, this went on for a few weeks, and I was really doing well under his tutelage, catching curve balls, fast balls, and all. I was pretty darn good. He took me to an adult league game, and the catcher on one of the teams became injured. He then volunteered me to take the injured players place. Hey I was eleven and these guys were grownups. Well, I got behind the plate and put on the catcher's mask. The chest protector would not fit so that was out. I caught four innings, batted once, got a walk, and finished out the game. I had not been this scared since Nu Nu saved my ass.

The coach approached mom with a deal that was too good to refuse. He told her that he has connections in Hollywood, and if she will agree to let him take me to Hollywood, he thinks he can make a child star out of me. I was not stupid, but I was interested. After all, I was in love with Margaret O'Brian. So, Mom said no, not a good idea. Thanks, Mom. A few days later the coach and I were playing catch at his place, and he invited me into his apartment for a coke, and then into the bedroom where he pulled out a condom (looked like a balloon to me). He started to explain safe sex to me and unwrapped the condom. I was starting to get edgy and asked to go get a drink of water. I was out the front door and never looked back. Despite his frequently dropping by looking for me, I never saw him again.

\* \* \*

Things at home got worse. It was early February 1949, and Dad was really into the booze. He came home one night, from where, I had no idea. He began to get on Mom's case about a bunch of irrelevant things. Mom started to cry, and I stood up and told Dad that enough was enough. He told me to mind my own business. I told him, "Mom IS my business." He got up and left. A week went by, and we had not heard from Dad, nor had any idea where he might have been. Mom checked around and none of the relatives had seen or heard from him. It appeared as though he had just disappeared off the face of the earth. Our family would not see or hear from my dad for the next 11 years. There is one exception to the previous statement. Dad sent my mom a post card addressed to my uncle Hershel's address in Richmond that was post marked March 2, 1949, Dallas, Texas. He was asking that my uncle go to a pawn shop, and tell them to hold his tools he had pawned. He did not say hello, kiss my ass, I love you, I am sorry, or how are you doing? Nothing. He was only concerned with his damned tools. I think Mom kept his location a secret all those years because she feared the County would go after him, and we would lose our entitlements. There was no Dad, no magic phone booth, no money, and no food. There was nothing. We were at the bottom.

Mom went to the Contra Costa County welfare department and asked for assistance. She filled out all of the paperwork only to find out we had not lived in the county long enough to get aid; however, the welfare authorities, God bless them, were willing to contact the welfare department in Modesto and see if we would qualify there because we came from Oakdale, Stanislaus County. In the meantime, they gave us enough money to purchase some food items that would last us one week. Within just a few days, we received word that we would be accepted back in Stanislaus County, and arrangements had been made for us to live in housing at White's Cabins in Oakdale. That weekend, my brother Marvin's in-laws had us all loaded up, miscellaneous junk in the trailer, and of course, and the infamous mattress on top of the car and headed down the road for Oakdale, which I hoped would be our very last move.

* * *

From the time I was born, 1937, to this move back to Oakdale, 1949, our family had moved a total of 20 times. Now those were short roots. White's Cabins were located on a two-acre site on Pederson Road in south east Oakdale, approximately 10 cabins of various sizes and design. Ours is very small, about the size of the place on A Street and Old Stockton Road. There was running water and electricity, but no heat or hot water. It was spring, so luckily we did not need it. The restrooms, including men's and women's showers, were outside and used by all inhabitants of the facility. There were also laundry facilities with washers that you paid $0.35 a load to use. Mom got the mattress settled in one of the rooms which was about 10' x 10'. She slept on a small cot on one side of the room with my little brother Jim while the rest of us five kids slept lying crossways on the mattress. The old standby coal oil two burner stove went up against the wall in the other 10' x 10' room, along with a table and four broken down old chairs. We were settled in. The very first thing on my agenda was to find Shorty. Mom swore she had no idea what Dad did with him, and I believed her. I promised myself I would find him no matter where he was or how long it took.

Our cabin at White's Cabins, Oakdale, CA 1949

\* \* \*

The White's place was clean and neat, and all of the cabins were occupied. Almost all of the occupants were out of work, looking for work, or on welfare. Mom somehow made her way to Modesto and got us signed up for welfare, made arrangements to pick up commodities at Wood Park in downtown Oakdale, and got a $25.00 a month county charge account for meat at Pigg's Market, next door to the H-B. The next day, she walked the two miles to Magnolia School and got Freddie, Sue, and I enrolled in school. Freddie and Sue went to Eastside School, which at that time occupied the whole block where Ryderz restaurant is currently located.

I enrolled in the sixth grade at Magnolia School. I immediately met a lot of my old friends including Larry Macken. I got a free lunch every day, I loved school, and I had not been this happy in a long time. Come Friday at 4:00 p.m., Mom and I made our way down to Wood Park to get our commodities, delivered to us from the back of a two-ton truck covered with a tarp. Potatoes, rice, corn meal, flour, beans, powdered milk, sugar, and lard. There were several other families there, but I did not recognize anyone. There was no way the two of us could cart all of this stuff two miles back to the cabin. While we were standing there, contemplating our situation, a 34 Dodge pickup drove by, made a U-turn, and came back. An old man got out (he looked old to me) and approached my mom. "Aren't you Dave Clark's wife?" he asked. "Why yes!" my mom replied. He introduced himself as Al Sipe and asked if we remember him from the hardware store across the street from our old house on Third Street. Of course we did.

"Well, where is old Dave," he inquired. Without going into a lot of detail, Mom explained he had left her, and we were living at White's Cabins on Pederson Road. He offered us a ride, and I got into the back of the pickup. "This is cool," I thought. He dropped us off, but not before I asked him if he could pick us up next month when we get groceries again. He laughed and said, "Probably not. You still got that lawn mower son? he asked. "No, sir," I replied, "We went off and left it at the house when we moved." "Your name is Pinky, isn't it?" I said, "Not any more. I am grown up now. You can call me Frankie, if you please sir." "Okay, Frankie it is," and off he drove.

The next day was Saturday, and early in the morning Mr. Sipe was at our front door. Beside him, he was pulling a Radio Flyer red wagon. "I have been trying to sell this wagon for years, and nobody wants to buy it. I guess it just isn't worth much. Tell you what, I will give this wagon to you and your mom, and you can haul your groceries home in it. That way I won't have to worry about giving you a ride." Only in Oakdale could this happen. "Mr. Sipe, do you know what a deal is?" I politely asked. "Yes, I think so," he said. "Well here is the deal. If you will accept it, we will take the wagon (I am the man of the house, so I can make deals), and when I have the money, I will buy the wagon from you for $3.00, deal?" Mr. Sipe stared at me briefly, kind of shook his head, extended his hand, and we shook. That same fall, I got a job at Oakdale Feed and Seed and did in fact pay Mr. Sipe. A month later, Mom, with me pulling my little red wagon, were headed back to Wood Park to get our monthly commodities. I hated this trip more than anyone could imagine. I was ashamed that we had to be on the dole, embarrassed, and hoping anyone we knew wouldn't see us. I silently made a pledge to myself that when I grew up I would never be on welfare or ask anyone to help me in anyway. To this very day, almost 70 years later, I still do not like to ask people to do much for me. I will accept their help, but I do not ask for it.

Things changed, and I thought we would only make about two more trips to the commodity truck when the county welfare began sending you a monthly check and did away with the commodity truck and Pigg's Market. They were also paying our rent to the Whites. I made lifelong friends with the White boys, Ralph, 21; Richard, 14; Roger, 11; Vernon, 9; and Eddie, 7. Ralph had very recently married and was living in a house he built over by the cemetery on J Street. The boy's father had passed away just months before we moved in, and Mrs. White was showing signs of dementia. The boys were really good, respectable kids, and despite having little or no supervision, they got along and helped out as much as possible. There was no garbage pickup at the cabins, so we put our garbage in a five-gallon bucket, just outside the front door, and Richard came by once a week to pick it up. He would then walk out into the field just south of the cabins and feed it to some pigs that lived in an enclosure. Any other trash was taken to an adjoining pit and tossed in to be burned at some time in the future.

\* \* \*

School was soon out and summer began. All of us boys were outside from daylight to dark playing baseball, football, basketball, or wandering off to the river to swim, fish or shoot birds with our homemade sling shots. On one occasion while at the river, we chose sides and decided to have a sling shot war. I think there were four kids on each side. Slings shots can be close to lethal, and if you have ever been shot by one you know what I mean. Rules were no shots above the arm pits. Try telling a bunch of kids how that's possible. Most of the kids were shooting rocks but some had access to more modern ammunition: marbles. They were more accurate than a misshapen rock. Well one of the boys, I think Joe Nunes, got hit right in the forehead. He was out like a light, and we could not get him to come around. Finally, he woke up, but he was goofy as all get out. In those days, there was no such thing as an emergency room, but there was a hospital just above the river at the west end of Walnut Avenue, maybe a mile from where we were. We were frightened, but Richard and I agreed to take him to the hospital to be checked out. Luckily, Doc Miller (Dr. W. D. Miller) was there and agreed to take a look at Joe, who was starting to come to his senses. Doc Miller examined him, decided he would probably be okay, and sent us on our way. No paper work, no bill, like it never happened. Those were the good old days.

That summer at the White Cabins was a bad time for all of us kids. There was an enormous fig tree just outside our front door that we loved to climb in and throw green figs at the kids on the ground below. My younger brother Freddie, who was about 7 years old, was at the highest point in the tree, and he fell. We thought he broke every bone in his body. The ambulance crew did not expect him to survive, but he was one tough little rascal. They rushed him to the local hospital, and the doctors there said they could not help him, so he was transferred to the Stanislaus County Hospital in Modesto. He slowly began to recover. Concussion, two broken legs, broken collar bone, broken arm, he was a mess. He spent the whole summer in the hospital. Mom went to see him as often as possible. She had to walk two miles to the bus depot, ride the bus to Modesto, and walk two miles to the hospital where she spent the day. I would watch the four kids at home until she returned late in the afternoon. Freddie came home at summer's end, none the worse for wear.

* * *

The White boys' fortunes took a tailspin for the worse. According to Richard, his father ran up some rather large medical bills prior to his passing. Everything but the house they lived in was sold to cover those medical expenses. His mother's dementia got worse, and Richard was left with responsibilities of trying to keep everything together. Remember he was only 14 or 15 years old. To make matters worse, the mother had a severe stroke and eventually was placed in the Stockton State Hospital, formally named the Stockton State Insane Asylum, where she passed away a few years later. Mom and our family moved out of the White's Cabins at the end of the summer. I will cover that a little later.

Richard and Roger joined the service, leaving only Vernon and Eddie at the house. My aunt and uncle Myrtie and Bob Crum bought the White place in 1955, but I am not sure if the cabins went with the deal. Eddie and Vernon left, moving in with a family out on Orange Blossom Road for about a year before they moved back to the house with my aunt and uncle. In 1959, my aunt and uncle sold the place. Vernon joined the Navy, and Eddie moved in with Richard and his wife, Shirley. Through just plain hard work and determination, Eddie finished high school and ended up playing college football. He went on to become a very prominent citizen and businessman in the Northern California area. Richard retired from Hunt Wesson Foods and moved to Tennessee. Roger worked for a large lumber company in Washington and retired a few years back. Vernon got out of the service and later retired from the City of Oakdale, public works department. Richard was, and has remained, my very best friend after all of these years. His family played a very prominent role in our family's life, and continues to do so.

* * *

On June 10, 1949, my mother got a strange letter addressed to our P. O. Box 835. The letter read:

*Dear Mrs. Clark,*

*My helpers tell me you are a very deserving mother of 12, with 7 children under 15 years of age. I understand that your husband has deserted you and that you are being evicted from your two room cabin. My helper tells me that if you had a down payment on a lot, or had any money at all, that your good neighbors would pitch in and build you a place to live in. That's a wonderful spirit, and to help it along---to fan the flame, so to speak---I'm enclosing a check for a hundred dollars.*

*Don't worry – the check is good. Just put it through at any bank, then the bank will check with my bank in Hollywood, and in a few days you'll get your money.*

*Tell your neighbors about it. I think they'll come through--- because, Mrs. Clark, there are a lot of Santa Clauses in the world.*

*Good luck,*
*Santa Claus*

June 10, 1949

Gladys Clark
PO Box 835
Oakdale, Calif.

Dear Mrs. Clark;

My helpers tell me that you are a very
deserving mother of 12, with 7 children under 15 years
of age. I understand that your husband has deserted
you and that you are being evicted from your two room
cabin. My helper tells me that if you had a down payment
on a lot, or had any money at all, that your good neighbors
would pitch in and build you a place to live in. That's
a wonderful spirit, and to help it along---to fan the flame,
so to speak---I'm enclosing a check for a hundred dollars.

Don't worry - the check is good. Just put
it through at any bank, then the bank will check with my
bank in Hollywood, and in a few days you'll get your money.

Tell your neighbors about it. I think they'll come through---
because, Mrs. Clark, there are a lot of Santa Clauses in the
world.

Good luck

*Santa Claus*

Santa Claus

Mom took the check to the bank downtown, and in a few days, they contacted her to come in and pick up the money. Well the word got out, and pretty soon several people contacted Mom, offering her assistance in finding a new home. Sometime in August a vacant lot was found at 351 South Fifth Street that was for sale, and Mom purchased it. My brother Marvin and his new bride Johnnie had been living in a trailer house in the Bay Area while he went to college. Having recently moved into an apartment, they no longer had any use for the trailer. Marvin towed the trailer to Mom's new lot and set it up, running west to east. Someone contacted Mom saying they had an old sheepherder's trailer on skids that she could have, and they were willing to deliver it. So, that got tied into the trailer, running north and south. It had a toilet and bathtub in it. We were moving up! Mr. Schiernbeck volunteered to hook up the electricity and Mr. Zakel to do the plumbing, if I would dig the trench from the trailer to the street. I did so under his supervision, and soon we were moving in.

There was no heat in the place, and I slept in the sheepherder's trailer. Mom and the five other kids were in the other trailer. It served as the kitchen, and Mom cooked on the old 2 burner coal oil stove. It wasn't long, and I am sorry I do not know who, but someone came along and poured a foundation in front of the sheepherder's trailer, framed it, put a roof on it, and Bingo! we had a living room. A few weeks later, Ralph White and some other gentlemen came over, and on the backside of the herder's trailer they poured a foundation, framed it, and on went a roof and now we had a kitchen and dining area. The old two burner coal oil stove was replaced by a nice antique cast iron wood burning cook stove, oven and all. By far the best place we had lived in in a long time. The gentleman who sent mom the $100.00 was correct; there were indeed lots of Santa Clauses. Life went on. Someone donated a refrigerator, delivered and installed it. First time my mom had ever had one. Cold Kool-Aid, homemade popsicles, iced tea, leftovers, and Mom made homemade ice cream in the ice trays.

Sheepherder's cabin and a house trailer, 352
South Fifth Street, Oakdale, CA in 1949

\* \* \*

I continued to work at Oakdale Feed and Seed, cleaning up around the store and unloading sacks of feed from rail cars. I was often called to help vaccinate chickens and turkeys, and clean out chicken pens. That was the worst job ever. You went into this long low silhouette building that has housed a zillion chickens who were being raised commercially. The floor was six inches thick with manure, which had dried out over the summer. You were given a shovel and a wheel barrow, fill the wheel barrow, wheel it outside, and dump it in a big pile. No respirator, face mask, nothing. The dust was unbearable, getting in your nostrils, eyes, and you could hardly breathe. This went on for a couple of weeks, but $0.35 an hour was better than nothing for a 12-year-old. Then there was force feeding sick turkeys, helping milk cows, picking peaches; I was never out of work very long in the summer. I almost always had a little pocket change. Mom was taking in ironing and also cleaning two or three houses in Oakdale, plus getting a little welfare stipend; so, while most people may have felt sorry for us, by our standards, we were pretty rich.

Next door to our house was a creamery. They processed milk and dairy products for home delivery. I think it was called the Oakdale Creamery and owned by a fellow named Gerald Clifton. I helped out over there periodically, and he paid me in dairy products, which was great to have fresh milk instead of that damned powdered variety. It was a particularly cold winter that year and we kids and my mom also, I am sure, were freezing to death in those two trailers which had no heat. Before we went to bed a night, mom would take her solid steel irons and heat them on the wood burning stove, then wrap them in towels or newspapers and put them in bed with us. They were life savers. Across the street from us, covering the entire block, was the Kaufman Brother's lumber processing plant. They took whole logs and cut them into lumber. We got all the scrap wood we needed, so fuel for the old stove was never a problem. Eventually, someone gave us a nice little wood burning potbellied stove that fit nicely into the living room. When we fired that little guy up before we went to bed, it kept us real cozy all night. Life just kept getting better.

In mid-October, Richard, Roger, and I were coming back from the river after unsuccessfully trying to spear salmon. We kept our spears hidden along the river. As we walked past the intersection of A Street and Yosemite Avenue, I happened to glance into the fenced yard on the corner. "Holy shit!" There was Shorty in the yard. I climbed over the fence, he recognized me immediately, jumped all over me, started yelping, licking me, and I was going nuts with joy. This man came out of the house and demanded to know what the hell I was doing in his yard with his dog. He was nasty! I went off the handle. Roger and Richard just stood there with their mouths open, as they knew nothing about the history of my dog Shorty. I was pissed. "Bullshit mister! That's my dog, and I am taking him with me." He grabbed me and said, "We will see about that young man. Mom," he yelled at the lady in the house, "call the police, and have them come down here." That did not scare me at all. "Fine," I said, "just let go of my arm." Shorty started to growl at him, which he could not believe. Well, guess who showed up in about 15 minutes, none other than Chief Dorrah. "What's going on here?" he inquired. "This little shit is trying to steal my dog." "Is that true, Frankie?" the Chief asked.

"That's my dog Mr. Dorrah, don't you remember giving us a ride home with the watermelon some time back?" The Chief scratched his head and said, "By golly, I do remember that." The Chief was, in many ways, a pretty wise old guy. "Tell you both what, we will put the dog over here by the tree, and both of you call him, and the one he goes to probably is the one he wants to be with and more than likely is the owner." "By the way," the Chief asked the man, "how did you come to own this dog?" The man replied, "About two years ago, an acquaintance of mine, Dave Clark, came by and asked if I would like to have this little dog. Well, our dog had been run over a few weeks before that, so we said yes." "Are you kidding me?!" I thought.

In Shorty's previous life with me I had taught him several tricks, nothing fancy, just some simple commands like roll over, stay, sit, fetch, stand, and to jump into my arms. So, the gears were really turning in my head. How do I stack the deck on this guy? Then the light went on. I called Shorty over by the tree and told him to sit. I knew he would not move until I said, "Okay." "I tell you what mister, to be fair, you call the dog first." He called, "Come here." The dog did not budge. He yelled at the dog, but he was still as a rock. Mr. Dorrah says, "Okay Frankie, your turn." I knew Shorty would not move until I gave the magic word, which I had done hundreds of times in the distant past. I looked at Shorty, and repeated the word, "Sit." He did not move a muscle. Then I said, "Okay!" He was off like a rocket, and without command, he jumped into my arms almost knocking me over licking me to death. "That's good enough for me," said the Chief. "Now, Frankie, you and your dog go along, and I will stay and have a conversation with this gentleman." I made it back home with Shorty, and it was a great family reunion for him with Mom, and all of the kids. I was not cold at night anymore with Shorty sleeping on the bed at my feet.

Training Shorty to stay

\* \* \*

I could never figure out just how mom managed to buy the property on Fifth Street with only $100.00 (two trailers), nor how she came up with the money to buy our house on Fourth Street a few years later. After lots of research at the County and old micro films at American Title, I put it all together. Mom purchased the lot on Fifth Street in October 1949 with the $100.00 from Santa Claus. In October 1953, Mom sold the property on Fifth Street to Carl and Dorothy Hofmann for $500.00. On November 27, 1953, she put down $100.00 on the house at 461 South Fourth Street, with a promise to pay another $400.00 within 30 days. Total purchase price: $3,900. Her payments were to be $40.00 a month until the house was paid off at 6.5% interest. The house on South Fourth Street had belonged to a member of mom's church, and her name was Polly Thomas. She told mom that if she ever had trouble making the payment, not to worry about it; she could just catch up later. Mom did in fact pay off the property in June 1963. The property consisted of four lots, and ran along the north side of J Street, from Fourth to Fifth Street. Mom sold the two back lots in 1965 for $1,000. In 1990, she sold the house and the two lots it sat on for $55,000 and moved into a senior housing project near Oak Valley Hospital. I would say she made a pretty good investment.

About the time we moved into the house on Fifth Street, Mom began going to the Pentecostal church on South Sierra Street. Previous to this, she had never mentioned or participated in religion in any fashion that I am aware of. Pure speculation on my part, but I believed that she did in fact pray to the Lord that somehow he could help us out of the mess we were in when we moved into the White's Cabins. Well, her prayers were answered on a gradual basis, and things did in fact get much better. There is no question she attributed our betterment in life to the Lord, and from that point on she devoted her life to Jesus Christ and the Lord. Without them, as devoted to her family as she was and the tremendous effort and hard work she put forth, we all may well have not made it. Mom devoted her life to Christ until her dying breath at the age of 96 years old. Thank you, Jesus and God for all you did to support our family.

Our home at 461 South Fourth Street, Oakdale, CA, purchased by Mom

\* \* \*

Sometime in July 1949, Mom was contacted by the Lions Club of Oakdale, and they told her they had been looking for two boys to sponsor for ten days at the YMCA camp,

Camp Jack Hazard, in Dardanelles, near Sonora Pass. They had selected me and another boy, Jimmy "Lizard" Adams. A couple of weeks later, a bus picked me up near Wood Park, and I was off to the Sierras. I remember looking out the back window and seeing Mom waving good-bye, like I was never coming back. This was the first time in our lives that we had ever been separated, except maybe for overnight. This event and trip proved to be one of the most significant events of my life. Swimming, fishing, baseball, capture the flag, and crafts. Late one night a few of us decided to have some fun. We took a bucket of hot water and made our way around to the different cabins. The cabins had open sidings, and it was hot at night, so the kids usually had their arms hanging out of the sleeping bags. We stuck their hands into that warm water, and Bingo! They wet their beds. It did not work every time, but often enough for us to think it was fun. While we thought it cute and entertaining, the camp administrators had a different position on the issue. As a result, five boys with an adult counselor were sent on a back packing trip to Upper Relief Reservoir for five days. We got back to Camp Jack Hazard, just in time to return home on the bus. This warm water event opened my life to the great outdoors. From that time until I was too old to do it (70 yrs.), I was an avid backpacker and outdoorsman. I passed this on to my children and grandchildren, and as a result, had many wonderful trips into the Sierra wilderness with them.

Apparently, the YMCA forgot about the "warm water incident", and the Lions Club was not aware of it because the next year they sent me again. My younger brother Jim always said it was a conspiracy between the Lions Club and downtown merchants to get me out of town for the summer. I spent 10 days as a camper and was asked to spend an additional 20 days working in the kitchen and doing various tasks around the camp. While wandering around Camp Jack Hazard, I came upon a rather large sugar pine tree that had been involved in a fire sometime in the far distant past. The base of the tree was hollowed out and burned inside but the tree otherwise seemed healthy. I began to dig in the hollowed-out portion of the tree, much in the same manner as I had in the basement of the burned out building next door to Third and E Streets in 1942. To my amazement, I began to uncover arrow heads by the handful. When I thought I had them all, I took them to my counselor. He told me not to mention it to anyone, as they might be sacred. He took possession of them, and I never said a word. I always wondered what Native American Indian had placed them there, and how long ago before I discovered them.

* * *

Before long, summer had come and gone, and it was harvest time. Richard, Roger, and I got a job knocking almonds on Roy and Grace Little's 40-acre almond ranch on south Crane Road. It was a much different process than we use today. Mr. Little had an old one lung John Deere tractor that you started by turning a fly wheel by hand near the back of the engine. Pulled behind the tractor was a wooden trough, about ten feet long. Attached to each side of the trough was a large piece of canvas. You pulled up next to an almond tree, spread the canvas around the tree, and then with a heavy mallet with a rubber head you hit the tree, and the almonds fell from the tree onto the canvas. With a long bamboo pole you knocked any almonds remaining on the tree into the canvas. Then you rolled up the canvas and the almonds went into the trough. We usually earned enough money to purchase a pair of Levi's ($3.00) and a couple of wool shirts for school.

School started in mid-September. I was in the eighth grade and had never in my life been happier. Good grades, girlfriend, playing basketball, still working once in a while at the feed store; so, I had a little spending money. Mom was still taking in ironing, cleaning three houses, and getting a little welfare. She was a wonderful, caring mother. She made sure we got by. I bought an old shotgun from Richard White for $5.00 and became an avid hunter. Season? What is a season? I hiked south for five miles along the Sierra Railroad tracks, looking for something to shoot and eat. I killed cottontails, pheasants, ducks, geese, dove, and an occasional pigeon. There was an abundance of wild game in the Oakdale area during those years; so, being a successful hunter was pretty easy, just look out for the Indian game warden, George McGladdery. I never met the man, but he was a legend in his time.

It was early winter, and little brother Jim had a .22 rifle. He and I were hunting rabbits along the canal bank at Warnerville and Fogerty Roads. I let him shoot the rabbit if it was sitting still, and I shot it if he missed and the rabbit ran. We spotted a little cottontail sitting by the hole in the embankment. He shot and missed. The rabbit took off running; I aim and fire. What a surprise. I guess this old shotgun had seen better days because a blast of powder and fire came out of the breach and almost tore off my forehead. Blood was pouring down my face, and a good portion of my scalp was missing just above my eyes. We got the bleeding to stop, and I walked over to the cement canal crossing. With the barrel in my hand, I beat that shot gun to death, and threw it into the canal, never to be fired again by anyone. We walked the three miles home. Mom put iodine on my wound and taped it up with Band-Aids. Boy did that burn. A couple of weeks later only a small scab remained.

Come about January, we boys got a call from Mr. Little; could we help him set out "smudge pots" in the orchard for frost protection? Come the weekend, we hitchhiked out to the ranch, set out and filled smudge pots. A smudge pot was a five-gallon bucket with the top cut out but retained to use as a damper. We went through the orchard, put a bucket between each tree, and laid the lid beside it. Next, we went down the rows behind the old John Deere pulling a 1,000 gallon-tank filled with fuel oil. We filled each bucket about ¾ full of oil and put the lid on it. We were drenched in oil by the time we were done. About February when the almonds were starting to blossom, Mr. Little kept a sharp eye on the thermometer. If it looked like it was going to frost, he came into town, picked us up, took us to his ranch, and put us up in the bunk house for the night. We kids hoped it didn't frost because we were warm and cozy and Mrs. Little had fixed us a nice dinner. We just wanted to sleep until we had to get up and return to school. When the temperature got to a certain level, say 31°, this would usually be about 4 or 5 a.m. Mr. Little would wake us up. We would put on our old oily clothes and head for the orchard. He gave us a torch, and we raced through the orchard, removing the lids and lighting the oil in the buckets. He kept an eye on the temperature, and when it started to rise, he had us race back through the orchard, covering the buckets with the lid about half way. That saved oil. When he thought the danger of frost was over, we raced through the orchard again, putting the lid over the entire bucket, suppressing the fire. We were exhausted. Remember, we were only 12 to 14 years old. We changed clothes, Mrs. Little fixed us breakfast, and Mr. Little took us back to school (We hoped no one would light a match close to us). This routine went on until the frost danger was over, and it could not come soon enough for us. We had no set salary; Mr. Little just paid us what he thought is right. He was a fair man.

Winter passed. It was nearing time to graduate from grammar school (eighth grade), and to get ready to be freshmen at high school. I was a straight A student, good athlete, and well-liked by my fellow students. Mom got dressed into her best church going clothes, and walked the two miles to Magnolia School to see me graduate. I looked out into the audience and saw my mother sitting there. I was so proud of her and thankful that she was there. The ceremonies were about to conclude, and it was time to announce the male and female outstanding students. They would receive the prestigious Stanley L. Collins American Legion Award for citizenship and outstanding performance as an eighth-grade student. Marsha Sibley got the award for the female student. I could not believe my ears when the master of ceremonies called out, "Frankie Clark." At that young age, I was very modest, not like now in my old age. I looked out into the audience, and my mom was wiping away tears. I thought I might cry, but before I could, all the kids on the stage gathered around, congratulating me and patting me on the back. There was a big graduation party at one of the other kids' houses, and I was asked if I was going, but I had to say no because it was getting dark, and I wanted to walk Mom home. I think it was Barbara Garat's mother who stepped up and said she would give my mom a ride home, bring me back to the party, and take me home afterwards. I had known Barbara's mom and dad since we first came to Oakdale. They were wonderful and generous people.

I was anxiously looking forward to summer, anticipating working at the feed store and saving some money for high school. Things took a turn for the worse. Mr. Wilson sold the feed store and the new owners were not interested in having a 14-year-old kid hanging around there, working part time. Look as I might, I could not find a job doing anything. Grandma would make up work for me and pay me a quarter here, a quarter there, but that was not going to help. I picked peaches for a few days at my classmate, Jerry Marquis's orchard, but that did not last long, and I only made a few dollars. Not to get bored, I began hitchhiking out to the swimming hole east of Oakdale, about five miles right off of Highway 108/120.

The place was called Seymour's because Sid Seymour owned the land you had to cross to get to the swimming hole. Seymour's was created in the late 1930s to early 1940s on the Stanislaus River by a giant floating gold dredge. This dredge was parked for many years in a large pond at Orange Blossom and Horseshoe Roads. I remember seeing it when I was a youngster. It was eventually sold to a Canadian gold mining company that dismantled it and moved it to Canada. Anyway, the river flowed into the hole from the east and exited it on the west where the river was just a shallow rapid. The hole itself was 30 to 40 feet deep and maybe 100 yards long by 50 yards wide, and its water very dark and scary. Right near the shore, the water was 18 feet deep, actual measurement, and as you dove near the bank you could see the claw marks the dredge made as it tore into the river bank. It was macho to dive to the bottom near the shore and come up with a little gravel in your hand. At this depth, when you came up your ears were ringing and hurting like heck. Early in the summer while fishing off of a big rock on the east end of the hole, I hooked what turned out to be a fish that I at first thought was a log or a tree root. I got off of the rock and walked the fish toward the shore. Finally, after what seemed like forever, I got it to the shore where I could see it. I had been fishing on the Stanislaus River since I was six years old, and I had never seen anything like it. It was ghostly, scary, prehistoric, and frightening. It was well over 5 feet in length, and based on what I know today, I estimate that it weighed over 50 lbs. Just as I was about to get it on shore, the line broke, and it swam away. No matter how many times I told the story, no one believed me. Thereafter, when I swam across the hole to the other side, I kept my eyes closed and swam as fast as I possibly could. I never again dove to the bottom along the shore. It was only years later that I learned that I had caught a sturgeon, somewhat common on the river but seldom caught.

\* \* \*

When I came home one afternoon, Mom asked, "Have you seen Shorty?" I had not, and Mom explained she had not seen him since yesterday. I said not to worry because he always came home. Next day, no Shorty. I combed the neighborhood but no sign of him. Days go by and still no sign of my beloved friend. We never saw him again; he just disappeared. I was so depressed, having never lost anyone so close to me. A couple of weeks later, I was back out at Seymour's for the day, still no job, no dog, I was feeling pretty low. There were a bunch of high school kids swimming and drinking beer, and it seemed to me they were just having way too much fun. One of them said, "Cheer up, Frankie," and offered me a beer. I turned him down; I was only 14 years old, and said I did not think drinking was a very good idea. "Have you ever had a beer before?" I said no, but I saw what drinking did to my dad. "Oh come on," he kept saying, "one little beer won't hurt you, and you will feel better. I guarantee it. Don't be a sissy. You are going to be in high school next year, so you might as well get ready now." So, I took the beer, Burgermiester as I recall. By golly it tasted pretty darn good on a hot day. I was feeling better already. Surely, if I drink another "Burgy" I will feel even better. Several beers later, I was laying on my side in the rapid at the west end of the swimming hole, passed out drunker than a hoot owl and only 14 years old. To think that only two months prior I was Magnolia's best.

Richard wasn't working either that summer, so we concocted this idea to hitchhike to San Francisco, and on the way stop by to see my brother Marvin in Richmond. Bright and early on Saturday morning, we were off. We both had begged, borrowed, but not stolen $10.00 each that would finance the trip. Our first ride was from just past the bridge in Oakdale headed north to Manteca. The nice old couple that picked us up wanted to know right away if we were running away from home. We got a kick out of this, so Richard said yes, we had abusive parents, and were running away to join the Merchant Marines in San Francisco. We intended to sail around the world and return to Oakdale in a few years, rich and famous. They let us out in Manteca after treating us to a coke and hamburger. Highway 120 at that time ran east and west, right through the middle of Manteca. We walked three or four miles west, until our next lift. It was a Hispanic guy who could not speak a word of English, and we thought he was trying to find the road to Salinas. He was terrible driver, 30 miles an hour then 70 miles an hour, and back and forth, swerving across the road on at least two occasions, scaring us to death. Keep in mind, Highway 120 at this time is just a narrow two lane road. There was no I-5 either. Somewhere just east of Livermore, we had had enough, so I started pointing to the next road headed south and shouted, "Salinas, Salinas," pointing in that direction. He turned and headed south. We went about 5 miles before we got him to understand we wanted out. It was 101°, and we had to walk five miles back to Highway 120.

Our plan called for us to be in Richmond in 2 hours because my brother said that's how long it took. What our plan did not call for was to bring anything to drink. We had been on the road for four hours. We were walking into Livermore when a guy stopped to give us a ride. We were just getting settled in when we both realized this guy is drunker that a skunk. His driving was so bad that the Hispanic could have given him driving lessons. When we got somewhere near Hayward, the guy spotted a bar alongside the road and pulled in. He invited us in to have a coke. We were so thirsty; I think we drank three each before he was ready to go. We asked to go to the restroom, which was outside. We disappeared, and then ran like hell for three or four blocks and hide behind a gas station. After 15 or 20 minutes, we came out to the front. Well, who was there getting gas? You guessed it. We hid until he left, then hoofed it back to the highway. We continued hitchhiking and finally got a break. A guy in a pickup gave us a lift. It was a miracle. He was headed for Richmond. He was a really nice guy and took us right to my brother's apartment.

It had been a long time since I had seen Marvin. He was now married to a really sexy, cute gal named Johnnie. We got the royal welcome, nice supper, a good place to sleep, and some wonderful stories about my family that I had never heard. Marvin was worried about us hitchhiking in the Bay Area, so he took us down to the bus terminal and bought us two tickets to San Francisco. We were very grateful and promised to pay him back (We never did however). We were at the bus depot in San Francisco by 10:00 a.m. and soon on a city bus in route to Fleishhacker Zoo. What a day we had, exotic animals, strange looking people, sky scrapers, humongous bridges, and the most fun riding the cable car. We were totally oblivious to the time, and all of a sudden, we realized it was 4:30 p.m. It dawned on us that there was no possibility that we were going to get home that day. We both had about $2.50 left, so we bought a hot dog and coke at a stand and sat down on a bus bench to mull over our situation. Clay Dorrah had mentioned to me on more than one occasion that if I was ever in trouble to go find a policeman, and he would help me. Richard and I went looking, and pretty soon we spotted an officer on a corner. I walked up and asked permission to speak with him. He removed his cap and very politely says, "Why of course young man." I explained that Chief Dorrah in Oakdale was my friend and what his advice had been to me. The officer wanted to know just what kind of trouble Richard and I were in. I explained everything to him from start to finish about our predicament and how we got into it. "Well," he said, "Chief Dorrah was absolutely correct. I get off shift in about an hour and I want you to promise you will wait right here till I get back." He was back in about 45 minutes, announced that he had spoken with his wife, and we were welcome to spend the night at his house. In the morning, early because he has to work, he would drive us across the bay bridge, and we could hitchhike back to Oakdale. Another good supper, watching TV, which we had never seen but only heard about, breakfast, and we were on our way home. I made up my mind right then and there that when I grew up, I was going to be a police officer. Our trip home was only four rides and about four hours long. What an adventure for two young boys from a very small town in the valley.

Richard and I finished up the summer knocking almonds at Mr. Little's farm. I went out for the freshman football team, and Richard became the Varsity yell leader. There were three high school football teams, "B" team which was comprised of little guys, too small to compete safely on the junior varsity, or varsity teams; junior varsity team, mostly guys who wanted to play football but were too big for the "B" team or not good enough for the varsity; and the varsity team comprised of bigger guys or those who were more talented. I was only a mediocre player, 120 lbs. 5-foot 6-inches tall, and of average speed. Certainly, I would never be a star, but loved the action, the fun of playing, and the comradery. Having never before participated in any sports involving physical contact, it was a painful experience. Keep in mind that in those days there was no pre-conditioning or physical training prior to the practice season beginning. You just walked onto the field after doing nothing all summer, or at best, working on the farm. By the end of the first week, you were so sore, you could hardly walk. Many young boys just gave it up, did not participate in any sports in the fall, but ended up in regular PE. Coaches had a different philosophy than their modern counterpart.

The tougher they were, the tougher you would be. It was still pretty warm in September at 5:00 p.m., but God forgive you if you ever got caught sneaking a drink of water. Drinking water was the worst thing you could do to your body during practice. Hydration was a word not yet invented. When practice concluded, you ran two laps around the track (½ mile) and lined up with forty other boys to get a drink out of the one water hose on the field. Football, if you applied yourself, taught tenacity, discipline, and teamwork, something to benefit you the rest of your life.

\* \* \*

When I graduated from grammar school, I was a straight A student, loved school work, completed all of my assignments on time, and I waited in anticipation for the school bell to ring to start the school day. I am still puzzled to this day about what went awry with my transition from grammar school to high school. I was just not interested. I liked my teachers, I loved my fellow students, but I just could not get interested in academics. My grades were okay, but certainly I was not living up to my potential. I got As and Bs, but then my first failing grade ever, an F in general shop. Just about everyone in our class disliked our teacher, poor old Chester P. Winston. If you crossed him, forget it, you were doomed forever. I did not like him from the get go, and he had reason not to like me. One afternoon, he was in the shop in his little cubby hole of an office taking a nap. Now, no one should ever build an office with a metal door and metal framing. A couple of us fired up the welding torch, welded the door shut, and just went off to the next class. Eventually, someone heard poor old Mr. Winston beating on the door, and with a cutting torch, let him out. I was not there, but I understood he was really pissed. Someone snitched on me and the other kid, and while we never admitted it, nor was it ever proven, we both got an F for both semesters and lost five credits. I grieved the matter to the principal and he changed the overall grade for the semester to a D-, and I got the five credits back.

\* \* \*

Football season ended, and we moved into spring sports. I loved baseball, and I was actually pretty good. I made first string on the B team, and I was enjoying going to school. I was not a bad kid. Really, I was just overly mischievous, sometimes. I had Mr. Bacigalupi for geometry, and he was a pretty good teacher. He was very amusing in class, and we liked him. Just as a practical joke, Doug Betz and I decide to play a little joke on him. Our classroom was located on the second floor of the old auditorium, next to the tennis courts. Doug and I got to class a little early and attached a rope to Bachi's chair. We were in the process of lowering it out of the second-floor window down to the tennis court when our lookout shouts "Here comes Bachi!" We let go of the rope, and the chair crashed to the asphalt below. Bye-bye chair. He did not find the missing chair, or pieces of it, until the custodian brought it to the principal's office. Why, I do not know, but the school made a big deal out of it. Everyone was interrogated, and someone must have cracked. Doug and I were the prime suspects, but we were confessing to nothing. We both got booted out of the class and got Fs on our report card. Hmm, does this sound familiar?

In the meantime, my girlfriend and eventually my wife, Carol Berg, were going steady. Holding hands every second, together every minute possible, nothing else but us mattered in the whole world. We went to as many school events together as possible. She lived five miles out in the country and I lived in town. No car, no way to see her, except at school. I couldn't wait until I was old enough to have a car. I had been driving, but with no license, since I was 14 years old, usually Richards's car, an old Model A Ford, or one of my other friend's, Henry Buie's parent's cars. Mr. Buie bought old cars and dismantled them for junk. They were usually drivable when he got them, so we had access as long as we did not go into town. Most of our travels were by foot however, to school, football games, Seymour's.

I wanted so much to go to the high school dances at the gym. Two things held me back: I could not dance, nor did I have clothes that I thought appropriate for the event. I was in an emotional melt down, knowing that Carol might be there (she was not) dancing with someone else. I was whining to Mom one night about not knowing how to dance, and Mom said, "Well, I will teach you how." Mom, teaching me to dance? I had never even seen her keep time to a tune. She could dance? Well, Mom taught me the Texas Two Step and the Tennessee Waltz. I was Arthur Murray/Fred Astaire all wrapped into one. I was really anticipating going to the dance and showing off my newly acquired skills. "Mom, what will I wear?" I asked. Mom pointed to a bunch of her customers' shirts hanging on a rack. We both smiled at each other. The ironing she takes in! What a selection. She found this great shirt that was a perfect fit. I was out the door and on my way to the sock hop. I was not in the gym door 10 feet when this kid came up and says, "Neat shirt, my dad has one just like it." Mom, we are busted. I danced the night away. Anyone could do the twist. They never did play the Texas Two Step.

\* \* \*

The summer of 1952 was long and, for the most part, uneventful. I had several jobs to earn a little spending money and purchase school clothes. I worked irrigating pastures on a ranch, relief milked twice a week on a dairy, bucked hay (I hated that job), picked peaches, and knocked almonds. I spent a considerable amount of time at Seymour's, but no drinking. I was back in school and playing football again on the "B" team. Never a great player, but still first string. We had a good team and may have won the league championship, I am just not sure. The coach knew I was a good baseball outfielder, so I was the punt returner in all games. We were invited by the coach of Hilmar High's JV team to travel there and have a game with them. They were a little bigger than us, but we were faster. Toward the end of the game, we were leading by a touchdown, and they had the ball but were forced to punt. No fair catch in those days, and a punt was a live ball. The kicker punted, and I set myself to make the catch. Here came the ball, way up in the air, and in front of me came a 250 lb. Hilmar player running right at me. Remember JV players were categorized by ability and skill, not size. I could see the train wreck coming. I gained consciousness on the sideline about 10 minutes later after getting hit and fumbling the ball. Luckily, we recovered the ball and went on to win the game. I fractured my ankle the next week during practice, and that was the end of my football career and the San Francisco 49'ers lost a good prospect.

\* \* \*

One of my very best friends in high school, who still is 65 years later, was Kathleen Holloway (married Bill Smith). We were never boyfriend/girlfriend, just really close "buddies". Kathy and her mom and dad moved to Oakdale in 1952 and settled on lower Horseshoe Road at the far north end. I believe Kathy enrolled in high school that year as a sophomore and was 15 years old. Their place was, I am guessing, maybe a couple of hundred acres of pasture with rolling hills in the background. The Oakdale Irrigation District north main canal was practically in their backyard. Her dad was an auctioneer, and her mom a school teacher. I thought them to be pretty well off, as they had three Hudson automobiles, a 1952 Hornet, and a brand new 1953 Hornet, plus an older model. The Hornet was the rage, stylish, winning all the stock car races, and the first car in America, as far as I know, with a stepdown floorboard. They were beautiful. Occasionally, I got to ride in it with

Kathy, who already had a driver's license at the tender young age of 14. One evening, Kathy, Jo Ann Verden, and I were headed for the rally at the high school when we realized we needed something that was at Carol Berg's house way out on the east end of Warnerville Road. So, we head out that way in the brand spanking new Hornet, Kathy driving, Jo Ann in the middle, and I was in the passenger's seat. Kathy was driving way too fast as we rounded the first two curves in the road. We sailed around the third curve and went into the next one just east of Stearns Road. I told her to slow the car down before we had a wreck. Kathy's infamous last words which I still remember from that night were, "You cannot roll a Hudson Hornet!" Next thing I know, we were off the road, through the fence, and rolling over three times. No seat belts, but we were lucky no one got thrown out. People popped up out of nowhere, and someone called an ambulance and the CHP. There was only room for two in the ambulance, so Kathy and Jo Ann were loaded up and taken to the hospital in Oakdale. I was just standing there in shock and bleeding from a severe laceration to my right arm, which had been bandaged by the ambulance driver, when C. C. Baxter, who lived nearby, drove up in his pickup and took me to the hospital. We were very lucky. Kathy, broken collar bone; Jo Ann, fractured ribs; Frankie, severe laceration of the right wrist and possible concussion. Hudson Hornets could be rolled over, and it was a total loss.

We were all together several weeks later at Kathy's place and decided to go horseback riding. I was deadly afraid of horses and reluctant to saddle up, but she assured me that old

*Apache* was gentle as a lamb. We didn't go 20 feet until "old gentle Apache" got a hair up his ass and decided he was *Man of War* and took off like a race horse. I was hanging on for dear life when Apache decided to run under a tree with low hanging branches. Boom! right in the head, and off I went, sliding through several piles of fresh cow dung before coming to a stop in a little creek. I was soaking wet, covered in cow poop, bleeding from my forehead and half-conscious when Kathy rode up. "Are you okay?" she asked. "Yes, Kathy, I am fine. I just wanted to give old Apache a little rest." Apache then meandered up and nudged me in the back, as though to say, "Hey, get back on cowboy." A few months later, Kathy's folks got rid of their horses, and sent Apache to a pack station in the Sierras.

Later that summer, three of us boys were at Kathy's, and her mom asked us to stay for dinner. We were always hungry, so we accepted. While sitting around the table, Kathy's mom, Connie, explained that she was having a real problem with her chickens roosting in the fig tree in front of the house and pooping all over the cars. "Sometimes I just wish someone would come along and shoot the darn things." Be careful what you wish for Mrs. Holloway! We took her seriously, and a few days later, we were out there with our .22 caliber rifles, ready to clean up. After knocking on the door and finding no one home, we slowly and methodically took care of business. Twelve dead Road Island Reds, that was four apiece, and we were on our way home. Mom made the best chicken and dumplings, so we invited the White kids over, and we had a great meal. We were so thankful to Mrs. Holloway. The next day at school, Kathy wanted to know if we were anywhere near her house yesterday. "Well yeah, we killed all of those chickens like your mom wanted." "Oh my God, you better stay away for a while, Mom was more upset than I have ever seen her."

\* \* \*

It was the beginning of school, September 1952. I was a sophomore and had a pretty easy schedule at school, but even at that I could only manage a C+ average with an F in geometry from Mr. Bacigalupi (that dammed chair). Mr. Weichert was our class counselor, and he called me in for a session. I remember his words, which were inspiring, but not followed up on for several years, "Frankie, you have a lot of potential, but you are just not living up to it." We did a bunch of testing and came up with some crazy results that showed I should become a banker. I accepted the results, but as I left his office, I was laughing to myself, "Yeah, right. This dumb little kid was going to work in a bank someday? Fat chance."

I loved and enjoyed school and would never think of dropping out. I had so many wonderful friends and got along with everyone. Mrs. Louise Ales was my very favorite teacher and I got As in English. My only A in four years of high school, except P.E. One day she said, "Frankie, the brakes have gone out on my car (1948 Desoto), and I know you have auto shop. Could you take a look at them for me?" Well, I wanted those As to keep rolling in so, "Of course Mrs. Ales." I was just a care free 15-year-old kid. So, I got the keys from her at 5ᵗʰ period and picked up the car. Best thing I have ever driven. I made a couple of passes around the campus (look at me) and then headed for the shop. As I pulled up to the large roll-up door at the auto shop, it was in the down position. I had completely forgotten what the hell I was doing. Brakes, what brakes? I hit the door going about 10 mph and knocked it off the tracks and 10 feet into the shop. Mr. Schott, our teacher, thought an airplane had crashed into the building. All of us kids and Mr. Schott gathered in front of the car and managed to straighten out most of the front end attachments, making it difficult to see any damage. She was out of brake fluid, so that was an easy fix. She got the car back before the period was over and was happy as a lark, and I got my A. I thought about my meeting with Mr. Weichert and promised to myself that I was going to try a little harder.

I had a literature class, and the teacher's name was Hypatia Hylman. I struggled in her class, but decided I was going to write the best darned paper she had ever seen. I put a lot of effort writing the paper, don't remember the subject, but I really thought I had done a good job. I even had Mrs. Ales review it, and she complimented me on a job well done. "You will get an A for sure." I presented the paper aloud to the class and they applauded. To my dismay, Miss Hylman said, and I quote, "That was the worst report I have ever heard." I could have literally "shit". The classroom booed her comments (first instance of civil disobedience at Oakdale High). I was devastated. No excuse, but I was devastated. I completely lost interest in school, except for baseball. My report card for that semester showed 3 Ds, an F, and an A in PE.

\* \* \*

It was November 1952, and I was 15 years old, still living on South Fifth Street, what a dump, but it was better than what we had been used to. Mom continued to take in ironing and clean houses. We were doing okay, thanks to her. Come December the only job I could find was occasionally working for Wilson Salyer, force feeding turkeys. What a messy job. You had to do it during darkness while the turkeys were nesting in the pens. They had some kind of avian flu and would not eat. There was a small pump with one end of a hose submerged in a tank of turkey food mixed with antibiotics, the other to a regulating nozzle. You held the turkey under your arm, forced the turkey's beak open, insert the nozzle way down into its throat and gave it a shot of the mixture. We were doing this all night long, then it was home, clean up, and to school. This went on for several weeks, as there were thousands of birds affected. Needless to say, most of the day I was very tired and sleepy, and there was no time for homework, but working was important. I was just thankful to have a little income.

# COOKIE WALTHER: FROM THE SERVICE STATION TO THE BANK: 1952-1956

Pete Willey, an old friend of my brother, Marvin, came by the house one day, and asked if I would be interested in working at a gas station in downtown Oakdale. Cookie Walther, owner of Walther's Shell Service, needed someone to help out on weekends at the gas station. I jumped at the chance to have a steady part-time job, and at $0.65 an hour. So, I started out on a new career that would last through high school and beyond. At this point I had little concept about the science of auto mechanics, customer service, selling of auto accessories, making change, etc. My hours were 9:00 a.m. to 6:00 p.m., Saturday, Sunday, and holidays. I was so excited that I showed up on my first day at 8:00 a.m. Mr. Walther was impressed (I will refer to him as Cookie hereafter) and told me if I wanted to come in at 8:00 a.m. that was okay. That's an extra $0.65 a day. My first day was pretty routine, cleaning windshields with a sponge and Bon Ami, checking the tires for the correct air pressure, water levels in the radiator, and the engine oil. I followed Pete Willey around and assimilated the service station vocabulary into my head. Regular, ethyl, cash, charge or credit card, TCP (an additive Shell Oil put in the gas); we called it "tom cat piss". After a couple of weekends, I pretty much had it all down pat. About the third Saturday of my employment, Cookie told me to jump into the company pickup, a cherry 1947 Ford, go to Ray Beaty's Auto Parts at Fifth and F Streets, and pick up some parts. I had been driving for two years around the outskirts of Oakdale, but had no driver's license, as yet. I jumped into the pickup, went to the auto parts store, got the parts, and started back to the station. Coming back, I stopped at the stop sign at F Street and Yosemite Boulevard, and as I came to a stop, some guy ran into the back of the pickup going pretty fast. There was minor damage to the pickup but it really messed up the front of his 1937 Terraplane. The police came to make an accident report, and I knew I was in big trouble for not having a driver's license. Officer Schmiedlen asked for my driver's license, and I replied, "I do not have a license with me." I guess a small lie, but technically correct. He told me that in the next day or two to come by the police station and give them the information on the driver's license, so he could finish the report. In 1953, Oakdale had a DMV office; so, on Monday, Mom and I, in Cookie's pickup, drove to DMV and got a driver's license. I had already had driver's education at school, so the whole thing was a snap. Tuesday, I dropped off the information for the accident report and never heard another word about it. "Whew!"

\* \* \*

When I first went to work at the gas station, I noticed, tucked away in a corner in the back of the tire shop, a vehicle of some sort covered with a canvas. I asked and received permission to remove the canvas and have a look. It was every boy's in the fifties dream car, a 1929 Ford Roadster, big tires in the back, little ones in the front. I asked Cookie for its background, and he stated the car belonged to Cecil Brown, who was in the Army in Korea, and the car was being stored there until he returned. "When would that be?" I asked. Cookie had no idea, but probably in a few months, as the war was at a stalemate. I just knew that in 1929, God had intended that someday this car was to be mine. I dreamed of how I was going to make this the hottest hotrod in Oakdale. I wrote down everything that needed to be done to get this beauty on the road, and it was a lot. First of all, no engine, no transmission, no floorboards, no seats, no gas tank, mechanical brakes, actually it was just a hulk. Come May, Cecil Brown returned from Korea and pulled into the station for gas. I immediately confronted him on his plans for the car in the backroom. He said I could have the car for $100.00. We went in the backroom, and I went over with him, in detail, what it was going to cost to get this piece of junk on the road. He came down to $50.00. We had a deal, except I did not have $50.00. What to do, what to do?

I talked to Cookie, and he agreed to buy the car for me, calling it a piece of junk that I would kill myself in. I was to pay him back $10.00 a month. I priced out and located all of the parts and accessories that I would need to get the car running, $150.00 plus the $50.00 I owe Cookie. This was turning out to be not-so-good of a deal, but I pressed on, determined to have my very own hotrod. I located a wrecked 1936 Ford at Fiez's Auto Wrecking Yard on Sierra Road, purchased it for $35.00, and towed it to Mr. Buie's backyard where I started to dismantle it. Engine ran good, seats were perfect, and the gas tank fit. Then it was off to the lumber yard where I purchased some ¾ inch plywood for the floorboard. The White boys and I removed the body from the chassis and cut the plywood to fit. We installed the seats, and they fit just perfectly. In went the gas tank, transmission, and engine. We put the body back on, connected the wiring, etc. and what do you know, VAROOM it runs! I cannot tell you the happiness and joy this little car brought me. It only weighed 1100 lbs., so with that little 85hp V/8, it was the hottest dragster in Oakdale. But alas, no top, no heater, no side windows, no radio, and I was beginning to fall in love with Carol Berg. I love you little car, but I love Carol more. So, I removed the body, and traded it for a 31 Ford coupe body. We channeled it, so it was only about five feet high. Really cool. Now, I could drive in the rain, and Carol was okay to ride with me.

I blew the engine racing Terry Jones and his 1952 Plymouth. I located a 1947 Mercury engine that was 110 hp but it needed to be overhauled. My Uncle Bob Crum offered to help me, so we got started. We stroked the crank, bore out the cylinders to max, polished the intake and exhaust ports, installed the most gas guzzling carburetor that Stromberg manufactured, installed the engine, and we were ready to fire that baby up. With great anticipation, I hit the starter, "THUD", IT WOULD NOT TURN OVER. So, we pushed it out into the street and towed it with Cookie's pickup. We put it in gear, and the rear tires just dragged. For some reason, the engine was too tight to turn over. My mechanic uncle had put the wrong size inserts on the crank and rods. He was apologetic, but I was out money for the correct inserts. Good-bye Uncle Bob. I fixed it myself, and it ran fine for a couple of weeks, until the engine started smoking. Shit, what now? To make a long story short, uncle Bob left out a snap ring on a wrist pin on one piston and it ground a channel in the side of the block. I took the engine out to Sundling Bros., and they sleeved the cylinder. That fixed the problem. I was on the road again and a happy camper. This whole love affair with a hotrod was both costly and a learning experience. It reinforced the old saying "you cannot make a silk purse out of a sow's ear". Carol and I still had no heater, no radio, and no windows to roll up.

* * *

It was early February 1954 while driving by C. A. Bowen and Son's Studebaker Garage on First Street that I spotted the most beautiful car I had ever seen, a 1940 Ford Deluxe coupe, heater, radio, Columbia overdrive, in perfect condition, asking price $400.00. It was way out of my price range, but I stopped in and talked to Mr. Bowen anyway. I had not talked to him in a long time. As a matter of fact, it was the previous summer when he caught us stealing cherries off his tree in the backyard on Eucalyptus Avenue. At that time, he said, "Just knock on the door, and you are welcome to the cherries." He also had a beautiful swimming pool, and he said we were welcome to use that, too, if we would just ask. He was a very nice man.

I had to have that car, and I had to have Carol. Mr. Bowen said he would hold the car for a week while I tried to come up with the money. I had no money and had not had any money since I got into the "hotrod business". I talked to Mom about it, but of course while sympathetic, she had no spare money either. "Why don't we borrow the money from the bank?" she suggested. "Mom," I said, kind of chuckling, "why in the world would the bank loan us any money?" We were always almost penniless, on welfare, and fortunate just to feed and clothe ourselves. "Well, it won't hurt to ask," she said. "Besides, I think it would be nice if we had a car our family could get around in and use when we occasionally have to go to Modesto. "Let's go to the bank tomorrow and ask." I chuckled to myself and under my breath muttered, "Yeah right, a bank was going to loan us money?" The next day at 10:00 a.m., we were standing at the front door when the First Western Bank opened for business. Mom looked nice, and I had on clean clothes. We both approach the receptionist, Mrs. Pearl

Titchenal. She said, "Hello," to Mom and "Hello, Frankie," to me (thank God no Pinky). We explained our mission, and she referred us to Mr. Joe Arbini, the bank's vice president and a lending officer. He was also one of my customers at Cookie's. "Hello Mrs. Clark, and hi Frankie. How can I help you?" We explained our mission and our hope, and why we needed to have a car. "Let me get this straight," says Mr. Arbini. "You want to borrow $400.00 to buy a car. Mrs. Clark, you are on welfare, and you iron a few shirts, including mine. Frankie, you make $0.75 an hour working at Cookie's. Is that correct?" "Yes, sir," I replied, "but I have no bills to pay, and I figure the payments, including 0.03 % interest would only be $23.00 a month for 18 months. I can handle that Mr. Arbini." He gave me a long hard stare and said, "Okay, Frankie. Don't let me down." He scribbled something on a paper, had Mom and I sign it, and said, "Give this to Mrs. Titchenal, and she will give you the $400.00." No credit check, no long forms, just a hand shake. "Oh, Frankie and Mrs. Clark, thanks for the business!" We walked the three blocks to Bowen and Sons and purchased the prettiest little car I had ever set my eyes on. I never missed a payment. I never changed a thing on the car. I just loved it the way it was. But like they say, you cannot have two loves in your life at the same time.

Carol and I broke up shortly after that, and I was without her for the first time since grammar school. I never had another girlfriend after that, always too busy working, playing baseball or drinking beer with the boys. Two of my good friends at that time were Jackie Rogers and Tony Rivera, both three years older than me. They graduated from Oakdale High in 1952 and were just hanging around waiting to go to Korea after having been notified they were being drafted and would be inducted in a couple of weeks. One night after work, around 10:00 p.m., they came by the gas station and asked if I wanted to go to the "cat house" with them. Well, I was only 17, but I knew the cat house was not the animal shelter. I had just gotten paid, so what the heck, I could afford $3.00. Besides that, I had in my mind that I had been a virgin long enough. The year before, Tony had taken me to the "cat house" at Yosemite Junction at Highways 108 and 120. I had drunk a couple of beers and was wearing this humongous cowboy hat. When we got inside, the madam, Ruby, asked me how old I was, and I answered, "18 years old, ma'am." "You are a long ways from 18, sonny. Take off that hat, and look at me. Are you shaving yet?" she asked. "That cowboy hat is not going to get you in here. Now get out before I call the sheriff." It so happened her boyfriend Dave Bonovia was the sheriff and later became her husband. I will say this, she had a great memory. Years later, she and the sheriff opened a restaurant at "The Junction" called Bonovia's. My wife Marilyn and I went there for dinner in 1965, and Ruby was the hostess. As she seated us she stared at me for a little bit, then asked if I was still wearing cowboy hats. "What did she mean by that?" Marilyn asked. "I have absolutely no idea," I replied.

We were off to the *cat house*, Banana Ranch, in Angeles Camp about 40 miles north east of Oakdale, and it was nearing midnight. I had had a couple of beers and was beginning to feel boisterous and more excited as each landmark passed. Knights Ferry, then O'Byrne's Ferry Bridge, on to Copperopolis, up the hill to Angels Camp, then a long narrow dirt road flanked by palm trees. We were there! My imagination was running wild. I had never had sex before (except with myself and that does not count, right Bill). Anyway, I was not sure how this was going to go, but I had great expectations and another beer before I went in. Several thinly clad, pretty, young girls came out and paraded around in front of us. Jackie and Tony had been here before, so they made their selections on a first name basis. I had only seen pictures of naked women, so the real thing was very stimulating. I selected this really cute little brunette who could not take her eyes off of me, and I knew she had the hots for me! We went into this dimly lit room that was perfumed to death but prettily decorated. I looked up on the ceiling, and there was a message, Go Mustangs the *Banana Man*. I asked her what that was about, and she had no idea, said it had been there for at least 10 years. She undressed both of us, and we had a short conversation, you know, names, how old are you, I lie and say I am 19; she smiles and knows I am lying. "Is it just straight sex, or do you want the 'around the world'?" she asked. I had no idea what she was talking about, so she explained "around the world" to me. That cost $2.00 more so we were up to $5.00. I thought about it, okay I say, "Let's try it," and I paid her before we got down to business. She asked if I was a virgin, and I said, "No," but she knew I was lying; she could tell a virgin a mile off. "I have done this, maybe 100 times," I told her. I had no idea where that number came from. So, to make a short story short, a few days later, things were not right "down there". Having had a class in health orientation from Mr. Vatone my freshman year, I knew what was going on. I immediately reported to our family physician Dr. Mundall for treatment. He asked, "Have you had unprotected sex recently?" I said, "No (beep! lie machine goes off)." He then asked if I had eaten any spoiled meat. Sounds like an out to me, so I say, "Why yes, only yesterday I ate some bologna that tasted bad." The doctor called in his nurse, Vivian, and said, "Give Frankie a shot of penicillin. He got ahold of something that gave him a urinary infection." "Frankie, stay away from that bologna," he says, "and don't try to give me any either." I never ate any bad bologna again, and I never ever went to a "cat house" again for the rest of my life. I am still curious about who the *Banana Man* from Oakdale might have been. Any clues out there?

* * *

I continued to work on weekends at the gas station and attended school full time. I was able to play baseball on the varsity team, first string, which was one of my most enjoyable times in school. We won the Valley Oak League championship that year, which was an event I have always cherished dearly. It was the summer of 1954, and I still only worked weekends at the gas station and spent a lot of time hanging out at Seymour's swimming and drinking beer. Just for a few weeks, I worked at Jake Lorang's swamping peaches and working in the dry yard along with a bunch of my class mates.

The big fall harvest party and dance was that weekend in Valley Home. Lots of music, girls, and drinking beer. Richard and Roger White and I decided we had to attend this end of summer event. My brother, Leroy, was home on leave from the army, and we asked him to get us a case of beer so we could party. He came through, we got our beer, and headed out for Valley Home. We were sitting in my 40 Ford, sipping a couple before we made our entrance to the dance when we saw headlights behind us. Some guy approached the driver's side of the car and flashed a badge. Busted! We were cited to juvenile court in Modesto, our beer confiscated (hope they enjoyed it). In Modesto we got questioned about where we got the beer. No one snitched out my brother and we were put on summary probation, whatever that was. It was only a few months later, November I think, when the White boys and I were once again sitting in my 40 Ford near the high school football stadium when we get approached by Oakdale PD. We had a couple of six packs of "Stout Ale" in those little 6 oz. cans, and at 6 % alcohol, they were pretty potent. Well, Sgt. Leply gets us out of the car, takes the beer, and starts the paperwork. I knew it was going to be 6 months in juvenile hall for sure. Holy Jesus, another miracle! Up drives Chief Dorrah to see what was going on. After he determined what was going on, he looked at Sgt. Leply, and to my amazement says, "For Christ's sake Dick, these little old cans of beer would not hurt anyone. You boys get on home, and Dick, you take these beer cans to the station and get back to work."

\* \* \*

Come fall, I started back to school, did not go out for football, but just took it easy, waiting for spring baseball. Come around Christmas, Cookie's fulltime employee quit, and Cookie asked if there was any way I could work fulltime for him. I thought he wanted me to drop out of school, but he very strongly emphasized that I had to continue school. I checked with my senior counselor, and he said I could graduate by only attending school half-a-day. That freed me up to work at the gas station from 2:00 p.m. to 10:00 p.m., five days a week, and on Saturday and Sunday from 7:00 a.m. to 6:00 p.m. I did not have time for anything but work. I was class president and could not participate in school activities like I wanted to. I made the best of it, and with Mom's encouragement, we moved ahead.

I was able to give Mom a little money, and our lives had never been better. We had a car, I had decent clothes, my little brothers and sisters were doing well, and we were becoming respectable; however, all good things must come to an end. Mom's welfare worker found out I had a job (Mom was just too dammed honest) and told her that she had to report that income, and it would be deducted from her monthly allotment. What to do, what to do? Do I quit my job and sit on my ass? Although I was making $60.00 a week, I still had expenses. Car payment, insurance, gas, school expenses, work clothes, etc. I detested welfare; although, I knew it was a necessary evil, and we could not get by without it. Being on welfare had embarrassed me my entire childhood. Please do not punish me for trying to get ahead. I drove over to the welfare department, unbeknownst to Mom, and asked to speak with the director. I was denied that request of course, snotty-nosed kid! I refused to leave until I spoke with her. Finally, the receptionist relented and announced my presence to the director. She invited me in, and I found her to be a very pleasant person who was willing to listen. We exchanged philosophies about welfare (I was only 17 years old). I told her where my money went and how I could not wait to get our family off of welfare. She listened but promised nothing. Did she listen? Did she care? I never heard back, but Mom's check remained the same, until I turned 18 years old.

Graduation picture, Frank Clark, Oakdale High School, 1955

\* \* \*

When I arrived at the gas station at 7:00 a.m. and opened up, there was usually not much going on; so, I read the newspaper and kept up on national events. I had long followed the Korean War, as my two friends, Jackie and Tony, were now deployed there. The Korean Armistice Agreement was signed by North Korea, South Korea, China, and the United Nations in July of 1953. The war had ended, but tensions were high, and the likelihood that it might reignite was very possible. This tension went on for several years, and of course, still exists today, maybe even more so. I had no desire to serve in the army, but realized that as I neared 18 years of age and things were as they were, there was a strong possibility that I would be drafted when I graduated from high school. I also closely watched the events taking place in Southeast Asia, primarily Vietnam, a country I had never heard of and had little knowledge of its history. There was a horrific battle going on, March through May 1954, in a little known place in Vietnam called Dien Bien Phu. The French, defending this outpost, were totally surrounded by Vietnamese Communist soldiers and cut off from any hope of escape. Facing annihilation, they surrendered after their commander committed suicide. This was, in effect, the end of the French occupation and eventual evacuation from Vietnam by the French, ending a hundred years of colonization. The 1954 Geneva Accords were signed by all participating parties, and Vietnam was divided into two separate countries, the north, Democratic Republic of Vietnam, and the south, State of Vietnam. Little did I know that 16 years later I would be right in the middle of the Vietnam War and spend 30 months in South Vietnam and other parts of Southeast Asia. We will talk more extensively about that later.

At the tender young age of 17, I joined the United States Navy Reserve in Modesto and was sworn in as Seaman Apprentice Clark. I was required to attend weekly meetings in Modesto at the airport. Our unit was an electronic unit, working with radios and other communication equipment. As a new recruit, I was required to attend basic training in San Diego. So that summer, a school classmate, Dwayne Pirkle, and I caught the train and were off to San Diego for two weeks. I enjoyed the training, military discipline, and especially the food. I had never in my life eaten so well. Dwayne and I decided to hitchhike back to Oakdale rather than take the train. We were given the money for a train ticket but chose rather to pocket that and use it for traveling expenses. I had two cousins who worked for the San Bernardino Police Department, and we had never seen the desert, so we headed in that direction. Being in uniform made getting a ride really easy. Keep in mind, we were only 17 years old and still green behind the ears. My cousin met us at the police department at about 6:00 p.m., and after dinner we got into the police car and started making the rounds of all the bars and honkytonks. We had a great time, free drinks, dancing, and all the snacks we could eat. At 2:00 a.m., we headed to my cousin's house and bedded down. After visiting my other cousin and my uncle (their dad), we were ready to head home. Ten hours later we were in Oakdale, tired and dirty, but with memories of a great experience. As long as I am on the subject of the Naval Reserve I will take the time to finish it off and then get onto my experiences working at the gas station.

I was loving the navy and had decided that if the draft got too close after I turned 18, then I would definitely join the navy. Well, a year went by and I kept going to the weekly meetings. I had become pretty good with Morse code and operating the other communication equipment. It was April, and the unit Commander announced that the unit would be going on a sea cruise to Vancouver, British Columbia aboard a destroyer or destroyer escort. We were excited. I had never been out of California and rarely out of the county much less another country. Time went by fast and before you knew it was June, and we were in San Francisco, standing in front of the USS George A. Johnson (DE-583).

This was the first time I had ever been up close to a warship, and I was excited that I was going to be sailing on her for 10 days to Vancouver and returning home. She had a crew of 186, was 306 feet long, and weighed 1,450 tons with a speed of 24 knots. The ship was commissioned on January 12, 1944 and served in WW II and Korea before being assigned to the 12th Naval District in San Francisco as a naval reserve training ship. She was decommissioned in 1957 and scrapped in 1965. I found a picture of her in the Navy archives that ironically was taken in Vancouver in June of 1955, the very time I was aboard on our cruise. Although I had never been to sea, not even in a fishing boat, I had made up my mind that this was my destiny. We boarded the ship at 7:00 a.m. and immediately were lead to the galley for a hearty breakfast of toast, eggs, and plenty of greasy pork sausage. We headed out under the Golden Gate and toward the Farallon Islands. This area can at times be some of the roughest waters in the Pacific, and it was one of those times. I was soon sicker than I had ever been in my life. There went the sausage, followed by the eggs and toast; just when I thought it was over, there it went again. I decided I would have to die to get better. I still had the dry heaves the next morning. "Well, boys," the old Navy Chief says, "today is the day we clean out and repaint the bowman's paint locker right up in the bow." This was of course the worst place in the world to be if you were sea sick. Do you think he knew that? After four days at sea and throwing up the entire time, I had changed my mind. Maybe being a ground pounder would not be so bad after all.

USS Johnson DE 583 Vancouver BC, 1956

We finally reached Vancouver. What a beautiful city and what wonderful, kind, hospitable people. I loved the place. After about four days, we headed back to San Francisco, and I had my sea legs. No more sickness, maybe being a sailor would not be so bad after all. Shortly after returning I dropped out of the Naval Reserve. I just quit going to meetings period. I received letters threatening me with the draft if I did not start coming to the meeting, but I was just tired of the whole routine. My buddies warned me that the draft was imminent. While that worried me, I did not care. I was trying my best to get into the air force and become a pilot. Well, time passed and I quit hearing from the Navy. Six years went by. I was married, had one child, and was working at the police department in Modesto. A registered letter came to the house from the Department of the Navy. I nervously open the letter and to my shock and surprise it was a letter from the Secretary of the Navy thanking me for my eight years of service in the naval reserve and better yet an "honorable discharge" also signed by the Secretary. Can you beat that? I guess I just fell through the cracks or the unit in Modesto wanted to keep its numbers up.

\* \* \*

Let's get back to Cookie Walther and my three years a pump jockey and grease monkey. In retrospect, I was really pretty lucky at this point in my life. Things were good at home, I had a good job, good car, and a great mom. I was out of school at noon and reported to the gas station where I worked until closing time at 10:00 p.m. Cookie went home at 6:00 p.m., so I was in full charge. I cleaned the place up, balanced the books for the night, so everything was ready at 7:00 a.m. when Cookie opened up. It was my understanding that Cookie's family came to the United States from Prussia around 1800 or so. They moved west and settled on 640 acres of land at the corner of Warnerville and Tim Bell Roads. I would guess they acquired the property from the U.S. Government, who acquired it from Mexico as a result of the Treaty of Guadalupe in 1848. Anyway, they dry farmed the land for wheat for several years before moving into Oakdale, and thereafter it was primarily used for cattle grazing. After Cookie's mom and dad passed away, the land went to Cookie and his brother Louis, who was in management with Shell Oil in Martinez, California. They leased it out for grazing and eventually sold it for around $500.00 per acre. That land today is worth at least $25,000 per acre and is now planted with almonds. Let's check my math. Value in 1965 when sold $320,000. Value in 2015 about $16 million. Quite a difference. Unfortunately, Cookie was an alcoholic and literally drank himself to death without benefiting from his inheritance at all.

Cookie's wife was a nurse, and they had two daughters just a year or two behind me in school. The oldest, Sandra, took care of all the bookkeeping and the posting of charge accounts at the station. In many ways, Cookie was like a father figure to me, giving me advice, listening to my teenage problems, and in general, teaching me the good and bad things about being a teenager. I was very fortunate to have him around during those formative years.

Having grown up in Oakdale, Cookie had a million friends, and many of them traded at the station. He put in tire recapping equipment and soon had another thriving enterprise. We sold and changed more tires than any other place in Oakdale. He was a hardworking man when he stayed off the bottle, and like many alcoholics, he would go months without a drop and then suddenly for reasons that only an alcoholic could explain, he was off and drinking again. When drinking, he would hide half pint bottles of Four Roses whiskey around the place and then sneak around taking nips out of the bottle. My hobby was to find the bottles and pour them down the drain and then discard the empty bottles. I bet I threw away a thousand bottles during the three and a half years I worked there. He knew what I was doing, but never ever said a word to me. Strange!

He was, when sober, a happy go lucky guy with a great sense of humor and personality. A real practical joker, he created a half wooden barrel out of an old 50-gallon wine container and made it into a cushioned chair. Inside the barrel he put a Ford model T coil hooked to a battery (all hidden from view) and when you sat on the cushion in the chair you got a real jolt. It was hard to get out of the chair as you were sitting back a ways, so you just sat there and got electrocuted. I remember seeing some people actually wet their pants while enduring this torture. There was one old gentleman called *Crippled Ed* who came to the station almost every morning to read the paper. He was elderly, walked with a very bad limp, and had to be assisted with a wooden cane. He had been severely wounded during WW I in France. As many times as he had been in the office he never sat in that chair nor had any knowledge of its potency. Well he finally sat in it and boom he could not get up. Cookie, while laughing his head off, grabbed old Crippled Ed and pulled him loose. Rather than thanking Cookie, old Ed hit him right over the head with that cane. I think it took about 12 stiches to close the wound. Anyway, Cookie quit laughing. That was the end of the chair. I never saw Crippled Ed in the station again.

I was about 18 and a half when one day Mr. Largent, who owned the Desoto Plymouth dealership next door (the one my dad should have owned but did not) came over and asked me to come over to his dealership, as he wanted to show me something. I went over a few minutes later, and there in the show room was a black 1954 Plymouth Savoy 2 door Sedan. Beautiful little car, but they only came with a very timid six-cylinder flathead engine. This was not something I was interested in at all. This was the era of the big V/8's the likes of Oldsmobile, Buick, Chrysler, Mercury, and yes, even Fords and Chevrolets. I started to leave and Mr. Largent said, "Now Frankie, just wait a minute. Take a look at this!" He raised the hood, and there before my eyes was the biggest V/8 engine I had ever seen. The carburetor was as big as my 40 Ford engine, I swear. A Chrysler 300 hemi engine in that little old innocent looking Plymouth. "Come by after work and take it for a spin if you like," he said. "If I like? Are you kidding me, I will be here at 5:00 o'clock sharp."

It was a rocket. The tires squealed when you poured the coal to it, and it almost threw you into the back seat. "Can we take it out to the Valley Home Highway?" I asked. "Sure, why not?" he replied. We kids in Oakdale had a quarter mile measured off and marked on the highway about a mile past Shively's that we used for drag racing on a regular basis. It hit a little over 90 mph in the quarter mile according to the speedometer. I HAD TO HAVE IT! Carol and I were still split up, and I had a little money saved; so, we worked out a deal. Goodbye 40 Ford, hello Mo Par. I had a lot of drag races in that car and never ever lost.

\* \* \*

Carol and I got back together, and the world was never better. She had a boyfriend while we were broken up who was a real jerk. He took it pretty hard when she left him. One day she and I were sitting in the Mo Par at the local drive-in called the Juke Box when he pulled in driving his uncle's new Ford Fairlane. Our cars were sitting side by side and he had been ragging on me and even threw in the middle finger a couple of times. I leaned over, kissed Carol, and hoisted my middle finger at him. He went off like a raging bull. He put that Ford in reverse and burned rubber across the parking lot. For some reason he did not see the monstrous Elm tree that for a hundred years had adorned its location in the lot. Dead center with the back of that new Ford. I swear the trunk lid was now in the front seat. We did not laugh then, but a few blocks later we pulled over and laughed ourselves silly.

Carol and I announced our engagement and set a wedding date of April 29th, 1956.

Carol was working at Bank of America, so we were really doing well financially, and neither of us had any plans to attend college. I was fully committed to becoming a police officer at some point in the future. I had my eye on the California Highway Patrol and took every opportunity to ride with my CHP friend, Earl Maddox. He was a great person and spent time working with me to have the proper background and training to be highway patrolman as soon as I turned 21. I was only 19, but I knew where my future lay. When I did turn 21, the CHP was not hiring; so, I resolved to the fact that I would have to put that goal off and be a police officer to begin with. That was exactly what occurred. I will get into that later.

Carol's parents and some of our other relatives thought it would be a good idea for the two of us to have some counseling by a "professional" person about all of the intricacies and emotions about marriage and raising a family etc. We made an appointment to see Doc Miller, a local physician who we had been told was just the person to provide this counseling. Doc was a great person and just about as down to earth as they came. We saw him, listened to him, but did not learn much that was new. About 30 years later, Doc was giving a talk to the Oakdale Dinner Club (Oakdale's finest and all male) when he brought up this counseling session of many years past. Jokingly, he claimed his marriage was on the rocks, about to go under when he talked to Carol and me, but he learned so dammed much from us about sex that his whole marriage turned around and was saved.

We were married as planned, and moved into a duplex at 124 West J Street in Oakdale. Nice little place, not very big, but for $50.00 a month it would be hard to beat. Our neighbor in the other duplex was a highway engineer with the State of California. He informed us that he was the head engineer on the Oakdale bypass that would be built in the next couple of years. It would have started just south of town near 26 Mile Road and then go across Wild Cat Canyon near Lovers Leap. The money had been appropriated and it was just tidying up the paper work, purchasing the property and we were a go. That was 1956. Here we were, 60 years later, and still no bypass.

Carol came home one day in September, and after a trip to Doc Miller confirms our suspicions, she was pregnant and the baby was due in June. Don't bother to count, that was 14 months after the wedding. Although not planned, we were elated. We both knew Carol would have to quit working for a while, but we had some money saved and we would get by just fine. Things were not going well at the gas station. Cookie was drinking more and more, I was getting tired of dumping bottles. His daughter was away at college, so I was doing the bookwork, also. Cookie decided to go on a fishing trip to Canada with some friends, one of whom had his own airplane. He left with little or no instructions. I guess he had confidence in me taking care of things or he didn't care. So, for about two weeks, he was gone. Things went well; although,

I had to pay myself cash out of the register. I hired a couple of kids from high school to help me out, and we got through the crisis for the time being. When he got back, he was a total drunk. His wife kicked him out, and he slept in an old ragged sleeping bag in a small room inside the station. To make matters worse, he brought his faithful, short-haired, pointer hunting dog, Maggie, to sleep with him. She crapped all over the little room. It was a real mess.

I was running the station full time, working 15 hours a day, and taking care of Cookie and Maggie. This went on for three weeks until his brother Louie showed up and put Cookie in rehab in the Bay Area. After a month he was back, and for once he looked really good, and I thought, "He's going to make it." He realized what a big help I had been through all of this, and gave me a $200.00 bonus. Well, things were back to normal, but I saw the handwriting on the wall. I knew this was not going to last, and I still saw reflections of my dad's behavior.

Some of our customers were regulars, and worked at the First Western Bank on the corner of Yosemite and F Streets, just past the station: Marge Montgomery, Mary McCallum, Pearl Titchenal, Betty Rydberg, Betty Nielsen, and Mary Grace Langford. I had been gassing their cars for a couple of years and had enjoyed their visits and our conversations. One day out of the clear blue sky, I think it was Marge Montgomery, asked me if I would be interested in working at the bank. That just floored me. Frank the grease monkey working at a bank; yeah, and I was going to find a pot of gold at the end of the rainbow! Then a light came on, a big bright light. I recalled that back in high school, my councilor Mr. Weichert had told me that I might have a future in banking based on the variety of vocational testing I had been given at school. I talked it over with Carol that night, and she said I should give it a try as it probably held a better future than the gas station. Best advice I ever got.

Well, as it turned out, a few, or maybe all of these ladies had suggested to the bank manager that he interview me for a job opening at the bank. A few days later Marge came into the station and said that the manager wanted to talk to me, if I was interested in a position at the bank. I told her I was, and she said to come into the bank and ask for Mr. Herb Barker. I did that the same day, and after the interview was offered a job as bookkeeper starting out at $250.00 a month. That was about $50.00 a month more than I was making at the station, with weekends and holidays off, 8:00 a.m. to 5:00 p.m., health insurance, and no more dirty grease or greasy clothing. While in many ways it broke my heart to tell Cookie I was leaving, I think deep down inside he was both happy for me and proud at the same time.

I had been at the bank for about 3 months and had just been promoted to teller when I was contacted by Mr. Waite Paul, the Shell Oil Company Distributor, and another man from Shell Oil. Mr. Paul said that Cookie was drinking again and in danger of losing the business. Would I be interested in taking over the station with the full financial backing of Shell Oil? I never batted an eye. I explained how much I appreciated the offer and opportunity, but I felt that would be disloyal to

Cookie, even though I realized someone else was going to take his place. "Sorry, but I will stay with the bank." A few weeks later, Cookie was gone, and the station was taken over by Bill Coppetti. Cookie's marriage fell apart, and soon he was just another town drunk living in a small room over the top of H-B Saloon.

In 1961, while a police officer with the Modesto PD, I received a call from the county jail that they wanted to see me. When I arrived at the jail, there was Cookie in the lobby, just being discharged after an arrest by the Oakdale PD for public drunkenness. After I got off of work at 10:00 p.m., I went to the jail, picked him up, and drove him to Oakdale. He borrowed $20.00 from me, I let him out of the car, and he headed up to his room. I went around the corner, came back, and saw Cookie walking into the liquor store next to H-B. That was the last time I saw him, until his funeral a few weeks later. Thanks, Cookie for all you did for me and my family.

# A LAW ENFORCEMENT
# CAREER BEGINS: 1956-1969

I began work at First Western Bank & Trust in the fall of 1956, and my first job was posting checks and deposits on this huge Burroughs bookkeeping machine. When I got to work, I would organize all of the checks and deposits from the previous day alphabetically. Then I would sit down at the machine, pull up a cart with ledgers of all the bank's accounts say from A to H, (there were three machines) and the stack of checks and deposits from the previous day, put the ledger by name into the machine, bring up the current balance, then subtract the checks or add the deposits, and come up with a new balance. This went on most of the day. Hopefully when finished, they balanced with the teller's tabulation sheet. I did this same thing every day for about three months (Cookie's was beginning to look a little better). Right after the first of the year, Mr. Barker called me to his desk and said he was impressed with my progress, and upon the recommendation of the operations officer, he was moving me up to a teller position working a window. This also included a $50.00 a month raise. I could not have been happier. "Mr. Barker, may I ask a question please?" He says, "Of course." "There are three other people working the bookkeeping machines who have all been here longer than I have. I can assure you based on my observations, they do as good of a job as I do. Why aren't they getting promoted?" I asked. "Well, Frank, quite frankly banking is pretty much a man's job; so, we promote men above women." While I did not think that fair, I accepted his answer.

At that point in my life, working at the bank was the best job I had ever had. Clean clothes, 8:00 a.m. to 5:00 p.m., Saturday and Sunday off. I had no idea life could be so good. Carol and I were together on weekends, going here and there, fishing, or just hanging out with Richard and Shirley, having a good time. I recall the bank's Christmas party at the Long Horn restaurant in Sonora. This was the very first time in my life I had ever eaten a steak. Talk about being a hick. Carol was getting bigger and bigger; so, I knew at some point she was going to lose her job because of her appearance, and there was no guarantee that she would get it back after she had our baby. Boy have things changed in the past 60 years, and for the better I must say. So Carol was laid off, and I became the sole bread winner. Right away I realized my black beauty, the Mo Par would have to go, as we could not afford the payments any longer. I traded it to an acquaintance in Concord and took his old Dodge in the deal.

Our first and only child arrived on June 8, 1957. Kurtis Browning Clark. I wish I had known then what a wonderful person he would grow up to be. It would have saved a lot of worrying. One of my favorite stories about Kurt was when he was two years old, and he and I were walking near the main intersection of town, and the train engine was crossing the street in front of us. The train stopped and Kurt and I walked closer. The engineer was Bill McCaulum, and his wife Mary had worked at the bank with me. Bill looked down at Kurt and asked if he wanted to come aboard. Well of course he did. Keep in mind this was 1959 or so, and it was a steam engine. He hoisted Kurt up on the seat, had him pull the chain to sound the whistle, and the train began to move. We went about a mile up the tracks and then returned. What a thrill for a little kid (and his dad, too). That kind of thing could only happen in Oakdale.

Upon turning 21, I had the opportunity to apply for the Oakdale Police Departments Reserve Officers program. I was accepted, and with no training whatsoever began riding around with the regular officers on their shift assignments. After a couple of months, I had the general jest of what police officers did; although, I was far from being qualified to be an officer on duty by myself. At this time, Oakdale had only four officers available for duty. One evening about 6:00 p.m., Chief Forbes called me at home and said someone had called in sick, and there were no regular officers available to replace that person. He asked if I could take the responsibilities for the swing shift. I was scared to death, but said yes. I put on my uniform, kissed Carol good bye, and went out the front door. The only weapon I had was an old Iver-Johnson .22 caliber single action revolver. I strapped it on and drove out of the police headquarters in the 1958 Studebaker Commander, ready to protect the world. It was not long before I got a dispatch from the fire department concerning a disturbance at The Club, which was a local pool hall and card room. When I walked in, I saw Smokey Jackson yelling and ranting, swearing, and in general, just being disruptive. I told him to calm down and come outside where we could talk. He told me to go fuck myself and asked, "What is a little shit like you going to do about it?" I weighed 150 lbs., and he weighed about 200 lbs. He said, "You know what Clark? I think I just may whip your ass. What are you going to do about that?" "Well, Smokey, I probably can't do much about it, but I do know that even if you whip my ass today, there is a tomorrow, and rest assured you will eventually go to jail, not for just disturbing the peace, but resisting arrest, assaulting an officer, and anything else I can think of. I am going outside, and I expect you out there in five minutes or I am coming back in, and we can go at it. Got that?"

In a few minutes, he came out and started to get into the back of the patrol car when I said, "No, get in the front seat. We are going to talk." I drove him home, gave him a lecture about his poor mom and his family and how embarrassed they would be about his arrest. He started crying and began to apologize for his behavior. I told him I would not arrest him providing that he went back to The Club the next day and apologized to the owner. He said he would, and he did.

I continued as a member of the reserve force until I went to work for Modesto PD in July of 1958. One of my most vivid impressions that remains with me today was the small town politics that went on in Oakdale during those times. Occasionally, I would accompany police Chief Forbes to the justice court in Oakdale to have morning coffee with Judge Vern Sawyer. The two of them went over all of the cases that would be appearing before the judge later that day. By the time we finished coffee, all defendants had been judged by the two of them and their sentences prescribed without them ever having an opportunity to be heard. My best friend Richard White became a regular police officer in Oakdale. He had arrested Bill Haslam, who owned the local Chevrolet-Buick dealership and was considered one of the towns leading citizens, for a DUI. Chief Forbes begged Richard to drop the charges, but Richard refused. Without any fanfare, trial, or legal process, the case was never heard. Richard resigned over the matter.

\* \* \*

Things could not have been better. Mr. Barker called me into his office and announced that I was in line for another promotion. There was one little catch; the job was in Sacramento, and I would have to move there or commute. I would undergo training to become a lending officer, handling auto and small loans. Well, there was no way I could drive to Sacramento every day, and I sure did not want to leave Oakdale and all of my friends and family. Carol and I discussed it at length and then made the decision to turn the promotion down. I got back to Mr. Barker the next day and told him of my decision. I made the mistake of going one step further (Honesty is the best policy, right?) and I told him that my goal was to seek a profession in law enforcement where my heart really lies. "Well," he says, "Then I guess there is no reason you should continue to work here. Thanks for your service. We will mail you your last check." Boom, I am outside looking in with no job. Kurt was nine months old, and thank God Carol was able to return to the Bank of America. My Aunt Alleene babysat Kurt, and I started looking for a job.

Patrolman Frank Clark, 1958

It was March 1958, and I put in applications for every law enforcement job I could find. I could not work for Stanislaus County because you had to be 23 years old, and I was only 21. California Highway Patrol (CHP) and the Modesto PD were not currently hiring; so, I submitted applications at every agency that was advertising for officers. I was not having much luck when I got a letter from Santa Barbara inviting me to take the examination for police officer. I took the Greyhound bus out of Modesto to Santa Barbara and took the exam. Luckily, my connections were such that I headed home without having to stay overnight. For whatever the reason, I got into Modesto about 2:00 a.m. and started hitchhiking to Oakdale. There was some kind of problem that kept Carol from picking me up. I hoofed it all the way out McHenry Avenue to where the old Stoddard School was (now a furniture store) before a police car came by headed for Oakdale. Sgt. Sam Riley, Oakdale PD had been in Modesto booking an arrestee and gave me a ride home, and was I ever thankful.

In a couple of weeks, another letter came from the City of Santa Barbara, and they wanted me back for an oral interview. These interviews were to take place on a Saturday; so, Carol and I were able to drive down and spend the night. The interview went okay, and about June I was told that if I passed the background investigation, I could expect to be offered a position with the City sometime in August. I was thrilled to death. The following day, which was in mid-May, I got an invitation to take the examination for police officer in Modesto. Well, to make a long story short, out of over 100 applicants, I got a job offer and subsequently told to report for duty on July 1, 1958. I was sworn in, issued my equipment, sent to Stockton to purchase uniforms, and began a career with the City of Modesto that would last until March 1969. The monthly salary was $341.00.

Lieutenant Frank Clark, 1965

\* \* \*

The City had hired four new police officers, and we were to spend the next two weeks going to an in-house orientation and training program. When that ended, we were to be assigned to a veteran officer for in the field training. Lucky me, at the conclusion of the training, I was assigned to the day shift, 6:00 a.m. to 2:00 p.m. and my training officer was one of the oldest officers on the department, Ernie Gansel, and his nickname was "Gunsmoke". I noticed the bill of his uniform hat was filthy. The only clean spot was where you grabbed the bill to take it off and put it on. I showed up at 5:00 a.m. bright and early Sunday morning, ready to eradicate all crime in Modesto, save all the women and children, and protect the elderly. We checked out the patrol car, loaded our equipment which consisted of what we are wearing, a billy club, handcuffs, revolver, twelve extra bullets, and a traffic ticket book (Ernie had a huge thermos of coffee which I could not figure out). No taser, portable radio, body cam, tear gas, bullet proof vest, just the bare essentials. I could not wait to get my hands on the steering wheel of the cruiser and start chasing down speeders, but no, Ernie drove.

We first headed for the Flakey Crème donut shop, three miles off of our assigned beat. Ernie went in and came out with a bag of something. Next, we went by Nichol's News on Eleventh Street where we picked up a Sunday Chronicle newspaper. Then it was on to our assigned beat on Scenic Drive and northeast Modesto. Ernie pulled into the cemetery across from the County Hospital, found some shade, turned off the police radio, and spread out the paper. He opened the bag and began to gulp down white powdery donuts, chased by black coffee from the thermos. He wiped out the cup and asked if I wanted some coffee and a donut. I was in shock. "What the hell is going on?" I asked myself. "Is this what I am to expect for the rest of my life?" Years later in Oakdale,

I became friends with Denny Armstrong who was a cattleman with a ranch in the LaGrange area southeast of Oakdale. When I first started on the police department in Modesto, I was given a traffic ticket book that had Armstrong written on the hard cover. I asked him if that was his and he said yes, that when he got out of the navy after WW II (he was a torpedo bomber pilot) that he joined the police department. "I had that book for three years and only wrote three tickets," he replied. He told me of the time he and *Gunsmoke* were sitting in the Needles Bar on I Street having a cocktail while in full uniform, and in walked the city manager Ross Miller. Gansel was about to faint and asked Denny, "What the heck do we do?" Denny ordered Mr. Miller a drink. He accepted it, sipped it down, and left for city hall. Nothing said.

Back to my training. This routine pretty much went on for the next two weeks. The training concluded, and I was assigned to the grave yard shift, 10:00 p.m. to 6:00 a.m. Shifts were assigned on a seniority basis, so I know these will be my hours for several months at best. There were five beats in Modesto, staffed by five officers and one sergeant. At times, there were only three officers working, so it was East, West, and Central beats. My beat was a nice residential area called La Loma beat 5. It also included Yosemite Boulevard where there are many bars and dance halls and the Modesto airport area, which was one of Modesto's most impoverished and a high crime rate area. I was not a big guy, barely 5'9" and 155 lbs. soaking wet. One morning while having breakfast at about 2:30 a.m. at Johnny & Mattie's café, this big boisterous, loud, obnoxious guy came into the café and just started raising hell. He was obviously very drunk. I got up and approached and immediately told him that he was under arrest for drunk in public and disturbing the peace. He shut up, looked at me, and laughed, then grabbed me by the waist, and literally threw me against the wall. I was dazed, scared shitless, and knew I was in for a rough time. With no portable radio like they have today to call for help, I was on my own. I pulled out my little 10" billy club and approached the man. Before I could get close enough to smack him, about three guys jumped out of their booth and decked this jerk. They held him down, and I put the cuffs on him. Case closed. Thanks for the kind of people we had around during that time period, who were willing to help an officer when he needed it most. Have times changed?

I loved being a police officer. For the next couple of months, I did routine police work such as traffic enforcement, neighborhood patrol, and investigating a variety of different crimes. I had never seen a dead person before; so, when I got the call to investigate a family fight about midnight on Los Flores Avenue, I had no clue what I was going to find. As I approached the front door, I heard a loud bang. No question in my mind; it was the discharge of a shot gun. I raced back to the patrol car and called for help, but was told it would be a while and the desk officer was trying to get help from the sheriff's department. I went back to the front door and then another blast. Once again, I was scared shitless, but knew I had to do something. I kicked the door a couple of times, but it did not budge. I tried the door knob, and the damned door was unlocked. I entered the house with gun drawn. Oh my god what a mess. Two victims in the front room, both head shots from a shotgun; one homicide and one suicide. The Crutchfields, a name I will never forget. I went outside and threw up on the lawn and waited for help; although, there wasn't anything anyone could do. I got a lot more calloused after that.

* * *

Long ago, I realized that if I were to get ahead in law enforcement, I would have to pursue an education, as well as prepare myself with on the job training. I enrolled at Modesto Junior College, taking three classes a semester and purchased several basic law enforcement publications. I went to school twice a week in the morning, and once in the evening before I went to work. This worked out okay the first semester, but come spring, Carol was getting a little tired of my absence from home. I promised that if I could enroll in the spring semester on the same schedule, I would drop school until I got on another shift. She was in agreement. So, it's back to school. Well, it did not work out; she was tired of not having a husband at home at night with his wife and young son. She wanted a separation and ultimately a divorce. I cannot say that I blamed her. My chosen profession was, unfortunately, more important to me than it should have been. I did not want to lose Carol, and I did not want to quit school. So, I decided to talk to the police chief, George Bowers, about my situation, thinking maybe he could give me some advice or better yet, get me temporarily on the day shift. The Chief who had become Modesto's top cop, about three years previously, was a very well educated individual whose career had been with the Berkeley Police Department. He was willing to get someone on the day shift to go on graveyard and put me on days. He promised that no one, not anyone, would know about this special arrangement.

We agreed to try this arrangement for 90 days and see if things could be worked out between Carol and me. Well, we could not work things out, and we both went our separate ways. At the end of the 90 days, the Chief, true to his word, called me in and asked how things were going. I said, "Not so well," but I thanked him for trying to help. Then to my surprise he said, "Officer Clark, I have a request of you if you are interested." I was flabbergasted! I mean he is the Chief; he can do anything he wants. He went on, "There is a position within the police department called the 'court liaison officer'. This position requires someone to get all of the reports together daily, and as defendants appear in Municipal court after an arrest, the paper work is all there for the judge to review. Judge Hanson has been in contact with us, and he would like to see someone younger, more energetic and have all the necessary documents available at court time, so that the process moves along without unnecessary delay. Would you be interested?" I jumped at the chance. I am now working 8:00 a.m. to 5:00 p.m. and learning so much about the legal and court systems that will help me professionally in the future.

Carol and I had gone our separate ways. I now had additional expenses, rent, child support, school; so, I had to look for a part-time job. Soon I found myself driving a school bus every morning and working weekends at Will's Texaco station on North Eleventh Street (hello Cookie). I was working my ass off but meeting my obligations. I rented a room from a wonderful elderly lady on Las Palmas Avenue. She was the widow of Dr. Edmunds who for many years had practiced medicine in Modesto. She was very lonely and having a police officer living in the house made her life much more enjoyable. When she had the gang over for bridge, she always enjoyed introducing me to the crowd as her protector. She was sweet.

After about six months, I was missing real police work, so asked to be transferred back to the Patrol Division. Over the objections of Judge Hanson, I went back on the swing shift as a patrolman. I loved it! It was the job I was always meant to have. I patrolled downtown Modesto, Tenth and Eleventh Streets, which were the drag strips for kids in those days. Loving to race myself, I would hide behind Will's gas station on Eleventh Street, and as the racers zoomed by, I was in hot pursuit. They got a ticket, and I had my fix. I met a lot of really neat young guys that hung out on Tenth Street around Burgi's Drive Inn. We also become friends on a social nature, and at times, went out of town to seek fun and adventure.

One evening while on duty, the dispatcher called and reported a burglary in progress at Needles Market on the north end of Eleventh Street. I was conversing with my friends (the Uptown Gang, as we police officers referred to them) when the call came in. My buddies also heard the call. I immediately raced to the market and parked a half block away and approached on foot. The front door was smashed in, and I could see a young man in his twenties rifling the cash register. I stood between him and the front door, gun drawn, and ordered him to the ground. He said, "Fuck you! You will have to shoot me first, and I am getting out of here." What to do? Kill some guy over a few bucks, confront him and lose my weapon and get shot myself? About then, in through the front door came five or six Uptown members who wrestled the guy to the ground, and I cuffed him and off to jail. Never would happen today or in a million years.

\* \* \*

Starr Hotel on J Street near Ninth Street. The hotel manager thought the guy in one of the rooms, who is a permanent resident, was ill, or something else was wrong. I got the call and met the desk clerk at the upstairs room in question. We opened the door with the master key; what a stink. If you have never smelled a dead person after three or four days in a warm room, please keep it that way. The body was bloated to twice its normal size, and the flies were swarming. It was all you could do to not vomit. Open all of the windows, the door, turn on the fan in the room, and call the coroner. While checking out the room I noticed a wine case size box in the closet. I took it down, no one in the room but me, opened it, and there were several stacks, I mean big stacks, of 20s and 100 dollar bills. Over $30,000 dollars when it was finally totaled. The coroner arrived, and I turned the money over to him. I followed up on my own initiative with the County to make sure that money went where it was supposed to go. I later told this story to one of our neighboring city police chiefs who came from the San Francisco PD, and he said I was crazy for not taking at least half of it, which no one would have missed. How did you sleep at night SFPD?

\* \* \*

When I came onto the police department in the summer of 1958, several things caught my eye that someday I would be in a position to change. During Xmas holidays each year, patrol Sergeant Smith would make the rounds of many of the bars and liquor stores in Modesto and ask for, or perhaps demand, a quart of booze. He would then brazenly bring it back to the police station and put it into his office. Bottle after bottle! Police officers could go to Smitty's Restaurant on Ninth Street at any time, day or night, and order anything they wanted and then leave without paying. Free coffee and donuts at Flakey Crème. This was all wrong and had to be corrected, but this practice had been accepted by the department as being okay for a very long time. God bless Chief Bowers, as he would change many of these things, as he moved toward the professionalization of the police department and the gradual improvement of police personnel through attrition, recruiting, and appropriate disciplinary action.

\* \* \*

I still had hopes of getting back together with Carol. We visited on my days off and went out occasionally, but I could see any opportunities fleeting away. One afternoon, she informed me that she had a friend, and they were just that, only friends. Carol asked me to consent to an uncontested divorce, and I agreed. Within a few months, we were officially divorced, and that was the end of a marriage that I thought should and could have been saved. She was no more to blame for it not being saved than I was. She was, and still is, a very wonderful woman.

\* \* \*

Back in patrol, I was in my element, chasing racing kids up and down Tenth and Eleventh Streets. Investigating a variety of crimes, having fun just visiting, and communicating with the populace. I enjoyed being a police officer and the respect the community showed us. One particular evening, I saw this cute little sports car speeding down Tenth Street, so I ran it down and pulled it over. The driver was cute and sexy. The passenger was even better looking. I recognized the passenger as being a gal I went to high school with when I was a freshman and she was a senior. I also recalled having some classes in banking at MJC with her when I worked at the bank. I gave them a lecture on bad driving and let them go without a ticket. A couple of weeks later, I was checking out a night club and dance place on Yosemite Boulevard, and who was dancing by as I stood there, but this same cute little lady who was a passenger in the sports car. She smiled and danced her way over to where I was standing. I thought she had had a couple of drinks, but she came up and initiated a conversation. She must have noticed my name tag "Clark" as she unexpectedly flipped the brim of my hat and said, "Hello Officer Clark" and danced away. I was embarrassed, and at the same time, also excited. Before I left, we talked, and I asked for her telephone number, that is, if she were unattached. "Well, that sounds like a police command," she said, and gave me her number. The lady was Marilyn Holman (Cudd in high school). That was the beginning of a wonderful (to date) 56-year relationship.

We began to date and were just crazy in love, spending every spare minute together. In July of 1960, we drove over the hill to Reno to get married. We took out our marriage license in Carson City, and because Marilyn's family were members of the Baptist church, we went through the phone book and found a Baptist preacher who was willing to marry us. We hurried over to his church and stood there before him holding hands as he prepared to administer the vows. "Have either of you been married before?" he asked. "Why yes, both of us have been previously married, and each have one child from those marriages," we replied. "Oh, I am so sorry, but I cannot perform this ceremony for divorced couples. I am sorry but you will have to find someone else." Back to the phone book. Screw the Baptists. Let's try a Methodist; they are a little more liberal. Bingo! We found a minister in Reno, and he said, "Come on up."

The next morning, we were at the church, but to our dismay were told the minister was ill, but no problem, another minister would perform the ceremony. Who was standing there as we walk up the aisle? It was none other than the Baptist minister from Carson City. He did not bat an eye, called on another couple waiting to be married to act as witnesses, and then he pronounced us man and wife. Hallelujah! We celebrated that night, and the next morning, headed to the casino for breakfast. We were both flat broke, except for just enough money for breakfast and gas to get back to Modesto. While waiting in line at the restaurant, Marilyn hit a $50.00 jackpot on a nickel machine. We have been blessed ever since.

We rented a nice little home at 211 Rowland Avenue in Modesto, and we, along with her son Ronald, moved in. Marilyn had been working at the Wells Fargo Bank in Modesto as a teller for the past three years and continued to do so. Life was good, could not have been happier. Come November, I got one of the shocks of my life: a notice from the local draft board that I was to report to the induction center in Fresno for a physical examination and processing for induction into the US Army. I gave Marilyn the bad news, but she just looked at me and broke into a big smile. She was pregnant! The next day we got a confirmation letter from Dr. Broderick, and I took that to the local draft board. I was reclassified and the possibility of being drafted was history. That was one of the many reasons that I love my son Greg so much.

Marilyn worked at the bank until policy required her to take a leave of absence, and we had to start spending our savings to keep up. I was driving the school bus for Modesto City Schools every day and working weekends at Will's

Texaco Service at Eleventh and M Streets. When school was out, I got a job at Stanislaus Foods, supervising women who were sorting tomatoes. Lots of work, but we were meeting our budget. Marilyn gave birth on August 12, 1961 to the cutest little guy you ever saw. Gregory Richard Clark (middle name for my best friend Richard White). In a couple of months, Marilyn went back to work part time at the bank and her sister, Twyla, babysat baby Greg. I kept working at the gas station but dropped my other part-time jobs. What a relief!

I had now been on the police department just over four years, and it was a job that I could not love more. I was working the swing shift, 2:00 p.m. to 10:00 p.m., so our home life was somewhat improved from being on graveyard. I came home from working at the gas station and started making preparations to go to work at the police department, and Marilyn said Captain Coulson's secretary called, and he wanted to see me when I come in and before I went on patrol. Captain Coulson was in charge of the Detective Division and number two on the department. I knew he was an ex-marine having served during WW II and participated in several landings in the Pacific. He appeared to be not only gruff, but also tough. I was a little nervous when I went into his office and unsure of why he would want to see me. We chitchatted for a few minutes, and then he explained the purpose of our meeting. Detective Larson was going on vacation for three weeks, and someone was needed to work plain clothes as his replacement. I was both stunned and elated to have such an opportunity to gain this new experience. I would be handling the bad check and forgery detail in Detective Larson's absence. If I was interested, I could start the day after tomorrow, Thursday, and work a couple of days with Eric (Detective Larson) and kind of get the drift of things. So, for the next two days I shadowed Eric and learned the ropes of being a bad check investigator. Eric was not enthusiastic about his job and had kind of a negative attitude about everything in general. I really learned little from him. That Monday, I reported for work in a new set of clothes, sport coat, tie, and new shoes. I was ready. During that first day, I made contact with Sergeant Jerry Starr at the Stanislaus County Sheriff's Office, who was my counterpart with that agency. In two hours, I learned more than I had the previous two days with Eric. Jerry was bright, hardworking, and had a sense of accomplishment about his job. When I got back to the office I noticed a top coat hanging on the coat rack, and for some reason I took a look at the inside pocket. I found a stack of checks three inches thick from businesses all over Modesto. These were bad checks picked up from the merchants by Eric over the past several weeks and months that have not been processed, cases opened. I walked into Captain Coulson's office and showed him the checks. He was beyond himself, "What the hell is going on here?!" he exclaimed. He took me into the Chief's office and threw the checks down on his desk. "Look at this Chief," he stated. The Chief looked at him and said, "Surprised Bill?" Just give them to Detective Clark (I loved those words), and he can just start knocking them off."

Well, I literally work 16 hours a day to resolve this situation. The layman has to understand the definition of *bad check*. Basically there are three types: The first is nonsufficient funds (NSF), when there is just not enough money in the check writer's account to cover the check. These made up approximately 60 % of the cases. The second, account-closed, when the check writer just keeps writing checks, and he knows his account is now closed at the bank, about 20 %. The third is out right forgeries, when the writer forges someone else's name onto a check, or they print checks on fictitious businesses, or steal checks from legitimate business and cash them at various locations, including even financial institutions. These are the real hard core criminals, and they make up the balance about 20 %.

While I do not want to be a collection agency, I had to eliminate this huge back log of checks turned into the police department by various merchants for some kind of assistance. I made contact with all of the NSF check writers I could find, and quite frankly, I gave them one week to make the checks good with the merchant or they were going to jail. Bingo! 90% were cleared up within two weeks. The *closed account* checks were a little different. Half of those made the checks good after a letter from the District Attorney and the remaining ones I went after, and they were arrested and prosecuted. Toward the end of my three-week assignment to the Detective Division, I had eliminated the backlog, and things were in pretty good order. It was gratifying to see what could be done by working 16 hours a day, 7 days a week and putting the police department into a better light. Several people, as I found out later, had complimented the Chief on my hard work and ensuing results. The owners of Modesto's three largest grocery stores were Rotarians along with the Chief, so he got it firsthand. My last day of working vacation relief in the Detective Division seemed to have arrived way too soon. I loved this job and was going to miss it.

On the last day, Friday at 4:00 p.m., I went into Captain Coulson's office to thank him for the wonderful opportunity he had given me and say what a gratifying experience it had been. I had never seen the captain smile before, but he was, as he pushed a police memorandum across the desk to me. I picked it up and began to read:

> *Effective January 1, 1963, Patrolman II Frank Clark*
> *is promoted to Detective and will report to Captain*
> *William Coulson for duty and assignment as directed.*
>
> *Congratulations,*
>
> *George C. Bowers Chief of Police City of Modesto.*

I thanked the captain for the opportunity and rushed home to share the news with Marilyn. We were the four happiest people in the world. What this meant was that with the $100.00 a month raise that went along with the promotion, we could now buy that new home over by Davis High. The next day, Saturday, we headed over that way and picked out the floor plan, signed the papers, and waited for it to be constructed. Three months later, we would move into our dream home.

1400 square feet, corner lot, big back yard, and lots of amenities. The payment was less than the rent we had been paying previously, and the down payment was only $300.00 dollars. My new work schedule was Monday–Friday, 8:00 a.m. to 5:00 p.m. with weekends and holidays off. Life could not be better. I could not wait to get started Monday on my new "permanent" assignment.

\* \* \*

One of my highest priority objectives was to establish a program to educate the merchants about how to reduce their risks when cashing checks and the things they could do to make it easier to apprehend and prosecute offenders. Having worked at the bank, I was familiar with the American Banking Institute (ABI) and there was also a state wide law enforcement professional organization called the California Check Investigators Association (CCIA). I was in touch with both organizations and they provided me a drove of information to help put together a professional education program for presentation to merchants and their employees. I began to have meetings with the employees of major businesses in Modesto and also prepared handouts on how to avoid bad checks to distribute to the smaller businesses. These two projects proved to be very effective and a gradual reduction in bad check offenses becomes obvious. These offenses, within a year, had been reduced by 50 %. Working with merchants, we also established a "check" hot line that you could call and get help or information on bad checks that were being passed.

The Modesto Police Department got accolades at the annual CCIA convention in Squaw Valley the next year, and several jurisdictions implemented similar programs. The prosecution of people who wrote bad checks was somewhat easier than, say, robberies or burglaries. You had a good piece of physical evidence in the bad document, an eyewitness in the person who took the check, and in many cases, a description of the identification used at the time the check was passed. Putting those together, preparing a report, interviewing all the witnesses and the suspects, and then getting a complaint from the District Attorney, an arrest warrant was very time consuming, but the conviction rate was high. I think in the long run, this served as a deterrent to others who either did not write bad checks, or when they did and were contacted, rushed down to the store and made them good. The most difficult cases to solve and make an arrest involved checks stolen from large businesses or checks that were copied (reprinted) from an original check of a large business. During this time period most people cashed their checks at grocery stores or other large businesses. If they had a check from Campbell Soup for instance, and their ID (usually faked) matched the name on the check, it got cashed.

My best remembered case, and I had literally hundreds of them, involved several brothers well known in Central and Northern California as the Morton Gang. This was a gang that involved themselves in burglaries, robberies, forging stolen checks, and almost any other crime you could think of. The leader of the gang was Jerry Morton, and he learned his trade at making checks in the print shop at San Quinton. His gang would get their hands on a check from a large, well known, legitimate business and print them up. Then they would go to the town where that business was well known, always on a weekend when the business and the banks were closed, and inundate the area with large numbers of checks. There were several cases where they were confronted by clerks, only to escape after producing firearms. On one occasion, they did shoot a grocery store employee.

They liked to hang out in South Modesto near Dallas Street where their parents and other family members lived They were on a roll, and half of the police in northern California were on the lookout for them. Someone in Manteca had gotten a description of a car and partial license plate number at a Safeway Market. While driving down Crows Landing Road, I spotted the car in front of me, and as it turned out, driven by Jerry Morton, the ring leader. We went a couple of blocks, and I pulled him over. Keep in mind, I was driving an unmarked police unit. The stop just happened to be next to an elementary school. Bad judgement on my part. I walked up to the car and asked for his driver's license which he produced. It read, "Edgar Williams from Sacramento." That matched the dealer's license plate frame. "Why are you stopping me officer?" he asked. "You failed to yield the right of way to that pedestrian a couple of blocks back," I replied. "I did not see any pedestrian." "Of course you didn't, or you would have stopped." We conversed a few minutes. I had his mug shot in the car, so I went back and took a look. "Yep, that's the bastard, and I bet he is packing." I asked for back up, but as usual it would be 15-20 minutes, if at all. I noticed the school principal wandering across the playground toward our location, and I motion him over. I knew the gentleman, and quickly and quietly told him what was going on, and that this guy was packing; so, there could be some fireworks. "Make sure no kids come this way." Thank God none were in sight. I was not scared, just anxious.

With the principal standing there, I asked Mr. Williams to exit the car, and as he did, I pulled my service revolver. I told him to spread eagle against the cyclone fence. When he did, I could see a bulge in his waist band, but I had the drop on him. I knew, based on his reputation, he would try to shoot me if he could, or escape if there was any possible way. I cocked my weapon and put it right up against the back of his head, while very gently removing a .45 caliber automatic hand gun from his waist band. Now came the time when I was most vulnerable. I had to hand cuff him, and that meant putting my weapon either back in the holster or my waist band, and I still had his .45 in one hand. I did a stupid thing. I took the .45, racked the action, and out came a round, a new one went in, and the hammer came back. I motioned to the principal to step over near me. I handed him the .45, asked if he had ever fired a hand gun before, and luckily he had. "I am going to handcuff this gentleman, and I want to tell you, he is very dangerous. If he makes just one little aggressive movement, I mean just one, blow his fucking brains out." The poor principal turned white, but aimed the gun at Morton, and I proceeded to handcuff him without incident. Morton asked on the way to jail, "Do you think he would have shot me?" "You know, Mr. Morton, I guess we will just never know."

\* \* \*

Being a detective was probably the best job on the police department. You worked days, weekends off, no subordinates to worry about, responsible only to the job and yourself. Late one evening, I was the detective on call when the phone rang. There had been a shooting at 3-B's Liquor on Yosemite Boulevard. Looked like a homicide. I got there about 1:00 a.m. to find the patrol sergeant and a couple of uniformed officers on scene. In the back room, I found the owner, Mr. Ed Davis, lying face down in a pool of blood, obviously deceased. I called the office and asked them to call Detective Gorman, who normally handled robberies and other violent crimes. He was there in 30 minutes. Mr. Davis, whom I knew very well, had been shot in the head several times with a small caliber weapon, as there were a few .22 shell casings laying around. The autopsy later confirmed 14 shots to the head. Someone really wanted him dead. The cash register was empty, and the cash box was missing. I determined later that a stack of bad checks was also missing. Harry and I collected Mr. Davis's clothing, the shell casings, and attempted to lift finger prints around the crime scene.

Keep in mind, in those days there were no fancy forensic units to analyze the crime scene and collect evidence, just gumshoe detectives. There were no surveillance cameras;

so, we asked the news reporters to put in their story to have anyone who might have been in the store that evening to contact Harry or me, so that we might speak to them. We got several names and a few leads. The next day Captain Coulson and the Chief called Harry and me in and said in no uncertain terms we were to solve this horrible crime. We were both to work full time on it until someone was arrested. Mr. Davis's clothing was examined in Sacramento, and lab tests determined that there were clothing fibers on Mr. Davis's shirt that came from someone else's garment, lots of them; so, there might have been a struggle before he was killed.

The murder weapon was a .22 caliber revolver, as there were no extraction marks on the shell casings. This suggested that the suspect shot Mr. Davis several times and then reloaded and shot him some more. Incredibly horrible! That was about all we had to go on. Several people came forward that were in the store that evening prior to the killing, but they were of little help, except for one Hispanic guy who must have been the last person served by Mr. Davis before he was killed. This little guy told us that there was a short, medium-built Caucasian smoking a cigar that was with Mr. Davis when he came in to get a six pack. No one of that description had come forward yet to be questioned, and he was our only possible suspect at that time. Why would the suspect take the bad checks? "For Christ's sake, wake up Frank!" I tell myself. "Only last week you went through those checks with Mr. Davis. There were over $500.00 worth of account-closed checks written to the liquor store from someone named Ronald Merman.

Marilyn and I bowled in a league every Thursday night at Modesto Bowl. Also participating was Ron Merman and his wife Kathy. He was short, a little overweight, and yes, he smoked cigars. We brought him in for questioning, and he denied being in the store that night. We asked about the $500.00 worth of bad checks, and he says he made them good. "When?" I asked. He replied, "About a month ago." "Bullshit," I said to myself. I saw those checks just last week. "This is the son of a bitch that killed Mr. Davis," I say to myself.

We went to District Attorney Alexander Wolfe and obtained a search warrant for Merman's house, car, and work place. In the house, we found a sports jacket that was the same color as the fibers found on the victim. We confiscated the jacket. We found a burn barrel in the back yard and rifled through it. We found remnants of checks that were marked *account closed* and signed by Merman. We found none that could be identified as being made out to 3-B Liquor. We were trying to contact Merman for further questioning when we determined he had been arrested in Manteca for the murder of his aunt. The police had also confiscated the possible murder weapon, a .22 caliber revolver. We had this weapon picked up for ballistic testing, and took it to Sacramento to be examined. The expert said he was 98% sure this was the murder weapon in the Davis case, but the bullets being of small caliber were badly damaged, and he just could not be absolutely sure beyond a reasonable doubt. In the meantime, our witness from the night of the murder identified Merman as the guy he saw in the store shortly before the murder. The criminal identifications department in Sacramento told us the fibers off of Merman's jacket and those on Mr. Davis were, without question, identical. We went back to the DA, and he issued a complaint and warrant for Ronald Merman, charging him with murder and robbery.

A couple of months later we went to trial, and after hearing all the witnesses and reviewing the evidence, the jury found Merman guilty of first-degree murder. The presiding judge, Superior Court Judge Dave Bush, announced a date for sentencing to take place a couple of weeks later. Harry and I were feeling pretty good, and so were the Davis family members. Come sentencing day, Harry and I were in the courtroom, along with Mr. Davis's family members. Judge Bush then reads a prepared document stating that he cannot agree with the jury's verdict and there was a lack of "preponderance of evidence" in this case. He was therefore overturning the verdict and ordering the case be set for re-trial. We were in total shock and disbelief! The family let their emotions flow, and we were all crying. We all just sat there as the judge left the bench. Merman and his wife hugged, and that bastard looked at me and Harry and smiled. Well, fortunately the Manteca police had a very good case, and he was later convicted for murdering his aunt. He was also more than likely guilty of killing a service station attendant near Auburn; although, he was never arrested in that murder. Several years later while serving a life sentence in San Quentin, he was attacked and murdered by other inmates.

* * *

A few months later Captain Coulson and I were sitting in the office eating our sack lunches, and in walked a records clerk who informed us that some guy was holding his wife hostage out off of Morris Avenue and was threatening to kill her. The clerk said two patrol units were on site trying to calm the situation down, but there was no supervisor available to assist at the scene. The Captain put down his liverwurst sandwich and bag of potato chips and said, "Come on Clark. Let's get out there and see what is going on." When we arrived, code 3 there were several neighbors in the street and two patrol cars in the driveway. The commotion seemed to be in the backyard; so, the Captain and I worked our way to the gate and entered the backyard. This guy had a woman on the ground, holding her tight with a large butcher knife to her throat. She was bleeding from a wound in her stomach and was hysterical. We tried and negotiate her release by pleading with the guy that things could work out; just drop the knife, and let the woman go so we can get her to a doctor. He was having none of that, and in a few minutes gave us an ultimatum: get out in 30 seconds or the woman is dead. Captain Coulson very calmly pulled out his service revolver, pointed it at the man, and shot him in the head. He was DOA. There was an ambulance standing by that immediately loaded both of them up and raced off to the hospital. We had already checked the guy, and no question, he was dead. The Captain and I returned to the station, went upstairs, and he finished his lunch. I could not eat right then. The Captain never discussed the matter, at least not with me. No one called in a psychologist to give us counseling, no chaplain. We did not go on administrative leave for two weeks. It was just another unfortunate situation that we had to live with. Case Closed!

\* \* \*

Things were running smoothly in the Detective Division, and in addition to handling the bad checks, I was now working a variety of cases to include robberies, burglaries, car thefts, and anything else that came my way. Captain Coulson called me in, and asked if I would like to go back to school? Well, school was nice, but how do I do that? He then informed me that the Chief had a good friend who was a professor at Berkeley and one of the country's foremost experts in the use of the lie detector, or better known as the polygraph. If I was interested, then the city would provide me the opportunity to undergo the training necessary to qualify as a polygrapher. I would be absent from normal duties for over a month, and would work with Dr. Albert Riedel for the next thirty days, or until he thought I had qualified. What an opportunity! I jumped at the chance. Mr. Riedel had a doctorate in psychology and had administered several hundred lie detector tests in his career. He would stay in Modesto during the week and work out of a rented office in the downtown area. There would be two other people attending the classes with me, one from the District Attorney's office, and one from the Sheriff's office.

Dr. Riedel had a very distinguished background working for the government, in the private sector, and currently at the University of California in Berkeley. For several years he was employed by the CIA, spending several years in Afghanistan during the 1950's. He traveled all over the world working for the Department of Defense (DOD) administering polygraph examinations to prospective employees, criminals, and foreigners. His best story, I thought, involved three air force personnel on Guam who were suspects in the murder and rape of a female Air Force nurse. The case was solved as the result of a lie detector test administered by Dr. Riedel. The suspect was seated in a chair, strapped down much like in an electric chair, and then hooked up to the polygraph. You have probably seen an electrical extension cord with a metal bowl like device on one end with a clamp. You usually clamp the light to the hood of your car, so that it shines light down onto the engine. Dr. Riedel removed the light bulb, plugged the light into the electrical outlet, and then placed the hood on the suspects head. He told the guy if he lied he would be electrocuted. The guy immediately confessed, even before the test could begin. He implicated two other guys who also confessed, and after a military trial, all three were put before a firing squad. Case closed. The guy must have been a real idiot.

We complete our training, and all three of us are now polygraph "experts", ready to put this valuable tool to work for our respective agencies. The polygraph is an investigative aid, nothing more, nothing less. I can unequivocally tell you that after personally administering over one hundred polygraph tests, they should not be, nor are they allowed as evidence in court. An example and true personal experience: John Doe took the test, and in my opinion passed it; he was telling the truth. First thing out of his mouth was, "How did I do?" I answer, "You know how you did. Why are you asking? You would not be here if you weren't guilty." He started crying and confessed to the crime. Was I a bad operator? No, he was just a very good liar. Conversely, I have seen people fail the test, but after working a little harder on the case, and not relying on the polygraph, the officer or detective found the individual innocent. They were nervous, maybe in bad health, or had other physiological problems. The polygraph measures heartbeat, breathing, and galvanic skin response (a change in electrical resistance in skin). If the polygraph detects and records a significant change in any one of these three, then the suspect may be lying. If the bell goes off on all three, then you can almost be sure the suspect was not telling the truth, but having said that, I believe that the polygraph, in the hands of a good operator, is 90% accurate. This experience was both educational and certainly enhanced my career.

\* \* \*

I had now been assigned to the Detective Division for 18 months and could not enjoy it more. Sergeant Smith retired, and there was an opening in the Patrol Division for a sergeant. I was working days, weekends off, etc. and the sergeant's job paid the same. Life at home, we could not have been happier. Why would I even be interested? I decided to talk to my friend Sheriff Dan Kelsay and get some advice from him. He asked me just one question, "Frank, do you plan on staying in law enforcement?" "Why, of course," I answered.

Actually, my long range plan was to be sheriff someday, but I did not mention that. He told me, "You cannot get to the head of the line without supervisory experience. Take the test for sergeant, and if you pass, and are offered the job, take it. That's the best advice I can give you." To make a long story short, I took the test, passed it, and I was offered the job. It meant going back to patrol, which I loved, but it also meant rotating shifts every three months. Marilyn and I talked it over at length and decided, if that's what I wanted, then to take the position.

July 16, 1964, I was back in uniform and assigned to the swing shift. This was going to take some adjustment. I had never supervised anyone, never had any training on the subject, but I would study, seek advice, and be a good sergeant, I promise myself. I loved being a patrol sergeant. You followed up on all exciting and interesting incidents, but you were not bothered with a lot of paperwork. I spent a lot of time reviewing reports, writing officer evaluations, and had gotten back into junior college. I saw lot of things I did not like as far as officer performance or lack of. I kept track of all this in a journal and knowing that at some point down the road, I may be in a higher position to correct a lot of things I saw as needing improvement. Time went by quickly, and after about 10 months as sergeant, the Modesto City Council approved three new positions of lieutenant for the department. We were to have a watch commander on each shift. I got really busy studying everything I could that I thought might be on the written examination. When the exam came, I was ready.

I passed that portion of the process to await the oral board exam. The chairman of the board was none other than Sheriff Kelsay. I was thinking to myself, "Sheriff, remember our conversation last year about getting supervision experience to move ahead?" I apparently did well on the oral exam, and on July 1, 1965, I was promoted to Lieutenant. Twenty-eight years old and the youngest lieutenant in the department's history. I was the watch commander on grave shift and in command of the police department from 12:00 midnight until 8:00 a.m.

This assignment turned out to be one of the most boring position I held during my tenure with Modesto P. D. You spent half of your time reviewing officer reports, making correction notices, and sending the report back to the officer for clarification and/or correction. If something really serious was going on, you would get in your unmarked police vehicle, go to the scene, and take command, if necessary. I put out an order on my shift that officers were no longer allowed to accept free meals at restaurants around town, no free coffee or donuts at Flakey Crème, no free booze from any bars or nightclubs. Several of the officers were not happy with this, but what can they do, complain to the Chief? I don't think so. The police department had never had a procedural manual or a code of conduct guideline book. With the permission of the Chief, I developed both over a period of a couple of months. This broke the boredom. They were approved and adopted by the City and put into effect, another step toward professionalism.

Just a few years back when an officer made a traffic stop and found even the smallest amount of marijuana debris on the floor of your car, you were busted for possession and usually received some time in jail. Second offense was prison for sure. Narcotics, specifically marijuana and LSD, were getting out of hand. Remember this was the Haight-Ashbury time, free love, screwy music, all that stuff, get loaded get loved, dodge the draft, and head for Canada, no Vietnam. Modesto PD had one officer working narcotics during the mid-sixties and it was far more than he could handle. In response to what we thought was a drug epidemic, the Chief established a Narcotics Enforcement Division within the Detective Division. I was asked to head up this new unit along with two detectives to be assigned under my supervision. I accepted the assignment with one caveat, I would have to be given time to come up to speed on investigating and prosecuting drug offenses. "We have taken care of that," the Chief said. "We are sending you to Monterey for a month to attend a training seminar presented by the US Bureau of Narcotic Enforcement." How sweet it is!

The month of October was a perfect time to be on the Monterey Peninsula. Marilyn came over a couple of times to visit, and the whole experience was outstanding. I got back to Modesto and found offices upstairs in the new police building. The neat thing about working narcotics and vice was that you had no set hours. You just worked to get the job done. Maybe 18 hours one day and 4 the next. Our unit was very successful and made several big arrests and confiscations of illegal drugs.

A joint drug task force was formed to include MPD, Stanislaus County S/O and the United States Bureau of Narcotics. The one and only time I ever fired my service revolver involved a young man from a very prominent family in Oakdale who became involved in selling and distributing heroin. His distribution base included the Bay Area, as well as the Stockton area and Stanislaus County. After the arrest of a low-level peddler, we were able to turn him, and he became our "snitch". Of course, we agreed to make sure he did not go to prison for the offences he was arrested for. Our mastermind from Oakdale drove a brand new Buick Riviera, paid for with cash, we determined. The night we were to arrest him and confiscate 2 lbs. of heroin that was to arrive, we were all on staked out in northwest Modesto near the Roseburg shopping center when the whole thing went down.

The task force was well spread out, and when we closed in, the Buick made a run for it. He was eventually forced off the road with minor damage to his car. Both individuals bailed, and the foot race was on. I was chasing one suspect with my weapon drawn, and when I caught up with him (I was younger then), I hauled off and hit him upside of the head with my weapon which discharged right next to his ear. He went down. I pounced on him and put on the cuffs. He was bleeding a little bit, but thought he was going to die. The guy from Oakdale was arrested, and as they did in those days, his beautiful car was confiscated, put on a trailer, and was in Sacramento the next day with a future ahead of it as an undercover drug car.

* * *

Probably one of the worst times in my history on the police department was just starting to show its ugly head. After six months of working untold hours of overtime and dealing with the lowest scum of the earth, I had had it. The whole damned world was going to hell in a handbasket. I could not see beyond a world of drugs and destruction for everyone in my Modesto, including my own children. I had to get my family out of there, before it was too late. Sounds crazy? It probably was, but not to me at that particular time in my life. I put in for a week's vacation and came home announcing to Marilyn that I was headed for the northwest, Idaho, Montana, Wyoming, to find a police job and a place where I could raise my family in safety. She also must have thought I was nuts, and I probably was. She flat out says she was going nowhere, not now, not ever! Well, I was going on a little vacation, and I wanted to take Ronnie and Kurt with me. "Fine," she said, "have a good time."

I had done a little research before I took off on this exodus and determined that maybe up around Missoula, Montana would be a perfect place to live with lots of hunting and fishing, hospitable people, great outdoors, low population density. That might just be the spot I was looking for. During our drive to Montana, we went through a little town in Idaho called Challis. Population just under 1,000 inhabitants, about 5,200 feet elevation, and next to the Salmon River. We stopped to have the car serviced, and as it so happened the service station owner was the Mayor. While we were there, the boys wandered off with their fishing poles to a little stream that runs through town. The Mayor and I conversed, and he learned of my mission. "I'll be damned," he said. "Our town is looking for a police chief as we speak." We get further into the subject. The chief was the only officer on the force. He used his own car, but the city provided the gas. The pay was around $500.00 per month. The kids came back, both with a stringer of fish that we put into the ice chest. I was so screwed up and disillusioned that I was actually interested. He said, "The job is yours. When you come back through next week we will introduce you to the council and make it official." I really cheered up as I looked at the big smiles on the boys faces. We make our way to Montana, going by Flathead Lake, Kalispell, and Whitefish (where I had a friend living). The country was beautiful, and I thought I had found heaven (Frank, ever been here in the winter?). We headed back for home, and spent the night in Challis, where I was fully anticipating meeting the city council the next morning. We went to bed, and I could not explain it but, I swear the room light went on all by itself. I laid there, and suddenly say to myself, "Are you crazy? What in the hell are you thinking? Half the pay I am currently getting, use my own car, 5,000 feet above sea level, the only officer for 50 miles?" It was 3:00 a.m., I wake up the kids, load the car, and we were on our way HOME. I felt bad about standing up the council and how embarrassed the mayor must have been, but I forgave myself, and I was never happier seeing my wife and my son, little Greg, that evening in Modesto.

I was home and back to work Monday morning when the department got word that Chief Bowers was retiring. What a shock! The city manager announced that a recruitment process would be made nationwide for a new police chief, and hopefully, we could have a new leader within the next 90 days. The City Manager, the Mayor, Sheriff Kelsay, and Chief Bowers screened the applicants and came up with four finalists, one of which was selected only by the City Manager. We will call him Mr. Roberts. All four were interviewed, and the panel made their selection. The City Manager did not like the panel's selection and was determined to hire Mr. Roberts. Sheriff Kelsay volunteered to have one of his best investigators do a back ground check on Mr. Roberts, but the City Manager said he would personally conduct the investigation himself. How he was qualified to do this was beyond me, but he proceeded. He gave Mr. Roberts a thumbs up and convinced the City Council to hire him. Chief Bowers and Sheriff Kelsay shook their heads, but the appointment was made.

Best I can remember this was early 1967. The new chief took charge and almost immediately had a sit-down interview with all of the command staff. This was a good idea, and we all expressed our opinions about the status of the department and in what direction we needed to be headed. About two weeks later, I was notified that I would now have a new title, Administrative Assistant to the Chief of Police, and would relocate my office next door to his. I would still have the narcotics division under my supervision, but he was bringing in an acquaintance from southern California with what he said was "a great background and experience to run the day to day operation." We will refer to him as "Ralph". We were told Ralph came from working at several police agencies in Southern California, primarily as an investigator; although, no one from our agency did a background check on him. He was just hired by the new Chief. I met with the Chief, and he had a list of priorities and programs he wanted to implement within the city. He gave these assignments to me and wanted to see progress reports over the next two weeks and implementation in 30 days. "Crap," I say to myself. "I can barely keep up with the work load I have now." Then he said, "I have a nick name for you that I will be using. I will be calling you my 'tool'." And he did, in fact, every time he called me he would say, "Tool, come to my office." It pissed me off, and I let him know it, but it did not change. I worked my ass off and put the programs together to his satisfaction.

With the Chief's approval, I put together a committee of 10 community members to help me develop a "crime stop" program for the city. We worked hard and diligently to meet the Chief's deadline. We called the new program *Citizens Operation Crime Stop for the City of Modesto*. It focused on crime prevention, education, community participation, creating a more favorable police image, and improving police training and education. The Chief liked the program, and we launched it with a big fanfare before the City Council. The Modesto Bee gave the police department a good write up, and the Chief got a lot of praise, as he should; he was the Chief and deserved the recognition. I spoke to every organization in the community, toting what the police department was doing and soliciting their support and cooperation. All went well, and sure enough the crime rate, albeit slowly, started to show a marked reduction. Many offences that previously, and rightfully so, had been classified as felonies, were now being classified as misdemeanors, at the Chief's instruction. These were primarily property crimes. The media paid no attention to this reclassification of incidents, nor did they have any way of knowing. The department was viewed in a positive light. Chief Roberts called me on the phone, "Come to my office Tool," he said. "Yes, Chief. What can I do for you?" "I wanted to let you know that the Stanislaus County Bar Association is awarding you the Liberty Bell Award this year." I was floored. It was perhaps the most prestigious award in the county that was given annually to the person who, in the Bar's opinion, had done the most to facilitate the community's understanding and appreciation of law and justice. I could tell he was pissed, as his face was very red. He came right out and said it, and I quote, "I deserved that award not you. I am the one who has worked so hard to make Modesto a better place to live," etc., and he went on and on. "Chief, I am honored, but it is not my fault they chose me instead of you. I will just turn the award down and tell them to give it to you." He was silent, thinking, but before he could speak, I said "No, I am honored to accept that award on behalf of you and the entire police department." I got up and left the room. I accepted the award on May 1st before over 300 people, including my family, and could not have been prouder.

With all of the other assignments the Chief had given me, I had not been paying as much attention to the narcotics unit, nor the new investigator, Detective Ralph, as I should have been. One of the other investigators in the unit came to me with a concern that Ralph was a lone wolf out in the community, on his own, and without much coordination with others in the unit. He had made lots of arrests, and I was aware of that and did review his reports, but there was usually not much corroborative evidence, other than a bag or two of marijuana, usually found under a car seat of the suspects. I did a little checking and found that Detective Ralph had a habit of checking out a couple of bags of marijuana from the evidence room, and then a few days later, checking it back in. I took a look at some of his arrests and found it was always two bags of marijuana confiscated when he made the arrest. I found this strange and talked to the Chief about it. He said to ignore it and that he would check it out with Detective Ralph.

A father of one of the arrestees made an appointment to speak with me about his son, whom Detective Ralph had arrested. The father was adamant that his kid did not, nor had ever used drugs of any kind. Yes, I had heard that story before, but for some reason, I believed this guy. A few days later Detective Ralph arrested a young lady, whom he met in a bar, for prostitution. His report said she propositioned him, and they went to a motel for sex. He gave her $40.00, and before they could consummate the act, another officer came into the room and searched her purse, finding the marked bills. She was booked in jail for solicitation of prostitution. Sounded like a good case to me. Who was the other officer? Well, as it turns out, although he was not identified in the report, it was none other than the Chief. I asked myself, "What in the hell is the Chief doing out after midnight and involved in a prostitution arrest?" I went to the jail and talked to the young lady. She said she met Ralph in the bar, they had a few drinks, danced, and then he propositioned her. She was drinking, having a good time, and he was cute. She agreed to go to the motel, but nothing was ever mentioned about money. They were getting ready to have sex, and then suddenly, a man came through the unlocked door, went through her purse, and came up with two twenty dollar bills that she claimed were not hers. Detective Ralph identified himself and arrested her. She was crying uncontrollably by now and pleading her innocence.

I began to wonder about the Chief's narcotics officer. I made a few calls to my police friends down south and determined that Detective Ralph was a real rat with a bad record. He had been fired from two previous agencies, convicted of filing false workers' compensation claims, and was unemployed when the Chief brought him to Modesto. I said nothing to the Chief because I thought he had to have known this when he brought Ralph to Modesto. I confided in Sheriff Kelsay about the situation, and we both agreed that while suspicious, there was not enough evidence to warrant any action just yet. He advised me to just keep my eyes on the situation, and if I did not mind, to keep him in the loop. That's what we would do.

For several weeks, I had been hearing that the son of a Stanislaus Superior Court judge was dealing marijuana. I kept this information to myself and one other detective in the division. I did not trust either the Chief or Ralph with this information. Finally, an informant was developed that came forward with information that it might have been possible to purchase marijuana from this individual. We provided him with some funds, courtesy of the Feds, and he purchased 2 lbs. of really good stuff, and we were able to record the transaction with a device hidden on the informant. Plus, we could observe the situation from some distance away. I contacted District Attorney Wolfe and requested a complaint and warrant for the judge's son who was about 20 years old.

I returned to the office and informed the Chief about the situation. He was a little annoyed, but I explained that it was just another case as far as I was concerned. He did not buy that, but that's the way it went. The next day we staked out the kid's car near Modesto Junior College, and when he left school, we followed. He soon realized we were after him and attempted to ditch us, but to no avail. He turned onto an irrigation canal and took off as fast as he could go, not realizing the canal was fenced off on the other end. He was trapped. We found two 2 lb. blocks of marijuana in the car, and he was arrested on the warrant and additionally charged with transporting narcotics with the intent to sell. Before the day was out, I received a phone call from the judge wanting to speak with me in his chambers. I told the Chief what was going on, and he instructed me to talk with the judge. I went there and listen to him tell me how this was going to ruin his son's life, embarrass the judge and his family, and create a frenzy for the news media. "Can't we work something out?" he pleaded. I told him I was sorry, but his son was old enough to know right from wrong, and he had to be treated like anyone else who sells narcotics. He was prosecuted, plead guilty to a misdemeanor, and got probation. This was a pretty lenient sentence in my opinion, but that was none of my concern.

The Chief spent, what appeared to me, a lot of time going to conferences and meetings out of town and for overnight or longer. I wondered about it, but really it was none of my business. That was between him and the city manager. Then one day, his secretary came into my office and wanted to talk. She handed me several letters that had been written to the Chief by three different ladies that lived in Modesto and one that worked at City Hall. She opened and read all of the Chief's mail before forwarding it to him. To make a long story short, he was meeting these ladies out of town, wining and dining them, and spending the night at a hotel or motel, whatever the case may be. His secretary provided me with copies of the Chief's expense accounts that he submitted to the city for reimbursement. He had charged the city for these little excursions and used a city vehicle, as well. It totaled up to several hundred dollars and a lot of time away from work. What to do, what to do? I went see my old confidant, the Sheriff, and we kicked the issue around. The Sheriff suggested that I discuss the matter with the city manager. "No," I say, "I think he would bury it, and then the Chief's secretary and I would be left hanging out on a limb." We finally concurred that the best thing to do was to talk to the District Attorney.

After contemplating the whole situation for a few days, I thought maybe the DA was the best route to go. I then talked with Detective Ray Coyle, who was also completely aware of some of Ralph's activities. We put together a case, and took it to District Attorney Wolfe. After a thorough review, he thought there was adequate evidence to take the case to the Stanislaus County Criminal Grand Jury. The Grand Jury impaneled and heard the evidence, subpoenaed the witnesses, and heard the case in secret for two or three weeks, then returned felony indictments against the Chief and Ralph. Both were arrested, booked in jail, and then arraigned the following week. They pleaded not guilty, of course, and a trial date was set. Both were suspended from their positions at the police department, and Captain Gerald McKinsey was elevated to acting chief. A superior court jury heard the case over a several week period and returned with a *not guilty* verdict. While they explained that both defendants exhibited very bad judgement, they really had no criminal intent. The city council ordered the city manager to instruct both defendants that for the time being they were on suspension from work with pay, until the council reviewed the matter.

I belonged to a duck hunting club in Los Banos, and one of my very best friends, Allen Corby, was also a member. One of his best friends was Mayor Lee Davies. I showed up at the duck club one Saturday morning at about 5:00 a.m., ready to go to my blind for the day's shoot. Allan said, "I have invited the mayor down for a little hunting. Do you mind if he shares a blind with you?" What was I supposed to say? "Of course not, glad to have him," I answered. Walking to the blind with the mayor, the gears were turning in my head, and I knew a lot more than shooting ducks was on his mind. He grilled me for over three hours about the Chief, Ralph, and a whole gamut of questions pertaining to both individuals. The mayor made me pledge silence about our conversation, and I promised him I would say nothing. He told me he was tasked with making a recommendation to the council regarding whether the Chief and Ralph should be given back their jobs or have their employment terminated. I knew I was in deep shit if the Chief came back; so, you know what I was hoping for. The council met, and a few days later announced that both the Chief and Ralph would be terminated. The Chief hired an attorney and sued the City and me. The case went to trial, and the judge or jury, I forget which, found in favor of the city and that was the end of a long, hard period of time for me and the entire police department. There was no appeal and the Chief's attorney later ended up suing the Chief himself.

Through all of this strife, I had made up my mind to leave the department, as soon as I could secure a position as chief of police in a desirable city, and one to which Marilyn would be willing to relocate. The Chief still had some local support, and I wanted to completely eliminate any suspicions that my actions were motivated by any hopes of personal gain or advancement.

The city hired a new chief from Sunnyvale named Jerry Ammerman. He seemed like a terrific guy and very professional. He and I had a long sit down discussion right after he arrived, and he wanted me to remain in my current position with the department. I was sure he was interested in getting to know me and make a determination on his own about my ability and dedication to the department. We hit it off right away, and I was starting to have second thoughts about leaving. Chief Ammerman did some reorganization after about three months. He wanted a new position, Patrol Division Commander. His request was granted, and he announced I would be filling that new position and would be third in command of the police department under him and Captain McKinsey. I had a really nice new office and enjoyed my position, but here I was supervising three other lieutenants, had more responsibility than they did, yet we were compensated the same. He realized this, but could not get an authorization for a captain's position. This grinded on me, so I started looking at the recruitment bulletins for chiefs of police.

# FOREIGN SERVICE OFFICER
# AND VIETNAM: 1969-1971

The year was 1969, and things were really popping in Vietnam.
I had never been in the service, other than my little stint in
the Navy Reserve, and this had bothered me for years. I just
could not shake the feeling that somehow I had not made a
commitment to our country that I should have. One of my
good friends and coworkers, Sergeant Gary Wiens, told me of
a friend of his who was home on vacation from Vietnam. He
worked for the Office of Public Safety (OPS), a department
within the United States State Department. The OPS provided
foreign countries throughout the free world with police advisors and logistical support for their police departments. We
met with his friend Bill, and I was totally fascinated and very
interested. Bill provided me with the information I needed to
find out more about OPS and the qualifications to become a
Foreign Service Officer.

Based on the information I had, I sent a letter of inquiry to the Office of Public Safety in Washington D.C. and asked for an application for employment. Within two weeks, I received an application and more details about the organization, its objectives, and its purposes. I discussed it with Marilyn and then completed all of the forms and sent them to the headquarters of the OPS in Washington D.C. I got a letter a month or so later from OPS asking if I could meet with Mr. Frank Walton, Deputy Director of OPS who would be in Sacramento conducting employment interviews. I did a little research and learned that Mr. Walton was the Deputy Police Chief in Los Angeles before his retirement, and he also wrote several books on law enforcement subjects.

One book that caught my attention was one on the use of police dogs. I had quite a bit of experience on this subject having headed up a canine program at Modesto PD and owned a wonderful and intelligent German shepherd myself.

I meticulously studied his book and thought that somewhere during the interview, I could interject the subject. So, I went to Sacramento, met Mr. Walton, and had what I thought was a good interview, making sure to mention my experience with the canine unit. This became a major part of our discussion and interview. I was very careful to make sure most of my comments were in concurrence with his theories on the use of police dogs. At the conclusion of the interview, he said his agency would be interested in taking me on board, providing the background check came out okay. We discussed salaries, moving, impacts on my family, career opportunities, and so on. Explaining to him all that I would have to give up and the sacrifices my family would have to make, we began to negotiate salary. I explained to him that I was making just a little over $11,000 a year at the police department. I told him I could not give up 11 years at my current position, and a great future for less than $20,000 a year. He kind of smiled and indicated that was not possible. I said, "Anything is possible, and you get what you pay for. I have a great track record and will commit to this Vietnam thing for the long haul, upset my family, and move them to a foreign country. Let's get realistic Mr. Walton, our effort in Vietnam needs me more than I need it."

My canine partner, Sam, 1966

He scribbled around on a pad, I think he was just doodling, but he says, "Okay, $18,000 per year. Will that work?" he asked. I stood up, shook his hand, and said, "We have a deal." Wow, a $7,000 salary increase. I could not believe it! On the other hand, as I would find out later, I had no idea what I was getting into. I informed Chief Ammerman the next day that I would be leaving the PD effective March 1, 1969. I knew he was sincere when he said that he hated to see me leave, but wished me all the luck and success in the world. He threw one heck of a going away party for me, both at the police department, and a smaller, more intimate one at his home.

A few weeks later, I received a packet from OPS containing airline tickets and instructions on reporting for duty in Washington D.C. on April 1st. I would be in Washington for three months, undergoing training at the International Police Academy, and then it was off to Vietnam. My job classification was Foreign Service Officer-R- Grade 5. The R simply meant I was not a full tenured employee, but rather classified as a reserve. While unusual, but not impossible, if I did well, and with the proper recommendation from my superiors, I could become a fully tenured Foreign Service Officer in one year. That would certainly insure job security. I was met at Dulles International Airport by a very nice young lady from OPS who informed me that accommodations had been made for me to stay at the Allan Lee Hotel in the Foggy Bottom section of Washington D.C. She commented that most people referred to my hotel as the *Allan Flea*. When I got there and checked in I could see why. What a dump. She apologized and told me that I would only be there a few days until an apartment was ready across the street from the State Department Building. It took about two weeks before I moved into my apartment that I shared with another OPS recruit, James Hoban, a retired Los Angeles PD police sergeant. He was a neat guy, and we hit it off really well right from the start.

It was on Tuesday April 1, 1969, April fool's Day that I started my new career. "Is that a bad omen," I wonder to myself? I, along with about 20 other new employees, were soon immersed in learning what the US government was all about, our purpose in the foreign service field, and cultural diversity. Most of the other new employees were going to be working for the Agency for International Development (AID) and in a wide variety of different fields. For example, there were advisors in the area of agriculture, nursing, animal husbandry, nutrition, and a whole host of other fields of endeavor. There were only four or five with OPS. We were indoctrinated in Vietnamese culture, language, history, and then the United States side for topics on U.S. Military involvement, government, and so on.

We spent two weeks at a fancy resort in West Virginia, along with a large group of Vietnamese military and civilians sitting in classrooms getting more indoctrination on the war and culture exchanges. We were all flown down to Fort Bragg, North Carolina for training in some military tactics and weapons. Do not ask me why. We fired M79 grenade launchers one day, then the next it was M60 machine guns, 4.2 mortars, M-16 rifle and the AK-47. Then we cut up nails and mixed them with plastic explosives, inserted a detonator, and blew those up. Lots of fun, but for what purpose? I think it was just something to keep us busy and entertained.

We were given a class on the purpose and use of the common compass. When the instructor thought we had got it, we were loaded into a helicopter and flown out to some vast expanse on the base, maybe 10 to 15 miles away in the woods and told to find our way home. There was really no problem, just a long ways and a lot of walking. Some old boy came along the dusty road we were on and said he was hunting tree squirrels, and did we want a ride. We jumped into the back of the pickup, he drove us to within about a mile of where we were headed, and let us out.

The instructor was amazed that we were able to find our way home so quickly. We told him we were just lucky, and he did a good job in the classroom. Time passed quickly, and before long, I was headed home for a week with the family before I headed out for Vietnam. I had not seen my family for over three months so Marilyn and I decided to have a nice party and get everyone together for a visit. Coincidently, it was mom's 65th birthday, so we planned a special party in San Francisco. Mom's last ride in an airplane was 1932 or thereabout in a Ford Tri motor passenger plane. Kurt had never been on a big airliner, so while Marilyn, Ron, Greg and I drove to San Francisco International Airport, we made arrangements for mom to fly there with Kurt accompanying her. We picked them up at the airport and headed for downtown San Francisco. Marilyn and I had made arrangements for everyone to stay at the Mark Hopkins Hotel on Nob Hill and have dinner at the Top of the Mark restaurant.

We were just getting ready to sit down for dinner and who walked in (pre-arranged) but my brother Marvin and his wife Johnnie. He was in town from Idaho doing some advertising work for his employer, Boise Cascade. What a surprise for mom! We had a great dinner and then we all headed for the top floor for the views and some after dinner drinks. There was a great band playing dance music, so mom and I decided to do the Texas two-step and Tennessee waltz. We cruised over to the band leader, and I told him we are there celebrating mom being selected the *Mother of the Year* in Stanislaus County. He stopped the music and made a big announcement. Mom got a standing ovation, and we continued dancing. Mom chastised me for telling such a whopper, but I explained that the family voted on it, and she won hands down.

Our family really enjoyed being together, and as I mentioned, I had been gone just a little over three months, and we had never been separated before. The State Department had a unique program that allowed, in some cases, for an employee's dependents to live abroad. In my case, I qualified, and the family had the option of living in one of three countries, but not Vietnam. Those countries were, Thailand, the Philippines, or Taiwan. Marilyn and I thought the Philippines would be the best choice because of similar customs, American influence for almost 100 years, and almost all of the people spoke English. So the decision was made that the family, our car, and our dog and cat, would be bound for Manila in three to four months.

Luckily, I had an acquaintance who worked for OPS, and his wife was currently in the Philippines; so, she would sponsor Marilyn and help her get settled in when they arrived.

The week passed quickly, and before long, Marilyn, our friend Felicia Corby, and I are standing curbside at San Francisco International Airport. I asked that we just say our goodbyes right then and get it over with. In all honesty, had Marilyn just cried a little more, or said, "Please do not go," then I would have gotten back in the car, returned to Modesto, and forgotten all about OPS.

I boarded the 707 that was headed non-stop to Tokyo, Japan. This was my first trip abroad and to Asia; so, I had no idea what to expect. When I got on the plane, there were only seven passengers aboard. I was told that this was not uncommon, that during the Vietnam situation these flights were on a rigid schedule and often were not carrying many passengers. I found a seat next to this guy and learned that he was a retired army sergeant and was also working for OPS in the logistics area. His name was Lee Aiken, and he was headed back to Saigon for his second tour of duty. He had spent quite a bit of time in Japan during his service years and said he knew his way around.

Now remember, I had spent almost my entire life in Oakdale and Modesto, the last thing you could call me was a world traveler. We arrived safely in Tokyo and took a taxi down town to our hotel before we headed to Saigon the next day. I was in total culture shock. We walked along the street, and I swore there were millions of people walking with us shoulder to shoulder, and that we were the only two Americans I would see until we got back on that airplane. Luckily, Lee spoke a little Japanese; so, we had a nice dinner, hit a couple of bars, fought off several cute little Japanese girls, and got back to the hotel safe and sound.

We arrived at Tan Son Nhut International Airport outside of Saigon at about 3:00 p.m. in the afternoon. It was 100 degrees plus and humidity was 95%. I walked out of the airplane and prepared to descend the gangway to the tarmac. It was like a ton of bricks hit me. I thought I was going to pass out. I will remember that day the rest of my life. I recall saying to myself, "What the hell have you gotten yourself into?" The guy I met in Modesto who got me into this whole thing met me inside the terminal, and we were soon in his National Police jeep headed for my hotel in downtown Saigon. What a ride! I had never seen anything like it. Taxi's, pedicabs, motorcycles with as many as seven people on them, army trucks, and military jeeps. It seemed as though everyone was honking their horns at the same time, shouting profanities at each other. More culture shock.

My new friend Bill, who spoke fluent Vietnamese, was cussing his best and blowing the horn just as loudly and often as the next guy. Bill helped me settle into my room, we chatted for an hour or so, and decided it was time to have dinner. We went to Maxim's, which in my opinion, was one of the finest restaurants in all of Asia. We had a great dinner along with some other guys from OPS Saigon, then headed for the cocktail lounge. I was just a country boy and familiar with

Bud, Miller, vodka and tonic, whiskey and soda, but I was not ready for what later was explained to me as my initiation to OPS Vietnam. The stuff that went down my throat that night! Things I had never heard of, Ba Muie Ba beer, Beer LaRue, Cognac, Cointreau, Drambuie, Grand Mariner.

I woke up the next morning, and I was not quite sure where I was. Worst hangover of all time. I threw up a few times, took some aspirin, and decided to head downstairs and get some coffee and breakfast. I found a seat in the restaurant, and a cute little waitress came over and said something to me in Vietnamese. I knew just enough Vietnamese that I learned in Washington DC to get me in trouble. I thought she said, "Good morning. How are you sir?" I said what I thought was, "I am fine, thank you, and how are you?" Well, by then she thought I was fluent in the language; so, she rattles off a barrage of sentences and syllables, and I had no idea what she said. I wanted to order breakfast, but could not. She was laughing as I tried to get her to understand coffee. "Coffee," I said. She got that and came back with this little cup full of heavy cream, sugar and coffee. I had never seen anything close to it in my life, nor thought that I ever wanted to see it again. She said, "coffe su," or something close to that. I said, "No, coffee American." She got it and brought me a fresh, hot cup of coffee that was the best I had ever drunk. I was embarrassed, but hungry; so, she and I walked around the other tables, and I pointed out what looked good, and then ended up with a nice breakfast, after all.

I presented myself to the receptionist at OPS headquarters, as previously designated. I was ushered into a classroom where there were about 20 other Americans, all there to be briefed and processed. There were four OPS guys there that I recognized from Washington, one of them being my roommate, Jim Hoban. We spent three days in Saigon for further orientation, and I gradually began to get acclimated to the weather and my surroundings. Then came the day we got our assignments. It could have been any one of 46 providences in South Vietnam. There was one OPS officer assigned to each providence, and he was attached to the Military Advisory Team (MACV) that advised their Vietnamese counterparts. In OPS, your counterpart would be the police chief of the providence to which you were assigned. Vietnam was divided into four Corps, I, II, III, and IV.

I Corp was in the northern portion of the country, and most of the war was being fought by Americans and South Vietnamese forces. II Corp was under the military control of the South Korean Army supported by U.S. logistics, air, and naval support. It extended from the South China Sea to Cambodia. III and IV Corp were the southern end of South Vietnam to the South China Sea, including Saigon and west to the Cambodian border. The military forces were Americans and South Vietnamese troops. So, we all sat in anticipation. Everyone hoped they got anywhere but Saigon. No one wanted to be in some isolated location next to the Cambodian border either, and the southern end of Vietnam was the delta, nothing but mosquitoes, swamps, and rice fields. My name came up,

"Frank Clark will be assigned to Khanh Hoa Province." "Oh my god," I say to myself. "You have to be the luckiest guy in the world."

Public Safety Officer, Vietnam, 1969

The province capitol was the City of Nha Trang located on the coast of the South China Sea. Wonderful weather, perhaps the most militarily secure city in Vietnam, beautiful beaches, seafood paradise, and you could drive almost anywhere with relative security (day time only). This was also the II Corp headquarters for MACV and OPS. The province was under very strict military control by about 10,000 Republic of Korea troops (ROK). There were almost no set piece battles, just an occasional night attack by small local Viet Cong units of 15-30 individuals.

The U.S. Military forces in the province were set in scattered locations, usually providing artillery, air, and naval support to Vietnamese and Korean units. Most of the heavy action took place in the mountains west of Nha Trang in Pleiku and Kontum Provinces. I was assigned to MACV Advisory Team 46, consisting of a retired Air Force Lt. Colonel, an active duty army Lt. Colonel, an army Captain, four enlisted men, and five other advisors from a variety of specialty fields. Our role was to provide "expert" advise to the provincial authorities in our own field of expertise, mine being law enforcement; although, I had to advise the fire department also, and logistical support. My office was adjacent to the provincial police chief's office and located about a mile from MACV. I had complete physical autonomy, except to report in once or twice a day and keep my supervisors, the two Lt. Colonels, apprised of my activities.

I moved into my office the first day of my arrival and met my counterpart, Chief Nguyen Tan Coung. He quickly let me know I may call him Charles, his French name. Charles came from a very prominent Vietnamese family and grew up in the resort mountain city of Dalat where most wealthy/ influential Vietnamese like to vacation because of the wonderful weather and surroundings. His mother was French and his father Vietnamese. He was extremely well educated, a devoted

Catholic, and father of six children. I liked him immediately. He gave me a little background on himself. He grew up in Dalat where his father was a wealthy land owner, and he loved to hunt, especially from the back of an elephant. He was part of the French military. He fought against the Japanese occupational forces in WWII, and was a POW for over a year until rescued by British forces near the war's end. He became a member of the National Police and rose through the ranks to his current position. He was about ten years older than me.

Next, I met my secretary Va Thi Minh. She was fluent in English, intelligent, and very attractive. I came to almost an immediate conclusion that she was a very fiery nationalist. She loved her Vietnam, and while she liked Americans and the United States, she was suspicious of our intentions in her country. "What do you want?" she asked me. "Are you like the Chinese who occupied Vietnam for over 1,000 years, or the French who colonized our country for 100 years and treated us like puppets and slaves, and of course more recently the Japanese?

Then America stands by, not only stands by, but finances and supports France's recolonization of our country. Would you be suspicious?" she asked. She went on, "You spend billions of dollars supporting the war, 50,000 of your young men are killed and hundreds of thousand wounded. Can you tell me why you would do that?" she asked. "What are the motives of the United States, and what do you expect to gain?" I asked myself, "How do I answer that? Would she understand the domino theory, as proclaimed by our politicians? I doubt it." So, I did not even go there. I told her that our country had long fought communism, and we wanted to keep it out of South Vietnam, and wanted the people to enjoy their elected democracy, as it was then. She laughed! "Democracy?" she said. "What do you know of our government? It is basically corrupt; elections are a sham, as you will find out. Do you know Mr. Clark, that every Province Chief, District Chief, Village Chief, is a military officer? How could you call that democracy?" But then she said she had said enough, and I would probably fire her for being so candid. I said, "No, I appreciate your honesty, and our conversation and all conversations that we may have will be held in confidence." I liked this woman!

My interpreter, who accompanied me everywhere when I was in the field or talking to my counterpart was Khiem, and he was about 5 foot 3 inches tall and weighed 160 lbs. He lifted weights for a hobby and was very muscular. He was very quiet and reserved, and embarrassed easily. He was, laid back, and did not seem to have any concern about the country's political/military situation. His English was okay, but I thought he translated lots of things that were not always completely accurate. Minh cautioned me to be careful, and if I was not sure to get a second opinion.

\* \* \*

Chief Cuong (Charles) and I hit it off great. Khanh Hoa Province was made up of five districts, each with a major city. Much like in the U.S. there was a state capital, Nha Trang, and counties (districts). Charles and I made it a point to visit each district, where he introduced me to all the major players, such as district police chiefs and the district chiefs who were much like a mayor in our government. We established a warm relationship hunting, fishing and attending social events. I had the run of the place, and Charles had no problem with me visiting the other police locations along with Khiem, as long as I let him know where I was going and gave him a report when I returned to Nha Trang. We never had a conflict, and he seemed to have complete confidence in me.

* * *

I lived in a very nice, extremely nice, three story villa about ½ block from the beach, along with four other OPS employees. Beautiful interior with dining room (although we never used it), gorgeous full 20 ft. mahogany bar (we did use that a lot), electricity, running water, air conditioned, two maids to do our laundry, housekeeping and a little cooking if we asked, and we had 24-hour security. We paid no rent, and as a matter of fact, I got $22.00 per diem, in addition to my salary, which I did not need and went to Marilyn. I spent most of my time in the field and ate almost entirely on the local economy. I was sick with diarrhea for the first three months I was in Vietnam and went from 186 lbs. down to 155 lbs. My system finally adapted to the local food, and I quit taking those damned malaria tablets. My weight stabilized, and I never felt better.

I spent most of my time out in the field visiting police loca-tions and learning as much as I could about police policies and operations, so that I could give advice that was both relevant and beneficial. Most of the police practices in effect were deep in tradition and hard to change, but where changes could be made and the chief saw a value, we incorporated new techniques or modified old ones. My traveling around the province had really been an eye opener. I came to Vietnam as one of the most hawkish people on the war that you could possibly have ever found. During my travels I encountered a lot of what we could call just average Vietnamese people: farmers, merchants, school teachers, policemen of course, and my eyes and ears gradually started to provide a different perspective on the war.

I gained a lot of trust with many different people and from many different walks of life. There was a common cord that ran between them. They all hated the war and most did not like America, and they were very suspicious of America's motives. They saw villages burned to the ground, their lives and families uprooted and relocated, some of them from lands they had been on for generations. "Why?" they asked, and I could not answer them. They did not like communism, nor what it represented or the North Vietnamese, but where could they turn? They only wanted their own country, and that included both south and north. They absolutely did not trust or have confidence in, nor did they support the South Vietnamese government.

\* \* \*

A GI at the mess hall one day mentioned that he had a German Shepard and because he was rotating back to the states he had to find a home for him. He only had one drawback according to the GI: he disliked Vietnamese! I had raised a German shepherd who eventually became one of the first dogs to be used by the Modesto Police Department on patrol. I took the GI's dog home, and he settled in. He could not stand to have me out of his sight. Wherever I went, he went. When I left the jeep, he sat behind the wheel and snarled at anyone that came near.

My Vietnamese police dog, Lobo

A favorite trick of V/C terrorists was to wrap a rubber band around a hand grenade, pull the pin, and drop the grenade into the gas tank of a U.S. or government jeep. When it exploded several days later, there would not be much left of the jeep or anyone who might be near it. The guards at home did not like Lobo, and he didn't like them much either. I loved that dog, and he slept outside my room every night. I flew to Saigon for a few days, and when I got back, no Lobo. The guards knew nothing, which did not surprise me, and my roommates said Lobo just disappeared.

Many Vietnamese, not the affluent ones, loved dog meat, and Lobo weighed about 75 lbs., so I figured he was a goner. I put out the word to all of the policemen and all my friends about Lobo's disappearance but heard nothing. Then a week after he disappeared, my friend Lt. Commander Murphy of the U.S. Navy thought he might have seen Lobo tied up at the Vietnamese navy facility near the port. Murphy and I went there, and sure enough it was Lobo. He barked, I untied him, he wagged his tail and jumped in my jeep. He was, I am sure, just about to be barbequed. The dogs to be eaten would be tied up out in the hot sun for two or three days with no water or food. They cleaned themselves out and then were given copious amounts of water and seasoned rice. Before it became excrement, the dog was killed and cooked in a deep pit covered with hot coals. Lucky Lobo. He lived a good life until I left Vietnam, and then one of the other guys looked after him. I do not know his final demise.

\* \* \*

I had met a couple of GI's, one a captain and one a master sergeant who were assigned to Ninh Hoa District, just outside of Nha Trang, about 25 miles. I saw them, maybe once a month when I made my rounds. Late in January 1970, they invited me out for a barbecue, some drinks, and a poker game. I was also planning on staying all night. We were quartered in the district military headquarters.

This facility was encircled in concertina wire (razor wire), about six rows of it, all around the compound. Additionally, there were claymore mines strategically located amongst the rows of wire and trip flares which would illuminate the compound if set off by anyone trying to infiltrate through the concertina. It was about 11:00 p.m., and we were sitting in our little block building playing poker when all hell broke loose. First thing we heard was small arms fire. So, we grabbed our weapons and hunkered down. More small arms fired, then several large explosions inside the compound near where we were playing cards.

We rushed out the front door, running toward the bunkers and ran into two guys dressed in black carrying satchel charges. The captain killed both of them before they could detonate their explosives. The place was really lit up from the flares which then started to go off. There were several men in black clothing running from building to building throwing satchel charges and blowing up everything up. When they blew up the ammo and weapons storage facility, I had never heard anything like it. My ears start ringing just thinking about it. Several claymores go off, and there was lots of machine gun fire coming from the National Police Field Forces (NPFF was a para military unit within the police department) and directed into and around the concertina wire.

This went on for about an hour, then all was quiet. It was finally over. There were about 15 Viet Cong dead inside the compound and another 20 or so dead, wrapped up in the concertina. Most of the dead in the concertina were young boys I guessed to be 12 to 14 years old. Conscripts by the Viet Cong. It really made you sick to see these kids laying there naked, just blown to bits. The technique used by the V/C was to have the kids strip naked and then attempt to crawl through the concertina while pushing in front of them a Bangalore torpedo. This was a 10 ft. long piece of bamboo 4 inches in diameter stuffed with high explosives. The kids pushed the torpedo in front of them, placed it under the wire, and then detonated it hoping to make an opening in the wire so the V/C can rush in. The place was a mess and most buildings blown to bits. There were 12 dead on our side, including the four police officers guarding the front gate.

At daylight, Chief Cuong arrived, and he was very pleased that I was okay. He surveyed the damage and carnage, gathered up all of police officers, and praised them for their defense of the facility. Next, it was Lt. Colonel Wilson from Advisory Team 46 who took lots of pictures and wandered around the scene of the carnage. Oops, he accidentally cut himself on the arm when he ran into some concertina wire, or so he said. Anyway, he went on his way, and I returned to Nha Trang, thankful to be alive. I was starting to have some serious reservations about this whole damned Vietnam War thing. A couple of days, later the leader of Advisory Team 46, the retired Air Force Lt. Colonel, asked me to meet with him and Lt. Colonel Wilson to go over an after action report on the incident at Ninh Hoa.

Nin Hoa, Vietnam Headquarters after V/C sapper attack

V/C cadre killed during attack on Ninh Hoa

When I got there, I was handed a document that was written in support of Lt. Colonel Wilson getting the Purple Heart while injured in the battle at Ninh Hoa. "Are you shitting me?" I asked. I was pissed, "You rotten fucker," I said.

"All those people killed out there, and you wander in 8 hours later, claim you are injured on some barbed wire, and now you want a purple heart? I will tell you something, you son of a bitch. I will go the highest level to make sure you do not pull this off." He was red faced and yelled at me that he was my supervisor, and I could not talk to him like that. He was putting me on report immediately and demanding that I be terminated. I told him to go ahead, as I was tired of the whole god dammed thing anyway.

My boss at OPS, who was the only guy who had any say about my future, was contacted by both of my bosses at Team 46. His name was Guenther Wagoner, and he was head of OPS for II Corp. He always seemed fair, and I knew he was tough as nails. He spoke with a little German accent. Guenther got me and the two of them together and listened to their complaint. He said to Lt. Colonel Wilson, "Now let me get this straight, you want to receive a purple heart for cutting yourself on some barbed wire at a battle location that you arrive at 10 hours AFTER IT IS ALL OVER. Is that correct? And you want me to discharge Frank here for insubordination, insulting an officer of the United States Army, and disobeying orders. Is that also correct?" "Yes," the two of them answered. "We cannot have our officers treated like that!" Guenther looked at me and said he wanted to apologize for not telling me sooner, but he only had it confirmed yesterday. "Mr. Clark, here has been promoted to Chief Operational Officer OPS II Corp, effective two days ago. He will be reporting directly to me. So, in effect, he no longer is under your supervision; therefore, your request is moot."

My head was swirling. I was having a hard time keeping up. Guenther went on, "…but concerning the Purple Heart issue, assuming you still plan on submitting your recommendation, and if it makes any difference, I plan on writing a letter to the Commanding Officer II Corp strongly protesting any such action on the Army's part. Good day gentlemen and congratulations Frank, not only on the promotion, but moving up to Foreign Service Officer 4 and to permanent status with the United States State Department." I do not know if they ever submitted the paper work for the medal or not. If so, they bypassed OPS. A couple of weeks later, Chief Cuong called me into his office to congratulate me and inform me that he also had been promoted and would be the new police chief in the 7th District of Saigon. He was happy about that, but sad to be leaving his beloved II Corp. I saw him off at the airport a couple of days later. I would not see him again for four years. That, however, is another story.

In the meantime, backing up just a little bit, Marilyn and the kids had settled in at Magallanes Village in Manila in the Philippines. I was allowed to go to the Philippines once a month at government expense to visit my family. My first visit was a great family affair. We had not been together for about 5 months, so we were really happy and enjoyed the weekend so much. The house they were living in was in one of the most expensive and prestigious neighborhoods in Manila. A beautiful two story, four-bedroom home with all of the amenities and all paid for by your U.S. government. Marilyn did have to pay for the gardener, the maid, and the cook.

We were living way above our former status. Greg and Ron caught a bus at 5:00 a.m. and headed for the nearest American-ran school several miles away. They got home at about 4:00 p.m., so it was a long day. It was a great cultural experience for the whole family. We could not get the pets out of quarantine until the maid let Marilyn know that you have to slip someone a couple of bucks and the doors would open. Bingo! The pets were home that night. We traveled all over the Philippines each time I came home. Corregidor, Bataan, Baggio, Subic Bay, and many of the outer islands like Leyte, Mindanao, and Luzon, and so on. But all good things must come to an end, and for a variety of reasons, after about a year we decided that the best place for our family was back in Modesto. The last time I visited them in Manila before they headed home to Modesto, we were at the airport, and I was headed back to Vietnam. Greg gave me a hug and said to me, "Dad, I love you. Don't go back over there." I was crying when I boarded the airplane and thought about it all the way to Saigon. By the time I was back in Nha Trang, I had made up my mind that when this tour was over, I was going to resign.

\* \* \*

I started my new job and found the responsibilities were so much more than I had as an advisor to Chief Cuong. I was supervising the operations of the public safety program for 13 providences and the work of 13 public safety officers. I traveled a lot, but in doing so, I had a helicopter and fixed wing aircraft at my disposal 24 hours a day. There is a district called Khanh Duong in Khanh Hoa Providence just west of Nha Trang that I fell in love with. The people who live there were called Montagnards. I can best describe them as being like Native American Indians in the early 1700s-1800s in America. They lived off of the earth, were very superstitious, many only wore loin clothes, needing nothing from the outside world but salt and iron, and they lived in pole houses. They were kind, down to earth, extremely honest, and last but not least, they did not like the Vietnamese. They were treated by the government much like we in America had treated Native American Indians.

I had a Montagnard interpreter named Anh who was pretty darned proficient in English, and how he did that, I will never know, except he hung out at our little American advisory post near the village. I made good friends with the village chief, E-Moe. He was elected or appointed by the villagers. He was a pretty neat guy, rotten teeth, bad breath, and always wanted to hug you. When I visited him once a month, he would bring out a big 35-gallon pot made of reeds which did not leak. You took the cover off to behold an exotic drink called *nampey*, an ancient Montagnard rice wine whose recipe had been passed down for literally thousands of years. It was potent, far worse than *white lightening*. So you sat around in a circle, took the lid off, some guy with a soda can in his hand stood by. You were given a reed straw three-foot long that went to the bottom of the pot. You started sucking, and the guy with the soda can full of water started replacing the liquid in the pot as you drank. You feel particles of who knows what moving past your teeth and into your mouth, as you sucked on the straw. When the guy with the soda can had emptied it, you passed the straw onto the next guy and the fellow with the soda can reloaded.

This went around the circle until the pot was emptied. Hopefully you were drunk if you get the straw after E-Mo. You either passed out or tried to find your way down the road to the American outpost, hoping you did not get shot on the way. Remember those five gallon jugs of water in the office that you turned upside down and the water ran into the cooler, and you put your cup under the spout and filled it with cool water? Well, E-Moe and I and a group of village elders were having a meeting, and at its conclusion E-Moe brings out this water jug. Inside the jug, and how they got in there was beyond me, was a deer embryo that had been fermenting for who knows how long. So, you put a small glass under the down spout and it filled with this cloudy liquid. You shot it down and passed on the glass to the next recipient. It was supposed to make you healthy and improve your sex life. We will have to wait and see if it helped me!

On another trip, I was visiting and a group of Montagnards approached our out of doors meeting. They had in tow a little girl about 12 years old that looked like death warmed over. It was very obvious that she was not well, one look and you could see the problem. She had a compound fracture of the tibia. The bone was sticking out a good four inches, the leg was swollen, and she had a high fever. We were never sure how this accident occurred, but we knew her parents were killed. She was living with her aunt and uncle. I could not do anything right then to help her, but my interpreter told the aunt and uncle to have her at the village chief's house the next morning at 10:00 a.m. When I got back to Nha Trang, I got hold of a doctor friend of mine who was an orthopedic surgeon.

The next morning, we flew by helicopter to Khan Duong, and thank goodness the little girl was waiting for us. Her name was Ha-Du, and she looked even worse now. Keep in mind, this little kid had never even ridden in a car, she was surrounded by a bunch of Caucasians, and they were preparing to take her away from the only world she had ever known, best described in modern terms as almost prehistoric. We boarded the helicopter and in an hour we were in Nha Trang at the U.S. supported hospital. My doctor friend infused her with antibiotics, a blood transfusion, and prepared her for surgery. She came through surgery just great, and the bone in her leg was aligned and pinned. She came home to our house to be spoiled rotten. The two maids could not understand why we were paying so much attention to a Montagnard child and kind of turned up their noses. Ha -Du got her own room, plenty of food, and get this, a television set. What a different world. She did well, and in about three months, the doctor said she could return to Khanh Duong.

Ha-Du and friends on her way home from the hospital

Frank and Marilyn, Ha-Du, and her aunt and uncle

I managed for Marilyn to come to Vietnam for a visit, so she was on hand to take Ha-Du back to her family. This little girl had stolen our hearts. We were going to miss her. We loaded Ha-Du into the helicopter along with Marilyn and flew her home. Marilyn surprised her with a cute, little, yellow, stuffed rabbit doll. She loved the rabbit, and when we drove her from the helipad to her village, she hugged it closely. The other kids gathered around to welcome her home. They also loved the rabbit, passing it around and laughing uncontrollably. We all headed for the village ceremonial lodge where a banquet awaited us. We had a great celebration and lots of nampey. Ha-Du cried when we left, and her uncle gave me a Montagnard sword that I still possess today. I saw Ha-Du only one time after that, and I asked her, through the interpreter, how the rabbit was doing. The village chief had it destroyed because he felt anything that made the kids laugh so much must have been full of evil spirits. I gave her a little kiss on the head, and away she went with a big basket on her shoulders to gather rice in a faraway field. I never saw her again.

* * *

I had really gotten into the swing of things with my new position, visiting all of the 13 provinces once a month and collating all of the OPS advisors reports into one that was passed through Mr. Wagoner, then onto Saigon, and eventually Washington D.C. I had a new interpreter named Tuan who, in the past, had been a high school teacher and also an interpreter for several years. His English was excellent, and he had a good grasp of American culture. Tuan was very savvy about Vietnamese politics and spent a lot of his time studying Russian. He confessed to me that he thought the war is a lost cause, and it was only a matter of time before the U.S. was out and the Russians were in. He was not happy with this, but like so many other Vietnamese, he was tired of the war, and even a communist government would be better than the current situation.

I was returning from the Post Exchange (PX) at the MACV compound, driving my jeep down a side street off of the main avenue, and approaching the local prison. The street was pretty narrow, just room for two vehicles and a little shoulder. When I was directly across from the prison, a figure popped up from behind a five-foot masonry wall topped by concertina wire and points an M-2 carbine right at me. The Vietnamese man holding the gun could not be more than 40 feet away. Why, I do not know, but I yelled at the top of my voice, "American, American" and he paused as I passed. The two Vietnamese naval officers behind me were not so lucky. He opened up on them, and the jeep they were driving careened off onto the side of the street. I stopped and with my own carbine (I preferred it over the M-16) cranked off a couple of shots in the direction of the prison wall. The guy disappeared.

One of the officers was dead, shot through the head; the other had a very bad wound in his forearm, and it was bleeding profusely. I got him out of the jeep, and we took cover. I made up a tourniquet from my handkerchief as best I could, and when we thought it clear, we made a dash for my jeep, and I rushed him to the hospital where he was hospitalized, treated, and later recovered. I relayed all of this over my radio to the command center as it was happening and time permitted. There was a takeover by the prisoners that went on for several days until the Vietnamese army and armored vehicles quelled the riot. That night, I thought a lot about the day's events. What the hell would have happened if I had been killed or badly wounded? Would my time and sacrifice in Vietnam have made any difference? Would it have made a difference in my life and my family's life? I decided right then and there that I was going to keep a low profile, stick it out until my current assignment was over, and get the hell out of Vietnam forever.

* * *

My nephew Michael "Mick" Clark, was currently in Vietnam serving with the 4th Army Division with an artillery unit and stationed in Pleiku, which was in II Corp, about 200 miles west of Nha Trang. I went there occasionally, but had not as yet met up with him. Finally, on one of my field trips, I managed to hook up and spend the night with Mick. I met the commander of the unit, Colonel Wright, who was from Texas; so, we spoke the same language. We had a great time that night with a steak barbecue; although, Mick was uneasy sitting down to dinner with a bunch of officers. A few months later, Mick went on R and R (rest & relaxation) to Australia for 7 days. The debarkation point was Cam Ranh Bay, just 30 miles south of me, and that's where he landed when he came back.

Unbeknownst to Mick, I made arrangements with Colonel Wright to allow me to pick Mick up and let him spend three extra days at my place for a real nice visit. Mick returned to Cam Ranh Bay and was just sitting there with some other GI's when I walked up and surprised him. "Get your shit together Mick, you are going to spend a few days with me in Nha Trang." He complained that he would be up for a court martial if he did not report back to his unit on time. "Are you kidding me, hell they will not even miss you."

For the next three days, we had the best time traveling around all the important places, shrines, monuments, and bars. Mick was worried about getting back to Pleiku and what sort of punishment was awaiting him. Finally, I told him that I had cleared everything with Colonel Wright, so not to worry. He was very relieved. I took him out to the airport at the end of his visit where he boarded a twin engine Cessna owned by the CIA. There were two pilots, and Mick was the only passenger. I had asked Colonel Wright to have someone pick Mick up at the other end, which he did. He still talks about the look on the jeep driver's face and the faces of his soldier buddies when they learned about his flight. Love that kid!

* * *

Guenther Wagoner announced that he had been reassigned to Nicaragua and would be leaving Vietnam on or about January 1, 1971. His replacement was to be announced within the next two weeks. He confides in me that he had recommended that I be elevated to the top spot but had heard nothing yet. A few days later, he called me in and told me that there was a reduction in force order for OPS in Thailand, and both the current Director and Assistant Director were being transferred to II Corp. The Director was kind of a milk and toast guy, or what I will refer to as a "career government employee who did not like to make waves".

A couple of months later on a Sunday, I was laying on top of our three-story villa, soaking up the sun and on my fourth beer when an OPS jeep pulled up to our front gate and the driver, the Deputy Director, started blowing the horn. The guard let him, in and he came to the top deck. He informed me that the Director was to be at MACV headquarters in an hour to brief the new II Corp commander, John Paul Vann (this position was usually held by a three star general but Vann was a civilian, and I will explain that later). Unfortunately, the OPS Director had taken ill and wanted me to brief the new commander on OPS activities in II Corp. I asked the deputy what was wrong with him doing it, as such a high level briefing is a little out of my league. He pleaded ignorance (under my breath I concur) and said he had paperwork to get completed. I finished my beer, (now just a little gassed) took a shower, and headed for MACV headquarters.

When I entered the briefing room, I never saw so much brass, several generals, high-level state department officials, and my boss from Saigon. I think by now a reader to this point knows what I was thinking about Vietnam and the whole situation. When I was called upon to speak I unloaded, and the audience was stone silent. Mr. Vann listened intently, but made no interruptions. When I finished, 15 minutes later, Mr. Vann, to my astonishment said, "You know Mr. Clark makes some very good points, points that we collectively have to address, if we ever expect to win this conflict. Do you have anything else Mr. Clark?" I thought to myself that I would never have a better opportunity; so, I told everyone that drugs in II Corp were running rampant amongst our troops, even out to the smallest fire base. This problem was critical and only getting worse. "Just talk to your own Criminal Investigative Detail (CID). They feel their hands are tied because officially, our government does not want to recognize the problem or address it. After all, most of the troops rotate out in six months or so; therefore, let them handle it stateside. Did you know, Mr. Vann, that the CID does not even have office space in II Corp? They work out of where ever they can find space. They get almost no support from their superiors. How can they be expected to do their job?"

I took my seat, and the meeting went on. While I was sitting there, an aide to Mr. Vann slipped me a note that said, "Mr. Vann would like you to have dinner with him at his villa this evening." What had I gotten myself into?

John Paul Vann was a quite remarkable man. He was an officer in the U.S. Army, stationed in, I believe, III or IV Corp, assigned as an advisor to the South Vietnamese Army. He made quite a name for himself as a no nonsense, ass kicking, and hard fighting individual. He was a Lt. Colonel, but rattled some of the higher brass, and knowing he was not going anywhere promotion wise, he left the army and got into government work in Washington DC. Somehow, he caught the eye of Richard Nixon and other government officials in Washington, and before he knew it, he was back in Vietnam as head of II Corps. He supervised all of the American war effort, and had several generals reporting to him. That must have really been a burr in their saddles.

We spent two hours dining and discussing the situation and circumstances of the Vietnam War, particularly as it effected II Corp. We focused in on the narcotic issue, and I explained that I did have a little expertise in the field. I went on to explain that with the cooperation of some of my Vietnamese police friends, I thought we had established where the snakes head was, and I thought it just a matter of time until we cut it off. He wanted more details but I said, "While I trust you, I do not want to compromise our plan." He accepted that, and our evening came to an end. He had no idea, nor did I want him to know, that his counterpart, South Vietnamese Army, three-star general Ngo Dzu, was believed by some in the Vietnamese police to be one of, if not the biggest drug dealer in all of Vietnam.

Quang Duc was a province in II Corp that borders Cambodia. It had long been the gateway for smuggling heroin out of Southeast Asia to many destinations around the world. I had an extremely close working relationship with the police chief there. He was a devout Catholic and an extreme patriot. He loved his country and wanted unification with the north and a democratic society more than anything else. Working secretly with him and other loyal and honest members of the National

Police, we were able to, without doubt, prove that General Dzu was the ringleader and profiteer of the heroin being smuggled into South Vietnam. The National Police in Nha Trang seized over 300 lbs. of uncut heroin being transported in a military C-123 aircraft at the airport and arrested several people. A shootout between the police and the Vietnamese soldiers was only averted by the intervention of some U.S. Military police.

There was a preponderance of evidence that General Dzu was the mastermind and profiteer behind this operation. John Paul Vann, as much as I liked him, intervened, and the case, along with the heroin, disappeared never to be brought up again. When I privately questioned Mr. Vann about this, he told me to get over it, and he wanted to hear nothing further on the subject. He went on to say that the whole event was actually helpful in the war effort, as now he had a hammer over General Dzu's head and could force him to become more engaged in pursuing the war. Later 27 officers under General Dzu' command filed a complaint with the Saigon government alleging several corruption and drug charges against him. These charges were discredited by Vann and Dzu was never held answerable. John Paul Vann was killed on June 9, 1972 in a fiery helicopter crash while flying to a U.S. outpost being attacked by V/C or NVA troops.

* * *

I reconciled all of the reports from the public safety officers in the other provinces, compiled the statistical data, and then interjected a long narrative of my assessment of the war. I did not see the United States making much headway, and I thought the war would be totally lost either through capitulation by the South Vietnamese government or negotiations in Geneva. No matter what, the South Vietnamese Government was not sustainable without our continued maximum support. Fifty-five thousand American servicemen and women dead, hundreds of billions of dollars expended, a major blow to our own economy back home, and almost an entire nation saying "Get out!"

My report was reviewed by my OPS supervisor who had no comments and was sent on to Saigon. It was back in a few days with a rather terse note that "a report of this nature and content cannot be forwarded to Washington. Shortly thereafter I was told to meet with the CIA Director for Vietnam, William Colby. We had a private meeting for over two hours. And while he could not or would not publicly say so, he agreed with me entirely. He later became head of the CIA. Saigon OPS said, "While some of the data and information is correct, it just paints a much too negative assessment of the situation. Please re-write and re-submit." My supervisor called me in and made some suggestions to soften the report; I refused to change a thing. He said I was really killing myself as far as OPS was concerned, and I said I did not care. I was going home in little over a month, and if they did not like it, they could dismiss me. He may have made some changes to the report, but I did not.

I packed up everything I owned and shipped it home to Modesto. Before you knew it, I was in sunny California for a couple of weeks and enjoying my family and friends. The Modesto Bee did a rather large article on my exploits, opinions, and anti-war rhetoric. I was off to Washington where I learned my request to be re-assigned to Latin America had been turned down, but rather graciously, and I received a little congratulations note for studying Spanish for two years at the MACV language school in Nha Trang. I would be returning to Vietnam and re-assigned somewhere in the country, location unknown at this time. I very graciously said, "No thanks," and tended my resignation.

Before I tended my resignation from OPS and returned home, I made it a point to call on my local congressman, John McFall, who was House Majority Whip. I went over my experiences in Vietnam and tried to convince him of the South Vietnamese government's unpopularity, and that the war was unwinnable. He was very polite and listened to me for over an hour. He had visited Vietnam, and told me when he was there and visited small villages that the people and children lined the streets waving American and South Vietnamese flags in support of both governments. I inquired of him, "Was it possible that all that support and enthusiasm might have been staged by the government." "Oh," he said, "absolutely not." I warned him not to believe everything he heard from the military and government bureaucrats who supported the war. We left on good terms, and I thanked him for his time. I was home after 28 months of adventure and education that I would not trade for anything. Marilyn and I had saved a substantial amount of money and could relax a little bit before I hit the road looking for employment.

\* \* \*

I will close this chapter about Vietnam completely by bringing you up to date on the travels and situation concerning Chief Cuong and his family as the war wound down, and they were forced to become refugees fleeing their homeland. You may recall that he was my counterpart in Nha Trang when I first arrived there in the summer of 1969. He was promoted and transferred to Saigon in early 1970. That was the last time I saw or heard from him. It was now April of 1975 and the fall of Saigon and the impending end of the war was near. Chief Cuong was desperately trying to get himself and his family out of Vietnam before it fell into the hands of the communists. With absolute certainty, he and his wife would face long terms in indoctrination centers (prisons). Some of these internments meted out by the communists were for over 20 years.

On April 30, 1975, North Vietnamese troops over-ran Saigon, and for all practical purposes, this ended the war after 20 long years of strife (1954-1975). Chief Cuong was able to buy passage on a small san pan for him and his family, and on the night of May 1st, they slowly started their way down the Saigon River until it joined the Nha Be River, which emptied into the South China Sea. They could travel only at night; so, it took almost three days before they reached the open sea. They had been robbed, of course, by pirates, but no one was harmed. They had been at sea for three days, and all of their food and water were just about gone when they were spotted by a large freighter. Painted on the side of the big ship was the word *Budweiser*. It would become the chief's favorite beer. They were taken aboard and eventually transferred to an American military ship which took them to the Philippines.

The family was settled into a refugee camp with several thousand other Vietnamese and had absolutely no idea of what the future may hold for them. The U.S. military housed them in tents and did provide the basic necessities of life, but for what had been a wealthy and affluent family, the situation was very demoralizing. Three months had gone by since the fall of Saigon and on this side of the ocean, I was wondering what had happened to my old friend "Charles". Is he dead, a prisoner of war, did he escape to France where he had friends? I had no idea, but I was determined to find out. I knew that most of the Vietnamese who got out of the country were taken to Subic Bay in the Philippines. I had little hope that he would be interested, but I put in a call for Congressman McFall, hoping that I could solicit his assistance in locating Charles and his family in the Philippines. I could hardly believe it, but the Congressman himself answered the phone. I understood that he was prone to do that on occasion. I introduced myself, and asked if he remembered me. Yes, he did, and he said he should have paid more attention to my assessment of the situation in Vietnam when we conversed. He promised to look into Charles's predicament and get back to me. This guy was the House Whip. So, I figure if anyone can help me and Charles, he was the man.

I was a little skeptical that anything would be done, but I was praying that he was a man of his word and would make a conscientious effort to locate the family. I heard nothing for a couple of weeks and then another miracle in my life occurred. Congressman McFall called me, and advised that they had located Charles and his family in the Philippines, and he was trying to arrange air travel to get them to the U.S. "Can they stay with you?" he asked. "Absolutely! We would be delighted to become part of his life again." But Charles had other ideas. He had friends living in a Vietnamese community in Maryland and felt he could better adapt to our country by going there. That was fine by me, and shortly thereafter he and his family were in America. They were hosted by the Catholic Church, and soon were living in a rented home in Maryland.

Mrs. Cuong spoke fluent English and French and had an extensive background in accounting. She found a good job right away. Charles, in the meantime did not speak much English, and he certainly could not be a policeman. However, he was ambitious and determined to make it in America. He studied his English and geography, and believe it or not, got a job driving a tour bus around the capital. In a few months, Marilyn and I flew back to Washington for a visit. We had an absolutely wonderful time and were treated like royalty by the Vietnamese community.

While in Nha Trang, my favorite restaurant was called, La Frigate. As it turned out, the lady who owned that restaurant was now in Washington DC and had opened a Vietnamese restaurant in Georgetown by the same name. We all went there for a big get together and the food could not have been better, or more authentic if you were in Saigon at Maxim's. Charles and his wife were in tears when they told me about the refugee camp. The whole family was sitting outside of their tent still pondering what would happen to them as time passed on. An American, who looked pretty official, walked through the area calling out "Nyguen Tan Cuong, Nyguen Tan Cuong?" Charles and his wife both raised their hands and start shouting at the man, "Here we are, here we are!" The man told Charles that he must be a very important man as the embassy had been trying to locate him and his family for over a week. "You are all going to America," he told them. The family met with embassy staff and learned that Congressman McFall had, through the State Department and immigration officials, made all of the arrangements for the family to be flown to San Francisco where they would be met by a gentleman named Frank Clark, and he would walk them through the government red tape, and then they would go to Modesto, California to live with Mr. Clark. The two of them were overcome with emotion and joy.

Well, Charles and the family, as you know, eventually ended up in Maryland, not Modesto. Marilyn and I have visited them several times, and their son Tuan spent one summer with us here in Oakdale and worked for me at Gallo. Charles is now 91 years old, and he and his family are doing well. Two of his older sons, who were officers in the Vietnamese military, both died in communist prisons. The other children, who came to America with their parents, have been very successful; one is a medical doctor, the other is in the communication and computer technology fields. God Bless John McFall for his efforts and help.

# E & J GALLO WINERY: 1972-1995

I spent my first couple of weeks home from Vietnam and Washington in Modesto at our home near Davis High School just relaxing and getting acclimated to the hot weather, visiting relatives, and taking the kids here and there. They were really happy to have their dad home, and I was happy to be with the family. I began my search for employment by going through a number of law enforcement professional magazines and publications, and by contacting the International Association of Chiefs of Police.

I applied for the position of Police Chief in three cities that interested me, Joplin, Missouri; Los Alamos, New Mexico; and Astoria, Oregon. I also wandered down to the Stanislaus County Sheriff's office and talked with my old friend, Sheriff Dan Kelsay. He offered me a job immediately, and said I could start the following Monday, if I was interested. That sounded good to me. So, I was prepared to become a sheriff's deputy, starting pay $636.00 a month, a far cry from my salary with the State Department.

The next day, I got a call from Captain Gerald McKinsey of the Modesto Police Department who told me that the Yosemite Junior College District was looking for someone to establish a public safety department for the college. The pay was $950.00 per month and no night or weekend work. It was a no brainer, so I contacted my old friend Dusty Rhodes whom I had known for several years and was the number two guy at the college, and he invited me out to meet the dean that was doing the recruiting. I left the college campus with the job in hand, Chief of Security and Safety, Yosemite Junior College, with campuses in Modesto and Columbia, California. What was I going to tell Sheriff Kelsay? He was very understanding, and said I would be a damned fool not to take the job. So, all was well, and everybody was happy.

The job at the college was going very well. I had an office, secretary, and three officers working for me. I went to school at night and received my Police Science Associates of Arts Degree. I was also very busy trying to get a working under-standing of fire protection-prevention, and employee safety, both of which I knew very little. I still yearned for a job with more responsibility, and of course, a higher income. Marilyn and I traveled to Astoria, Oregon where I interviewed for the police chief's job, but came in second. As in many cases when making a selection, the City Manager went with the current second in command. There was less risk of making the wrong selection and usually less turmoil within the city and department. I turned down an interview opportunity with the city of Joplin, and I was still waiting to hear from Los Alamos where I had a sincere interest.

I had been on the job at Modesto Junior College for about 6 months when one day, I got a call from Bob Gallo, the son of Julio and a vice president with the winery. He said he had read about me in the newspaper recently, and he recalled me going dove hunting a few years back with him and his brother-in-law Frank Damrell, who is a longtime friend of mine. He said that there may be a job opportunity for me at the winery, and if I was interested, I could come in and talk to John Bodily, who was the vice president of Industrial Relations for the winery. I had always had a great deal of respect for the winery and the founding brothers, so I said why not, and made an appointment to see Mr. Bodily.

The interview went well, and he told me the Winery was looking for someone to take charge of the Security Department. "Is the person currently in charge being terminated?" I asked. He replied, "No, the company just wants someone with more experience to reorganize and make an assessment of the current situation." We did not talk salary or benefits. I told him that I would get back to him in a few days, after I thought it over, and gave him time to see if he was really interested in me. I called Bob Gallo back the next day and expressed my concerns. First, I could not work for Mr. Bodily because for some reason, and I could not explain why, but I just had a bad feel for the man. Actually, I went on to say I didn't think I liked him. Also, being "head of security" as Mr. Bodily described the job, did not ring well with me. As a former police person, the term security officer reminded me of some old guy walking around with a flashlight and ring of keys checking buildings. This was an incorrect perception, but at the time, that was what I thought.

A month went by, and I got a call from Jesse Nelson, Bob Gallo's secretary, and she said Mr. Gallo would like for me to come in and meet with him personally. I agreed to the meeting, and listened to what Mr. Gallo had to say. He informed me that Mr. Bodily was no longer with the company, and if interested, he would like to discuss the possibility of my employment with the winery. He went on to explain that I would be working directly for him and in charge of security and safety at all Gallo production facilities and ranches. The winery currently had no one overseeing industrial safety on the corporate level, and I would be taking on that responsibility. My title would be Director of Corporate Safety and Security. If I was interested, then he would arrange for me to have lunch with him and his dad within a few days and see if we could come to terms of employment.

A few days later the three of us gathered at the Sundial Restaurant for lunch and further discussion. Bob said that the he would like to make me a job offer, if I was interested. "Well, a lot depends on the salary," I said, and Bob asked, "What kind of an offer would make things work." I had decided that I really wanted this position with the winery, but if I asked for too much, I could lose the deal. I had absolutely no idea what a position like this should pay. If I asked too little, I could be making a big financial mistake.

I went back to the last time I negotiated a salary, and that was with Mr. Walton in Sacramento when I went to work for OPS. I shot for the moon and came out pretty darn good. So, I said to myself, "I am currently making a little over $11,000 a year, which is not bad, but I know I can do better. What if I double that? Would I scare them off?" Neither of them had asked what my current salary was, and I hoped that they would not. I started out by explaining that the job at the college was short term, that my intentions had been to become the police chief in a large city somewhere in the western United States with a salary comparable to what I was making with the federal government. "And what was that?" asked Bob. I replied "$22,000 per year," and held my breath. Bob looked at his dad and asked, "What do you think dad?" His dad thought for a moment and then replied, "That sounds about right to me." Oh my God. I asked myself, "Can this all be happening?" Then Bob throws this in, "And you will be needing a company car, so I will arrange for that." "Are you kidding me?!" I asked myself. I was thinking that I was the luckiest guy in the world, as I headed for the college to inform them that I would be leaving as of March 1, 1972.

\* \* \*

I reported to the Gallo Administration building on Wednesday, March 1, 1972 at 7:00 a.m. Jessie Nelson came in at 8:00 a.m. She informed me that Bob usually appeared at about 9:00 a.m. and worked until 6:00 or 7:00 p.m. Then she sent me over to Personnel in another building to fill out a bunch of paperwork, get photographed, and get an ID card. When I got back to Bob's office, he was there. He took me around the various offices and introduced me to family members who were there and to the various vice presidents. We then settled down in his office for the next three days from 9:00 a.m. until he left the office late afternoon. We got to know each other better, and I learned what his expectations of me were.

On Monday morning, I showed up at my office, which was located in the very corner of this cavernous wine warehouse. I introduced myself to Howard David, who was the security manager and supervised the security department in Modesto. I had previously worked with Howard at the Modesto Police Department, until he left a few years back. There was a young lady who worked and sat in my office across from me at another desk. I could see that any privacy was out of the question. She handled all of the paper work for the department and took care of any required typing. The security sergeants and squad room were in the office next to mine and were separated by a wall with a 4ft. x 5ft. sliding glass window in the center with no curtains. The secretary, who wore mini-skirts, chose to crawl through the window when she needed to go into the squad room rather than go out our door and through another door to the squad room.

To the disappointment of others, I put a stop to that practice immediately. I instructed Howard to arrange for me to interview all of the security personnel, including the supervisors. I wanted 20 minutes with each one, beginning the following Monday at 8:00 a.m. There were 35 officers and four sergeants. I told him I would conclude the interviews with a final interview lasting as long as necessary with him. At the conclusion of the interviews, I was appalled at the quality of these people. I realized they were not paid a salary comparable to, nor received the benefits, that the winery union employees enjoyed. This had to be corrected. I also determined, after a month of observations and interviews, that the department was grossly overstaffed. I spoke with salaried supervisors in other departments in the winery, and it was very obvious that they had little respect for our security department.

When I thought the time was right, I presented a new organizational chart to Bob Gallo. It called for the elimination of 18 positions, reducing points of entry by vehicles and personnel into the winery. I also recommended that we took this savings made by the reductions of personnel and give the officers we kept a wage and benefit package at least equal to the union employees. Bob agreed to the plan, and we laid off 18 officers. Two days after they were gone, we announced the new benefit and wage package to the remaining officers. Morale skyrocketed. I visited the wineries at Livingston and Fresno where the security was on a contract with a security company out of Merced and Fresno. The security supervisor at each location was a Gallo employee.

I spent a day at each location and additionally interviewed the two supervisors. I intended to recommend to Bob that we terminate the contract with the security agencies and hire our own personnel, but before I could do that, fate stepped in. Ernest and Julio had driven together to the Livingston

Winery on a Saturday. They pulled up to the entrance and are stopped by a gate and a contract security guard. When the guard inquired of their business, Ernest tells him that they were the Franzia Brothers, and they would just like to come in and check things out, compare the two operations, Gallo vs Franzia. The guard said he thought that would be okay and allowed them to drive in. Julio called me on Monday morning, and he was absolutely livid, but before we were through talking, he had calmed down, and was laughing a little bit about the stupidity of the guards. He told me maybe it was time to put our own security at both Livingston and Fresno. I informed him that I had already put that proposal forward to his son. Within about two months, we had our own security at both locations.

* * *

During the 1960s and 1970s, there was a lot of publicity being given to a host of radical organizations. The Manson's, Patty Hurst, the Black Panthers, the Weathermen, and so on. I had a deep concern for the safety of the Gallo families, as there was no security whatsoever at their homes, not even an alarm system of any sort. The decision was made by the families at my suggestion that we had a security detail dedicated to protecting them. Around the clock security at each home was put into effect, which meant hiring an additional 20 security officers. Between the 20 officers already working at the winery and new recruits, we came up with a pretty good group of people. There were retired police officers and military personnel and also some exceptional young people who were seeking a career with Gallo. I had an understanding with the families that they could utilize these officers in any way they wanted, as long as the tasks and duties given to them were in no way demeaning to the officer, for example, no lawn mowing, house cleaning, gardening, cooking, etc. This arrangement worked out very well.

When I first became involved with Gallo, I was not sure just how much emphasis was being put on product security. Gallo produced and shipped around 80 million cases of product annually. It was hard to imagine that some of it was not being misappropriated somewhere along the line. All vehicle entrances in and out of the winery and Gallo Glass, with the exception of three, were eliminated, and all vehicles coming and going were to be inspected. There were literally hundreds of trucks coming and going daily through the scale house entry. Trucks moving product were not weighed, but only inspected. Only trucks carrying the materials for glass bottle manufacturing were weighed. Just how much wine went into a truck or trailer, and did it match the bill of lading? This was pretty much monitored by the shipping foreman on the docks or the clamp lift driver doing the loading. Not a good situation.

Working with the shipping and billing department, we came up with a new bill of lading. When a truck entered the winery for product, it was weighed, and when it was leaving, it was weighed once again. The security officer printed on the bill of lading the trucks weight when it entered the winery.

The weight of the product that was supposed to be on the truck when it left was also on the bill of lading. Adding these two together, the security officer came up with a net weight for the truck. If those figures did not match, the truck was pulled aside, unloaded, and bill of lading checked for amount of product that was supposed to be on the truck. When this procedure was first implemented, it created a huge backlog at the exit gate, as many of the trucks were carrying more wine than they should have been. This procedure virtually stopped the theft of wine created by collusion of Gallo employees and truck drivers.

Internal theft was another problem. One of the supervisors of the bottling department was an elderly gentleman who had been with Gallo for many years. His counterpart in the shipping warehouse was of the same type. When I asked the bottling room supervisor if he thought there was any theft going on, and did the inventory every show a discrepancy, he kind of chuckled and told me confidentially the following: the supervisor at the shipping warehouse took inventory, and if there was a shortage, the bottling supervisor chalked it up to "breakage", thus always a balance. "Incredible," I thought to myself. The warehouse manager was leaving the winery one Sunday in his vehicle, and the security officer stopped him, and as the new procedure called for, told him to open his trunk. The manager was outraged, and refused to do so. He was an old time employee and friend of Julio. He asked to use the phone, and he called Julio at home to protest. I was told later that Julio simply told him, "Pete, times are changing, and you will just have to adjust." Julio told Pete to put the security officer on the phone. Julio told him to check the car, then let Pete go, make a report, and see that he got a copy. He also told Pete to open his trunk, which he did. There were four cases of wine. The officer lets him go, and I never heard anything else about it. Pete, to my knowledge, never took any wine out of the winery again.

\* \* \*

I thought we had a very dedicated and honest security department after all the discharges and moral boosting that went on, but I was never sure. I had been provided some training in the art of phone tapping with my previous employer; so, I took advantage of that knowledge. Periodically, I would listen in to the phone traffic at the security gate nearest the shipping warehouse. One evening, and I spent a lot of evenings at the winery when I first got there, I was listening to the security post, and I heard a conversation between the officer and someone in the warehouse. It went something like this, "Let me know when the patrol officer is busy. I am going to sneak my friends some wine down Fairbanks Avenue on the clamp lift and put it over the fence." "That's interesting," I thought; so, I sat there for another couple of hours and listened, but mostly, there was no phone traffic.

Just when I was about to give up, the security officer made a call and told whoever answered to tell Lucius happy birthday. I got hold of the security supervisor, but told him nothing. We waited behind the wine tanks on Fairbanks Avenue, and sure enough, here came the clamp lift with a pallet of wine. About the same time, a pick-up pulled up on the other side of the fence, ready to take possession of the wine. We let them get it loaded and then bounced out, guns drawn, and arrested both of them. The security officer involved was given the option of quitting or being arrested as an accessary. He quit.

\* \* \*

I had long been suspicious of the trains that went into the warehouse on Sundays and picked up loaded rail cars of wine for shipment to all across the country. There are no Gallo employees working in the warehouse on Sundays. So, one Sunday, I contacted the security supervisor, told him of my suspicions, and a plan to investigate it. The train engine entered the warehouse and picked up 15 or 20 railcars. Keep in mind, Gallo shipped about 80 railcars a day. When it exited the warehouse, I had instructed the security supervisor to park the patrol car across the tracks and stop the train. The train stopped, and the engineer got out and wanted to know, "What the hell is going on?" I informed him that we were going to search the compartments on the engine. He said, "Over my dead body. I will just run over your god dammed car, and see how you like that." We also locked the gates on the railroad track and called the railroad company supervisor, whom I happened to know very well. That was better, I thought, than the police. The supervisor got there shortly, and we searched engine. Twenty-two cases of wine and champagne! A new train crew was called in, and later all of the employees involved were fired.

* * *

The summer, fall, and winter of 1972 pretty much came and went, and I had spent most of my efforts in the area of security. By the spring of 1973, I thought things were going well with the security programs the winery had implemented, and I began to concentrate more of my time and efforts in the area of industrial safety, of which I knew very little. Many departments within Gallo organization had no formal safety programs, with the exception of the winery, which was only marginally better than the other entities. There were few regular safety meetings, safety committees, or workplace safety inspections and trainings.

There was a very large void that had to be filled. I traveled to San Francisco where I met with Gallo's worker's compensation underwriter to explore ideas for meeting all statutory requirements and the process for implementing sound safety programs at all locations. They were extremely helpful. I next met with local members of CAL/OSHA and established a good rapport that later would prove invaluable. I must say that every department in the Gallo organization was extremely supportive, especially Bob Gallo. Job and task procedures were written, safety steps for each task were documented, and monthly safety meetings were made mandatory. Boy, was I getting an education.

Within months, the accident rate began to decline, and the days missed from work because of accidents was seriously reduced. Soon, Gallo was leading the industry in employee safety. That credit goes to the various department managers throughout the company. Gallo reduced their insurance costs significantly to the point that it became more economical to become self-insured, which they became. The next thing I knew, I had my office location changed from the dingy little room in the warehouse, to the "temple" with an office right next to Bob Gallo. I was not sure if it was a promotion, or if he wanted to keep a better eye on me (kidding). I also had a new secretary, Mary Inglima, who was one of the most efficient and wonderful people you could have ever met. We hit it off right from the start. After about four months, I went to Bob and told him I needed to relocate, so that I would be closer to the people and departments that I supervise, so he set me up with another office in the operations building. This worked out much better; so, after having two offices for a few weeks, I finally moved everything into the operations building. Mary Inglima also went with me.

Bob called me one day and said he had both good news and bad news for me. The bad news: his secretary was leaving the winery, and he was going to have Mary take her place. The good news: I could have anyone I liked that applied to take her place and work for me. Word got out, and soon I was interviewing about six ladies who thought they wanted the job. They were all well qualified and currently working in the same capacity somewhere within the organization. I settled on this nice looking, pleasant, well qualified, young black lady. Her name was Pearl Cooper, and she would be my right arm for the next 20 years.

You could never get away with it today, and maybe I should not have in 1975, but my interview with her went something like this: "Mrs. Cooper, I am going to be honest with you. I am not sure I like black people. I had a lot of problems with them as a police officer, and it may be hard for me to get past that." Her reply, "Well, Mr. Clark, (she called me that for 20 years) black people are no different than white people, some are good and some are bad. If I get this job, I am certain I can change your perception of black people, if you really have a negative one." I was just testing her; maybe that was okay, maybe not okay, but I was impressed with her answer. You could not have asked for a more wonderful person, ever so faithful to me and to Gallo.

I could tell you lots of stories about Pearl, but the one I like best was the one about Gallo's ad in newspapers, seeking qualified applicants for the position of security officer. This guy from Oakland called, and Pearl answered the phone. He wanted to know if the position was still open, and if so, he would come to Modesto and fill out an application. Pearl assured him that the deadline had not closed. He went on, "You know, I am just surrounded by niggers up here and, well you know how they are, I just have to get out of here." Pearl replies, "Oh yes, I know exactly how they are. I come from the South and have lived around them all my life. When you come down, please ask for me personally, so I can help you with the application." He made an appointment to see Pearl, showed up at the personnel department counter a few days later, and asked for Pearl Cooper. He turned pale when she greeted him and kind of stuttered, "Does it make any sense for me to fill out an application?" "Oh absolutely, and I will give it my personal recommendation." He left without filling it out. Have to love that woman. To this day, Marilyn and I are still very close with Pearl and her husband, Jerry.

\* \* \*

While Gallo had perhaps the best employee safety programs in the industry, it was not without tragedy. Pruning the grape vines was an extremely important part of the wine making process. At Gallo we used pruning machines. These machines were comprised of a motorized vehicle that had two long, extended arms that ran horizontal on both sides of the machine. An operator was seated on the machine. Each arm was 20 feet long and had five to six pneumatic pruning shears, each operated by an employee as they moved down the rows of vines. When not in use, the arms were raised and secured to the pruning machine, extending 20 feet into the air. On one particular day, the motorized machine hit a hole or bump, and the arms went up into the air and right into some high voltage lines that were overhead. Had the driver simply kept going and then gotten off the machine he would have been alright, but when he tried to get off, he was electrocuted and another employee coming to his assistance was also electrocuted. The first fatal injuries ever recorded on the ranch. CAL/OSHA was contacted and the accident reported. The Regional Director of CAL/OSHA reported to the scene to initiate an investigation. After going through all of the details and inspecting the equipment, he and I retired to the ranch manager's residence, which was located on the ranch, to discuss the matter. Let's call the OSHA guy Oscar. Well, Oscar liked to drink and I knew that because we both belonged to the Oakdale Golf and Country Club. So Oscar, I, and the ranch manager had a few drinks, and the manager decided he would review the case to determine if Gallo was at fault. I said, "Oscar let's play a round of golf tomorrow, and we can discuss the issue in a more relaxing environment." He said okay and I made a tee time. Oscar and I had a round of golf, and he beat me; we had a few drinks in the bar, and he told me the accident was unavoidable. Case closed. I am not saying this was the right way to handle things, but that was what happened.

* * *

Harvest season at the ranches was fast approaching, and there were dark clouds on the horizon as the United Farm Workers (UFW) were attempting to unionize our ranch employees. Gallo's employees were already the highest paid in the industry, and in Gallo's case, received other benefits not given to most of the farm workers in California. Half of our workers lived in housing on the ranch provided by Gallo, and the other half lived in the surrounding areas. During harvest, a large number of grape pickers come to the ranch from Texas, as they had for a number of years. Perhaps as many as 50% of our workers were of Portuguese descent and lived in and around the area. Most of the Hispanic employees decided that they wanted to join the UFW. An election was held, but the results were contested by Gallo and the UFW. The majority of Hispanic employees walked off the job and went on strike. The Portuguese employees and some of the Hispanic employees continued to work.

The UFW called for a national boycott of all Gallo products. Gallo was the largest winery in the world, and the UFW hoped the boycott would be supported by people across the nation, bringing Gallo to its knees. A lot of sabotage occurred, vines cut, irrigation pumps turned on flooding vineyards, and buildings vandalized. Because it appeared all of this damage was occurring internally, a decision was made to eliminate all employee housing and the structures leveled. I was instructed to organize a security force for the ranch, in order to protect our property and employees who were working. I hired 40 security officers to make sure our workers were provided a safe place to work. The Merced Sheriff's Department put 20 deputies on the picket line, and Merced Superior Court issued an order that restricted the picketers from coming within 60 feet of our employees while they work. The Teamsters Union decided it wanted to organize our employees, so they showed up on the scene, demanding new elections be held. This increased the tension.

While conversing with the teamster organizers one day, they happened to open the trunk of one of their vehicles, low and behold, 10-15 baseball bats. I questioned this, but was told they practiced softball at the end of the day. Think what you like, but from personal experience, the UFW at our ranch in 1974 were nothing more than a bunch of gangsters. They threatened and intimidated every employee at every opportunity. Breaking car windows, going to their homes threatening the families, and continuing to damage ranch property.

On one occasion, I was being followed consistently, everywhere I went. I was nicknamed *Raton Blanco*, the White Rat. Once, while being followed across ranch property (private), I sped up to 60 miles an hour, and the union organizers were right on my tail, I mean four or five feet behind my vehicle. I threw a cardboard carton out the window to distract them, and then hit my brakes. The ensuing crash totaled their car, while causing minimum damage to my pickup which had an iron bumper. This went on all summer and we continued to harvest the grapes. The picketers, as many as 100 at times, were there every day, yelling and shouting, and occasionally throwing rocks at our employees. Finally, near the end of the harvest, the UFW picketers rushed the field and began beating the workers. What a mistake! The workers were ready for them. Clubs and wire cables came out of the grape gondolas, and the UFW made a hasty retreat. That incident led to many UFW supporters being arrested and soon thereafter, the end of the picketing.

\* \* \*

I received a radio call a few days later to report to Ernest Gallo's office. I was exhausted after a whole summer 5:00 a.m. to 8:00 p.m., seven days a week. My emotions were running high when I walked into the conference room, filled with all of the family members, and most of our legal staff. I was asked to give a situational report on the strike at the ranch. I did so and told them we would get through the harvest in good shape, and I thought we had taken the wind out of their sails. Ernest announced that there was concern about the national boycott and consideration of the UFW's unionization offer was being kicked around.

I broke down and with tears in my eyes I asked, "How in the hell can you let down all of the employees at the ranch who have stuck by us, been subjected to violence and abuse, came through by harvesting our grapes, live in the area, and have been so supportive?" What kind of message was that? You help us and we will screw you. We will put your lives and jobs into the hands of a bunch of socialistic bastards, who every time you get out of line will, come after you. This boycott will pass believe me, even if it ever gets off of the ground. Please, I beg of you, do not turn your back on our employees." I turned and left the room. Gallo never capitulated! Did I make a difference? Who knows?

A few weeks later, the harvest was over, and I was walking up the sidewalk by the administration building, and here came Julio. He stopped me and thanked me for all of my work at the ranch. "Frank, I want you to take a week off and along with Marilyn, take a little vacation. Take her somewhere nice okay?" "Julio, I have no idea where to go. Do you mean like San Francisco or Monterey?" With a smile he said, "No, damn it. I mean any place in the world, okay?" I told Bob what his dad said, and Bob said, "Okay but don't overdo it." We spent a wonderful, relaxing week in the Bahamas. Was Gallo a great company to work for or what?

When I left the winery in 1995, I had been responsible for seven different departments and had been promoted to vice president. There is an interesting story behind each acquisition. I was having a meeting with Bob Gallo in his office in late 1973 and the phone rang. The caller was the Director of Engineering and Planning. Reporting to him was the Landscape Maintenance Department. He informed Bob that the employees were petitioning to join the union. Bob was not happy to hear this, as the winery was interested in keeping salaried employees out of the union, and any movement in that direction, if it caught on, could affect several hundred employees. I volunteered to look into it and he gave me the green light and told the Engineering Director about my involvement.

The landscaping Department was located off site, but just across from the winery on the north side of Yosemite Boulevard. This street was one of Modesto's busiest, and our employees were, on a daily basis, put in a very dangerous situation just trying to get across the street. They were housed in the basement of the old Gallo credit union. The place was a dump. No heat, or A/C, one old broken down toilet, and a picnic table for a lunch room. They must have figured the company did not care, so why should they. They did little to make things better and added to the clutter and unkempt look of the place. They were underpaid, in my opinion, and had no benefits. I interviewed every employee and found almost all of them to be good, hardworking individuals who wanted to do a good job. They, for the most part, had only minimum education and no high expectations for advancement beyond their present station in life. They did, however, like what they did.

Bob and I discussed the issues, and I gave him my take on things. He put the department under my supervision, asked that I do a salary and benefit assessment, and look for a better location to house the group. Gallo had just recently purchased an old gas station on the south side of Yosemite, and it was currently not in use. Arrangements were made to build a new facility to accommodate the employees and functions of the landscape department. The pay was improved, and they received benefits. The thought of joining the union never came up again. Twenty years later when I left the company, five of the original nine employees in that department were still with the company.

* * *

The mail room distribution center consisted of five employees who picked up the mail daily, sorted it, and then delivered it to the various locations in the company. Also delivered were interdepartmental mail, office supplies, furniture, and other needed materials. Having a background in narcotics, I became suspicious of one of the employees and had a hunch he was delivering more than office materials and mail. Bob gave me permission to put an undercover narcotics officer on the mailroom staff. It only took about two weeks until the guy I suspected was arrested for possession and distributing cocaine. Several employees were fired. I was then given the responsibility for that department, as well as the entire shipping and receiving (non-product), the nationwide point of sale distribution, solid waste management and recycling, and surplus property disposition departments.

I later got involved in managing the company's hazardous waste, purely by accident. One day while browsing through the Federal Register (a book put out monthly by the government describing new environmental laws and regulations that were going into effect), I came upon an article discussing bricks from glass furnaces that contained an element called hexavalent chromium, or more commonly, chromium-6. It is an extremely hazardous carcinogen, requiring very special handling and disposal. Gallo had five glass furnaces, and they all contained chrome bricks. Each furnace had a life of five to six years and then had to be torn down and rebuilt. Where did the old bricks go? I asked that question, and a lot of people at Gallo were upset because I did, but in the long run, it saved us a great deal of agony. Historically, I discovered these contaminated bricks were dumped on Gallo property just north of the winery, pushed around with a big D-8, leveled off, and forgotten. The company apparently was just ignorant of the hazard they posed. Bob informed me that during the last furnace tear down, the bricks were dumped on a ranch southwest of Modesto, which Gallo later purchased, and took remedial action to clean up the property. I checked that location and found that a large area had been dug out by a D-8 or front loader leaving a very large hole in the ground maybe 10 feet deep and 150' by 150' and the bricks were dumped in there. The water table in that area was very shallow so the bricks were actually in contact with the ground water. This meant that the contaminated water was probably forming a plume underground and headed for the Tuolumne River a few miles away. I arranged to have all of the bricks dug up and hauled to a Class 1 hazardous waste dump at Kettleman City, off of Interstate 5. Next, experts were brought in to determine the scope of the problem, and sure enough, a plume had already developed and was moving toward the river. Several wells were dug, the water pumped out of the ground, and circulated through equipment that removed the chromium-6.

Gallo ended up buying the property, and I have been told while the plume was no longer moving but actually being reduced in size, the water was still being pumped and treated. This was over 35 years later. The California Regional Quality Board was involved in the whole cleanup process. They also wanted us to address the bricks dumped near the winery. I had soil tests taken, and they showed a particular level of chromium-6 in the soil. This substance is naturally occurring in the soil and sometimes, even though natural, it could exceed the PPM government standards. I had soil samples taken as far as two miles away from the winery and those samples in a natural state were higher than the samples where the bricks were buried. With this information in hand, the Water Board backed off and bricks near the winery were deemed not to be a health risk.

Thereafter, I supervised the removal and transportation of all hazardous material from the winery and glass plant to a class one dump for disposal. Keep in mind that when a furnace tear down was done there were 80 to 100 truck and trailer loads of bricks that had to be transported to the dump. These were stockpiled on site until the bricks were all in one big pile. Then the trucks were called in, and they were hauled away.

* * *

One of my favorite little jobs was selling scrap metal, surplus equipment, doing demolish jobs, and selling that junk. Before I got involved, the process was pretty simple. One local scrap metal dealer would simply leave two or three 20-yard scrap bins on site, and when they were full, he would be called, come in and pick them up, and send Gallo a check for what he said it was worth. I put it out to bid and wanted prices on iron, stainless, copper, brass, and copper wire. I wanted bins placed on site for each different commodity, so they could be weighed separately. When the bids came in, a different vendor was selected. The first year saw Gallo net a little over $65,000 more than they had made the previous year. When you tore down a glass furnace, there was quite a bit of scrap generated. One metal that was found in the electrodes or igniters is called molybdenum. Depending on the price, there could sometimes be $25,000-$30,000 worth of this scrap metal in a scrapped furnace. When asked where this metal went after a tear down and if we paid for it, no one could answer the question. I made it a point to have this metal delivered to my scrap yard to be sold at a later date. Perhaps my funniest story during my time in the scrap business involved a gentleman named Sam Haar, who owned Haar Scrap Metal.

Sam bought a lot of scrap from us, and one day while we were going through the scrap yard at the Livingston winery, we came across two heat exchangers. These were 10 to 15 feet long and were in tubular shape with a cap on both ends. The interior was comprised of numerous copper tubes. Sam could see the copper as the caps had been removed; so, he was interested in purchasing them and a deal was struck, at so many cents per lb. at our scales. Sam used to throw a saying around, "Sometimes you make a little money in the scrap business, sometimes you lose a little, but you cannot cry over it." Six months later, we repeated the scene on two more heat exchangers, but these two still had the caps on them. I told Sam that if he wanted them, he would have to pay cash in this one particular case. We weighed the exchangers, agreed on a price, and Sam picked them up the next day, dropping off a cashier's check at the security station. Maybe a couple of months later at Sam's scrap yard, he pulled the ends off of the exchangers. Two hundred gallons of water and sludge ran out onto the ground. Sam had been screwed, and he knew it. When he complained, I simply repeated his old slogan,

"Sometimes you make a little money..." He chuckled a little, and got over it, I'm sure.

\* \* \*

I had previously mentioned that Gallo had purchased a service station at the corner near the winery. Gallo had hundreds of vehicles of all types. Cars, trucks, scooters, family vehicles. I mentioned to Bob that a couple of hundred employees were running all over the place on company time, buying gasoline, getting the car serviced or washed. The scooters were contracted out to J.M. Lift for service and repair at about $45.00 per hour. I suggested we reopen the gas station and do all of the above in-house. He agreed, and I hired a manager and a mechanic. Both of who were really good employees. Another real bonus was that I hired a bunch of high school kids or just out of school kids to pump gas and ferry vehicles. The ones that were exceptional, and there were many that fit into that category, eventually worked their way into better, more responsible positions at the winery or glass plant. This arrangement saved a great deal of time and money for the company.

\* \* \*

When I had just turned 42 years old, I noticed that my eye sight was starting to act peculiar. My optometrist at the time suggested I make an appointment at the ophthalmology department at Stanford University to see if they could make a better diagnosis than he could. After several visits, I ended up having cataract surgery on my left eye. That seemed to correct the problem, but a couple of months later, my eye went haywire, and I had very distorted vision in that eye.

I now had a new optometrist in Oakdale, Lee Scaief, and he was sure I had a detached retina. He also suspected that something far more serious was going on. He suggested I get back to Stanford immediately and on an emergency basis. I called and made an emergency appointment for the next morning at 8:00 a.m. Another miracle! The ophthalmology department had a brand new department chairman, and it was his first day on the job. Dr. Gaynon was a graduate of John Hopkins Medical School, and for his doctorate he had studied a rare eye disease called Wagner vitreoretinal degeneration, also called Wagner's Disease. The disease is inherited and often found in several members of a family. The only other people in our family that have been diagnosed with it is my cousin Cindy and her son Sammy. Dr. Gaynon identified the problem almost immediately, and after seven hours of surgery and eleven days in the hospital at Stanford, I was discharged. I had to remain on my back and as immobile as possible for fourteen days after I got home. The back of my eyes had hundreds of small holes in them and the eyes were degenerating rapidly.

Dr. Gaynon did over 100 laser treatments on each eye and put a one inch "patch" over the back of my left eye. The miracle was first that Dr. Gaynon was there, and second, that after 40 years, I have almost normal eye sight in my right eye and not bad in the left one. They say in the medical journal that there is no cure for this disease. I guess they never heard of Dr. Gaynon and Frank Clark. After almost a month away from Gallo, I was ready to return with no idea of the new job challenge that I would be taking on.

* * *

I do not recall the exact date, but I was called up to the front security desk where the union employees entered and left. There I found a young storeroom attendant had been detained by the security officer and the sergeant. During an exit inspection of his lunch pail the officer noticed he had a rather large thermos so he took it from the employee and opened it. Inside he found numerous parts, nuts and bolts, and an array of items from the storeroom. When threatened with arrest he allowed me, the sergeant, and his supervisor to go to his home where we found several thousand dollars' worth of stolen Gallo property.

The following day, I asked for and received approval to interview all of the employees assigned to the storeroom. To the very last employee, they all agreed that taking things from the storeroom was not stealing, but more like a fringe benefit that went with the job. They also told me that some of the supervisors were the worst offenders and often took or asked to be given parts that had no connection to jobs at the winery.

The next day, I met with Bob, and we discussed the storeroom issue in depth. Here was a department that cared for and managed over five million dollars' worth of inventory on any given day. The department, Maintenance, was the department that stored, inventoried, and used these commodities. To me that made no sense, as there were no checks and balances.

In a couple of weeks, Bob informed me that the storeroom would now be reporting to me. This was a critical part of the winery function. The winery was a 24-hour operation, and there were machine repairs, breakdowns, and new installations in progress continually. You have to have the parts, tools, and equipment available without delay.

Within six months, we had all new employees, the old ones either leaving or gone for disciplinary reasons. I had a very bright, energetic, young lady working for me in Point of Sale Distribution that I thought had a lot of potential. Her name was Deana Landingham. I transferred her to the storeroom as assistant manager. The employees spent a lot of time taking inventory manually, and there were many times we ran out of parts. Sometimes these were parts critical to the bottling operation. I requested and received permission to have IT come up with a proposal for a Material Management Inventory system (MMI). Deana was the brains behind this new system, but it had a hefty price tag on it. Bob wanted a briefing before he would approve it. Deana and I prepared for the briefing, and when we arrived to brief Bob, his dad was also there. Poor Deana, briefing Julio Gallo, she was nervous, but did a great job. Julio asked if I thought a woman could do this. "Yes," I told Julio, "I am very confident everything will go just fine."

The system was put into operation, and in just one year, the inventory was down to less than two million dollars. Rather than keep a large inventory ourselves, our vendors were notified of what parts they must keep on hand and made available on a 24-hour basis. Deana was later promoted to storeroom manager. In the meantime, I had a serious problem in the security department. One of the officers had circulated a petition asking for a vote on unionization. This hit me like a bolt of lightning; although, I had heard rumors, I had not seen evidence of such. Enough signatures were gathered to certify the NLRB to hold an election. The election was held, and the majority of the security officers rejected joining or forming any kind of union. Now what do I do with this bastard who started all the trouble? I could not fire him because that would be deemed retaliatory. What to do? Bob had a crazy idea. When the next opening came along for security supervisor, offer him the job. "He is sure to take it," Bob said. "Are you serious?" I ask, "Promote that bastard for all the grief he has caused the company and particularly me?" Bob went on, "Wait until just before his probation is up, and then fire him on the basis he has not made the grade." I took a hard look at Bob and said, "You sly son of a gun." An opening for sergeant came up a short time later, and I made the offer. He accepted it with the understanding he would be on probation for six months, and if he completed his probationary period satisfactorily, he would get a permanent position.

About three months later, the matter resolved itself. One of my female officers reported that the new sergeant kind of crowded her into a corner at the office and began groping her breasts. I had the matter investigated, and our Human Resources Department said there was probable cause to terminate the sergeant, which I did. We never heard another thing from him.

I never enjoyed having to terminate any employee; some were just easier than others. Because I had several departments under my direction, there were many instances when troublesome employees from other departments were sent to me for job reclassification and/or re-assignment. For whatever reason, I was told to eventually get rid of them as gently as I could. Two of those instances come to mind that are of interest. The first was a long time vice-president who headed up wine production at all facilities, and additionally a good friend of Julio's. This employee drank a lot, but when on his game, he was one of the best in the industry. Somewhere in the fermentation process he, or his subordinates, made a major screw up and tried to hide it. He refused to let the winemakers take samples from the wine tanks for analysis. He believed he could correct whatever the problem was before anyone up top could become aware of it.

It did not go that way, and the winemakers reported it to Julio. While infuriated, Julio still had a soft spot in his heart for the man. He knew for integrity's sake he would have to remove him from his position. He notified me that on a particular day, this man would report to me and be under my supervision. "Find something for him to do, keep him busy, but do not humiliate him." Well, this man and I had always been good friends, so the transition went well, but I understood what I was expected to do, and I think he saw the handwriting on the wall. As gently as I could, I made his job uncomfortable, and after six months or so, he resigned.

The second employee worked for Ernest as his right-hand man, his "gopher", his driver, and anything else Ernest wanted handled by a servant type employee. We will call him Mack. Mack drove Ernest everywhere he wanted to go both day and night and usually in a limousine. He ran errands, went to the bank, picked up things at the store, dry cleaners, etc. He had worked for Ernest for several years. When he was not busy with those chores, he came to the operations building and found a desk and took a nap. It always irritated me to look out and see him snoozing away, but this was not my concern. Ernest decided to travel to South America, and he took Mack with him to facilitate all of his personal needs and travel necessities.

Ernest called me and said "Frank, you know my driver, Mack?" "Yes sir, I know him well. Why is there a problem?" "Yes, there is," he replied. "I want you to find me another person to take Mack's place. Eventually when the time is right send him on his way." "May I ask what the problem is?" I requested. "Yes, I will tell you, but it is a confidential matter, please. You are aware, I am sure, that I just spent two weeks traveling in South America on a pleasure and business trip correct?" "Yes, sir," I replied. "During that trip, Mack sat near me, ate in the very best restaurants, and had the best of food and wine. First class travel everywhere. When we went fishing he was there, pole in hand getting as much enjoyment and pleasure as I was, but of course it was costing him nothing, and this trip was not inexpensive. When we got back to the winery, he submitted an expense report, which was a little irritating, but when I saw he was asking several thousands of dollars in overtime, I was totally beside myself. The vacation of a lifetime for him, I was sure. Anyway, take care of the problem." The only place I could use Mack was to replace the person I sent Ernest, and that would to be a security officer. He quit a couple of months later.

* * *

I retired from the winery in 1995 as Vice President of Special Services and for a variety of reasons, but still in good standing. My retirement party was attended by over 350 people, including the Gallo family. Ernest, up until just a couple of years before he passed away in 2007, invited me to have lunch with him at the winery once every year. I am still puzzled by his invitations. I guess he just liked me for some reason. I loved that man, not only a marketing genius, but a good soul. There is no possible way I could every repay or thank the Gallo Family enough for all they did for me and my family during the 23 years I worked there. They afforded me an opportunity that I would never have found anywhere else. Gallo made it possible for me and my family to live a very comfortable life, helped to provide my children with good educations and successful careers, and made my time at Gallo interesting and productive. Thank you, Ernest, Julio, Bob, Joe, and David. I can never thank you enough.

# JULIO GALLO: A TRIBUTE

Julio Gallo. Who in the world could you compare him with in the history of the United States, because he does indeed belong in the history books? Two young guys, Julio and his brother Ernest, with just a few thousand dollars borrowed from a relative, were able to create the largest, most productive, most prestige's winery in the world. Phenomenal, unbelievable, incredible; yet, they did it and kept the entire business within the family.

The first time I set eyes on Julio (excuse me for not addressing him as Mr. Gallo) he was speeding down Grand Street headed for the winery at about 8:30 a.m. in 1958 or so. I was a young officer on the Modesto Police Department, and although I knew the man I had stopped was an important citizen, he was going to get a ticket. I asked for his driver's license, which he provided. Same old question from me, "Do you know how fast you were going?" "Yes, officer, 45 mph," he replied. "Do you know the speed limit?" "Yes, officer, it is 25 mph." He went on that he had a lot on his mind, was late to work, and afraid he might get fired." That set me back, and I had to laugh. He was the consummate gentleman, and I will never forget that first meeting. No way could I give this gentleman a ticket. I gave him a stern warning (I could never do that again) and sent him on his way. I asked him about this incident many years later, but he did not recall it.

The next time I met Julio was during my interview for the job at Gallo. We had minimal contact during my first few years at Gallo, but when we did, he always called me *Clark*. I was sitting in my office in Modesto, and the phone rang. It was the security desk. The officer said that Mr. Gallo (Julio) had contacted him and told him to tell me to get to the Livingston Ranch pronto. I was there in 30 minutes (talk about getting a speeding ticket). Over the radio, he said to meet him, and the ranch manager, Bill Heuer, at the Caldera vineyard. When I got there, he was upset, I mean very upset. He started in with a real ass chewing. "Are you head of security?" he asked. "Yes, sir," I replied. We were standing in the middle of the vineyard and he starts in. "Look at this. Someone has come in here and picked all of the grapes off of about 10 acres." "How could that go unnoticed with the size of the security we have? None of the vines have a single grape on them."

In protest, I tried to explain, "Even after the grapes were picked there were always a few bunches left on the vine," and, I went on, "and if you look around under the vines, you will see that there are no foot prints, no gondola tracks, or other indications that these grapes were picked." He stroked his chin and then asked Bill, "What the hell is going on here, Bill?" Well, Bill fessed up that the ranch's viticulturist had conducted some experiments with growth enhancing chemicals, and, apparently, it resulted in the vines not producing. Well, now Julio was really pissed, not at me, but poor old Bill. Bill was one of Gallo's most tenured employees and Julio's fishing buddy. He was not going to get fired, but the viticulturist was terminated.

There are so many wonderful stories about Julio that I could go on all day, but I will just say a few words and tell a few stories and then move on. He was one of the most generous persons you could have ever met. On many occasions, he called me and directed me to help some unfortunate person or family that he had heard or read about that were down on their luck. A bike here and there to some poor kid, temporary housing for someone burned out, funeral expenses under certain circumstances, or perhaps an airline ticket, if the situation warranted it. He would always conclude his instructions to me with "Now, I do not want anyone to know who did this."

* * *

The Howard Training Center in Modesto is a non-profit organization that provides jobs and job training for people who have learning or developmental disabilities. The Gallo organization has long supported those efforts. I cannot recall who called me, either Julio or Bob, to say that there was a young man at the Center that they wanted to provide a full-time position at the winery. Would I please talk to him and see if I could fit him in somewhere? His name was Chuck Caldera. Nice and polite, but very shy, and you literally had to pry every word out of him. He had a severe intellectual disability, but was neat and pleasant. After he went to work at the winery, he opened up more, and in many ways was smarter than a lot of people I have met. I assigned him to the Landscape Department where I thought he could be given a routine job that was repetitive in nature and would not require a lot of decision-making. Also, he would have the close supervision of his coworkers. Gallo swept all of the streets adjacent to the winery and glass plant with a mechanized street sweeper and a driver that received union wages and benefits. About the time Chuck came along, the street sweeper had broken down and was on its last leg. Bids were out for a new one, $50,000 plus. I told purchasing to hold up for a couple of weeks until they heard back from me. The landscape department came up with a push cart, big dust pan, and a large push broom. Let's just see how much territory Chuck can cover in a day or two in comparison to the street sweeping machine. He did a terrific job, and really seemed to love it. Good by street sweeping machine! There was only one little incident where he was told to sweep in front of the winery on the main thoroughfare, Yosemite Boulevard. When someone noticed that Chuck was still on Yosemite but two miles east of the winery still sweeping and apparently headed for the next town. Well, we got that straightened out and never had another problem. For the next twenty years he replaced that street sweeper and the higher paying position the driver had held. About 10 years into the job Chuck's mom, with whom he lived, passed away. His aunt and uncle stepped forward to take custody of Chuck. Almost immediately they announced they were moving to Florida with Chuck and wanted to withdraw his Gallo pension funds. The pension probably amounted to around $15,000. We were all suspicious of this matter and I had one of our investigators look into the situation. It became apparent that their intentions were very simple, get Chuck's pension. During this time one of Chuck's cousins and his wife contacted me and wanted Chuck to live with them and continue to work at Gallo. They were asking nothing in return. In checking them out we found they were a very solid couple, church going, and loving of Chuck. The aunt and uncle went to court to get custody of Chuck. The cousins of course were in no financial position to oppose this move and things looked pretty bleak. I explained the situation to Bob Gallo and he told me to contact our legal department and have them intervene as a friend of the court. That was what occurred and in the end the cousins were given custody of Chuck. Thanks Gallo for doing the right thing! He continued to work at Gallo for another 15 years and recently retired with a nice pension check. He was a very nice young man, well-liked by everyone, and an asset to Gallo.

* * *

Even as a child, I had always been very prolific in spearing, grabbing, or shooting frogs. To me they are the most delicious and delectable food item you would ever find. One evening, after having a dinner of pressed duck at the production vice president's house at which Julio attended, Julio said, "Jack, that was one of the best meals I have had in a longtime." I popped up and asked Julio if he had ever eaten deep fried frog legs? "It has been ages, so long, I really forget what they taste like" he replied. "Tell you what," I said, "I will visit the local irrigation canals and ponds and come up with 200 frog legs, and we will have some guys from the winery over for an old-time frog fry." He said he was looking forward to it.

Toward the end of irrigation season, which kind of coincides with grape harvest, my best friend Richard White and I had collected the frog legs, and we set a date. This dinner at our house on the golf course in Oakdale turned out fantastic. It was so good that for the next 21 years we enjoyed *Frank's Famous Frog Fry* on an annual basis. A funny little side story. Gallo was preparing to begin distributing a new varietal wine from the gewürztraminer grape. It was kind of a secret, and while a few cases had been produced it had not been released. Julio told me to pick up a couple of cases in the warehouse and we could try it at the frog fry in a couple of days. "Let's see what the boys think about it." Well, we tried it and loved it; it really went well with frog legs, that's for sure. Julio's son-in-law was at the frog fry, and while he said nothing to me, he was surprised to see the wine surface that night. The next day, his vice president of bottling was in my office, demanding to know how I got my hands on that wine and by whose authority. I told him I had no idea what he was talking about. He went into a tirade, but I did not budge. "Were you at the event?" I asked. "No," he said, "but I heard about it." "Well, I am afraid you heard wrong. Now, if you please, I have work to do." He left in a storm. I told Julio the story, and he got a big laugh out of it.

* * *

Bob Gallo has a cattle ranch near Livermore on Corral Hollow Road. Each year he has a roundup, and I usually helped out. I had previously told Bob about my mom's background with cattle in Texas, and he said "Bring her along. Better yet, drop her off at dad's house, and she can ride up with mom and dad." I do not remember mom ever having a better time. She and Aileen Gallo had a very enjoyable day visiting with each other.

Now, I am afraid of horses. Bob promised me a gentle horse, and that the horse would do all of the work. I got on this horse, named *Snelling*. I was not aware that Snelling was seldom ridden, and when ridden, the rider usually went flying. The horse, I found out later, had been treated very badly by its handler, and did not like people very much. Snelling and I went riding off into the wild rangeland looking for strays. Straight out, I repeat, I do not like horses, I am scared to death of them. I still remember "Apache" from when I was a teenager. But we made our way across the hilly landscape, and off in the distance in some pretty rough terrain I see 10 or 12 head of cattle and some calves. Snelling was a lot smarter than me, I assure you. Between the two of us we "head 'em out", and soon we were at the corrals, none the worse. The other "cowboys" there could not believe their eyes. When they told me of their amazement and Snelling's reputation, I could not believe how lucky I was. Thanks, Bob!

\* \* \*

My assistant Pearl buzzed me on the phone and said, "Julio is on the phone." He began by saying something like this "Clark, I understand that you are a fisherman, is that correct?" "Well, yes sir, I do enjoy fishing very much," I replied. He went on to explain that he was planning a fishing trip to Canada in late May, and asked if I would I like to come along? Also going were my good friends Bob Slayton, who managed the Fresno and Livingston wineries and Bill Heuer, who managed the ranch in Livingston. "Okay, block out the last week in May, and I will plan on you joining us." Well, needless to say, I was ecstatic, not only about going to Canada, but going with Julio. That evening, I informed Marilyn about the invitation and that I had accepted it. She said, "You know, that is going to be pretty expensive. Can we afford it?" "Well, you are the bookkeeper and can answer that question better than I can." Well, I was determined to go even if I had to borrow the money. I called Bill Heuer the next morning and told him about Julio's call and my concern of the expense. He laughed and told me not to worry, as Julio was financing the trip. I did not think that fair and told Bill so. He just laughed again and said, "For Christ's sake, Julio can afford it, and besides, he likes the company."

The end of May was there before I knew it, and Julio called and said be at his house at 8:00 a.m. and we would take the helicopter to San Francisco and catch a flight to Vancouver. We were headed for a place called Stuart Island which was about 30 miles off the east coast of Vancouver Island. We landed in Vancouver, then onto a twin engine turbo float plane for the ride to the resort. What a magnificent place. I had only dreamed of being in such surroundings and scenery. Lots of great food, wine, and perfect accommodations. The fishing, clamming, getting oysters, I tell you it was a sportsman's paradise. Out fishing at daylight, big breakfast, fishing, back for lunch and a nap, back to fishing, come in for dinner, and then back out fishing until dark. I never thought I would, or could, get tired of fishing.

For the next four years, this fishing trip became an annual event. On the fifth year, Julio arranged for the wives to accompany us, and that turned out to be one of the most memorable trips ever. The fishing started to peter out. The salmon were just not there anymore; so, Julio informed the three of us that he would not be going fishing in Canada that year. He did, however, want the three of us to go, "So go fishing and enjoy it for the last time," he said. He paid for that trip also. His generosity was unbounding. Thanks, Julio. You were a great friend.

Julio Gallo at Stuart Island with a big salmon

# DAN DONNELLY

Much later in life one of my very best friends relayed a story to me about his aviation teacher at Oakdale High in the late 1930s. Yes, it was none other than Chester P. It seemed, according to my friend Mr. Dan Donnelly, Chester was totally against drinking and alcohol in general. During prohibition, Dan's dad ran one of the finest and most notorious stills in the entire central valley, located in the Orange Blossom area. People came from far and wide, including the sheriff, judges, and even people all the way from San Francisco, to taste and purchase his wares. Prohibition ended in 1933, but Chester had a good memory, and was not about to pardon the Donnelly clan for their insidious operation. Without good cause or any rationality according to Dan, he kicked him out of his class. Dan was heartbroken because he had a childhood ambition to become an aviator.

Without delving into a lot of detail and history, let it be known that by about 1940 or so, Dan was, in fact, a U. S.

Navy Ensign and pilot. Mr. Winston had arranged with the commander of the navy base, near Livermore, to fly over to the Oakdale airport, located at Albers and Warnerville Roads, and let his students inspect the aircraft and talk with the pilot. Sure enough as prearranged, the little navy trainer appeared out of the sky at 10:00 a.m. sharp and landed at the field. Mr. Winston and 25 very excited students rushed the airplane as the base commander and his Ensign pilot climbed out of the cockpit. The commander introduced himself to Mr. Winston, and then he introduced the young aviator with him, who had not been recognized. Mr. Winston. "I want you to meet Ensign Donnelly, one our very finest young pilots, oh, excuse me, but of course you already know him, don't you?" Chester's jaw dropped, Dan's smile was wider than the airplane's wing.

I want to talk further about Dan Donnelly and his impact on Oakdale and particularly his impact on the U.S. Military. Dan was already in the navy and a pilot at the outbreak of WWII. He was such an exceptional pilot that it was determined by the Department of Navy that he could better serve his country training young pilots, rather than flying off to some combat assignment. I think he did that for the better part of the war. As the war began to wind down the United States was flying B-29's from several islands in the pacific to bomb mainland Japan. The Japanese had gun emplacements on several islands along the route the B-29's took on their return from the bombing runs and were taking a toll on our airplanes and their crews.

Dan was just one of a handful of navy pilots selected for a very secret mission. I think this project could very well be described as the advent of the United States entry into the guided missile age. Dan was sent to a secret base in the Pacific where he underwent training in this new, innovative, state of the art warfare project. Dan was seated in the pilot's seat of a Grumman TBM-3 Avenger with two technicians in the rear seat. Sitting across the runway 100 feet away was a Cessna twin engine civilian type aircraft. The two technicians were watching a TV screen as Dan taxied for takeoff. Simultaneously the technicians were controlling the pilotless Cessna, which was taxiing remotely. It was loaded with 10,000 lbs. of high explosives.

Soon, both planes were airborne, Dan flying the TBM, and the technicians flying the Cessna. Dan's co-ordinates were an island about 300 miles away which was the location of a heavily armed Japanese gun emplacement. Dan, under heavy enemy fire, flew his TBM right at the gun emplacement, and the technicians directed the Cessna to the same co-ordinates. They flew the Cessna right into the guns, and there was a terrific explosion. Direct hit. Dan performed this exercise several times more in a few short weeks until all of the gun emplacements were obliterated. The B-29's flew unabated to Japan, dropped their deadly ordinance, and returned safely until the war ended. Keep in mind this was 1945. The guided missile era was here but little noticed.

Dan returned to San Diego just before the war's end and was flying the Consolidated PB4Y-1 four engine bomber (army version B-24). Old habits are hard to break. Dan made his way across the border to Mexico and bought a plane load of liquor. He somehow got it loaded onto his PB4Y and was preparing to fly his next mission to China. Word came that the war was over. There will be no flight to China. Dan told me back in 2005, as far as he knows, that airplane was still sitting on the runway in San Diego.

Dan's 90th birthday was approaching, and as we always did on his birthday, a group of us and Dan's family were preparing to go to Lake Tahoe to celebrate. I thought it would be great to do something special for Dan; after all, 90 years was pretty darn significant. Dan had always had an extreme interest in aviation, and after all the Oakdale City Airport is named after him. I wrote a letter to my congressman, and asked that he arrange for Dan to be invited to Lemoore Naval Air Station near Fresno to take short ride in a navy trainer aircraft and have lunch at the base. A few weeks went by, and I received a letter from Lt. Commander Corrigan that my request was not possible, as it was just far too dangerous to have a 90-year-old man flying around in a navy plane. Request denied. I thought about this for a few days, and the longer I did, the madder I got. I noticed on the commander's letter that he had cc'd Admiral Williams, Commanding Officer CINPAC, United States Navy, Pacific, Hawaii.

I sent the following letter and a copy of Lt. Commander Corrigan's denial letter to Admiral Williams:

*Dear Admiral Williams,*

*With all due respect sir, this is horseshit. Commander Donnelly spent 8 years in the United States Navy, almost entirely away from his loving family. He trained many heroic pilots who fought for this country in WWII. He flew several very secret and dangerous missions, risking his life for his country. Lt. Commander Corrigan, in all due respect sir, does not have the foggiest idea of what "dangerous" is. The Navy had no problem asking Commander Donnelly to make the sacrifices he made, nor would they even had to have asked. He would have volunteered. I cannot tell you just how disappointed I am. By the way, Mr. Donnelly has no idea I had made this request. Thank you and all of the military for what you do. God Bless.*

I also sent a picture of Dan loading a 90lb sack of feed into a pickup. A couple of weeks later a letter came from CINPAC Admiral Williams. I opened the letter expecting a final denial, but to my surprise:

*Dear Mr. Clark,*

*First, I want to express my personal thanks and the thanks of the United States Navy for Mr. Donnelly's service to his country. Please contact Miss Nancy Marrieta at the U.S. Navy Facility, San Diego, 1-858-245-7845. She will make arrangements for you and Mr. Donnelly to be my guests on the USS CVN Abraham*

*Lincoln for a few days. I will have my aircraft pick you up and fly you out to sea for a landing on the Abraham Lincoln. Good sailing, and if I can be of further assistance please contact Miss Marrieta.*

The Donnelly clan and 20 of Dan's closest friends were in Tahoe for the annual gathering. We had just finished dinner and were getting ready to head out for a night of gambling and revelry. I stood up and tapped on my wine glass with a knife to get everyone's attention. I then read my letter to our congressman and the reply from Lt. Commander Corrigan. The audience was a little disgruntled, and a few negative comments were expressed. I then read my letter to Admiral Williams, and there were a few "Atta boy Frank. Glad you told them off, etc." Then I read the admiral's letter and invitation. The family and guests reacted in disbelief. I think in reality even they thought Dan might not be up to it.

Dan still had not gotten it and came up to me and said, "Did you say you and I are going to fly out to an aircraft carrier?" "Yes, Dan, get your bags packed we are back in the Navy again." Now, an unexpected situation developed a few days later. I was telling my fellow Rotarian, Rich Paddock, about Dan and our impending trip, and he looks at me in disbelief. He explains that his brother, Jack Paddock, was also going out to the Abraham Lincoln on exactly the same day as Dan and I. He further explained that the executive officer on that ship was Jack's best friend. Jack had made a fortune in the film industry by inventing and patenting specialty cameras for filming movies. A few days later, Rich called me and said if Dan and I could meet his brother in Burbank, we could fly with him in his helicopter to San Diego. Wow, we jumped at the chance!

Dan and I flew to Burbank via commercial air and met Jack. We jumped into this beautiful black helicopter, the three of us with Dan as the co-pilot, and in a couple of hours, after a beautiful flight along the coast, we were in San Diego. We took a taxi to the Navy base and got out at the security station at the main gate. While we were waiting to get processed I took the young petty officer aside and briefly explained Dan's status and his leaving that airplane on the runway 65 years ago loaded with booze headed for China. He smiled and said, "I get it. Watch this." When he started to process Dan he hesitated a minute and asked, "Mr. Donnelly, were you ever in the Navy and stationed at this base?" "Why yes," Dan replies rather proudly, "I was here about 65 years ago." "Well, Mr. Donnelly, our records go way back, and when checked, I found that you were attempting to bootleg booze to China. Is that correct?" Dan did not know what to think, and looks a little queasy. "I am afraid we are going to have to take you into custody," and he gently turned Dan around, handcuffed him, and called two MP's over who take hold of Dan.

At this point, everyone busts out laughing, including Dan. We were then driven over to a hanger and boarded a neat little twin engine turbo-jet. We flew three hundred miles out to sea where we spotted this magnificent nuclear carrier gliding along in the splendor of the Pacific Ocean. The pilot made a couple of low passes so we could enjoy the excitement of the moment. He said, "Okay boys, make sure you are tied in good, we are going to land, and if you have never done this before it should be exciting." We were doing about 130 miles an hour when we hit the deck and the "hook" grabs us. We were dead stopped in three seconds. What a thrill!

Dan Donnelly and Frank landing on the deck of the
USS/CVN Abraham Lincoln, January 2006

It was almost dinner time so we got situated in our quarters five levels below the flight deck and made preparations for dinner. We were ushered into the Captain's mess along with Jack, his friend and the other officers. The Captain introduced us to the officers, and we indulge in a very special and delicious dinner. The Captain requested each of us give a brief bio, and then he asked Dan to comment about his experiences.

The table was stone silent. Those officers were hanging on Dan's every word. They heard things about the service they would never hear again. After dinner we were taken to an area where the pilots congregate while not flying. In a matter of minutes, everyone to the man, was gathered around Dan and listening intently as he spun a web of excitement and adventure. We then assembled on the flight deck and witnessed night time take offs and landings of the jet fighter aircraft. Unbelievably exciting!

It was off to bed and an early rise for breakfast in the officer's galley. Although we were escorted, we had the run of the ship all day. I will forever remember Dan sitting in the Captain's chair in the command center, staring off into the horizon. I had always wondered what he was thinking about at that particular moment. Of course, I will never know, but I do know he was as content as any man I had ever seen.

The next morning, we boarded the Admirals twin engine plane and hooked to the catapult ready for launch. The pilot said to just sit back hard in the seat and relax. This would only take a few seconds, then wham off like a rocket into space. What a thrill, zero to 100 mph in about two seconds! We were headed home. The rest of the trip home was uneventful, and Dan got a great view as we flew over downtown Los Angeles in the helicopter. Soon we were back in Oakdale. What a trip. When I got out of the car at Dan's house, he looked deeply into my eyes, and with tears, said, "Thank you, Frank. I will never forget this." "Neither will I Dan! Nor will I ever forget you."

# THE BOYS AND I GO
# FISHING AND HUNTING

From the very first time I was exposed to the great outdoors
(Camp Jack Hazard in the Sierra's) I have had the greatest
respect and appreciation of what God has given us. It is something that cannot, nor should ever, be taken for granted. I would
like to be called and remembered as being an environmentalist,
but certainly not to the extreme that some people go. Common
sense has to be a part of the formula with a balance between
wild life and humans. From the first shot fired to the first line
cast, I was adamant in making sure our boys, Ron, Kurt, and
Greg, shared my feelings and adhered to the same high standards
and values that I have, and with pride, I believe I can say they
have. Firearms safety was an absolute as I recalled my early
days with Mr. Pollard. My kids were always gun safe. Their dad
being a police officer when they grew up, the boys were always
around guns. They often accompanied me to the police range or
to shooting events. As a matter of practice, when I came home

from work, I would deposit my revolver on the coffee table in the living room and point out to the boys that it was there. They were aware of the potential danger guns presented. Never once did they even think of picking up that weapon (It was unloaded of course). Kurt lived with his mother and her husband several miles out in the country. I knew it was going to be difficult to get him to a California Fish and Game certified instructor in order to get his hunting license; so, I took all of the courses, paid the fee, and became a certified instructor. Kurt was my one and only pupil ever.

* * *

*Hunting*

You may recall that I owned my very own .22 caliber at the very young age of seven. I roamed the waters and shoreline of the Stanislaus River for five miles above and below Oakdale. I was totally unsupervised. No instructions, no training, no education whatsoever relative to fish and game laws, firearms safety, hunting etiquette or the environment. Perhaps it was divine intervention, but as I grew older and progressively more involved in hunting, I just seemed to get it right. Do not shoot anything just for the fun of it (except pesky ground squirrels), eat what you shoot, do not shoot more than you can put to good use, and obey all fish and game laws. I believe I followed those rules all my life, and I believe my kids did also.

My personal hunting experiences began during the mid-1940s, and the boys began to accompany me and occasionally shoot in the late 1960s. Clear up into the late 1980s, there was an abundance of dove, pheasants, ducks and geese in the Oakdale area. As a boy, if you wanted a pheasant, you just took your gun and walked the railroad tracks right of way in and around Oakdale and without question, in only a few minutes or miles, you had a couple of birds for dinner. Our favorite hunting spot was the Kaufman Ranch, just south of Oakdale, past the Hershey candy plant. There were about 240 acres of clover and a small duck pond on the property. We would get six to ten people together, including my kids and my brother Jim and some of his friends and break the hunting area up into 50 acre blocks. We surrounded the area and gradually worked toward the center. As the noose tightened, up to 200 pheasants would get up at one time. There was no problem for each of us to get our two bird daily limit (ten per season).

My dog Max and his mother on the right

The ranch was only ten minutes from our house; so, during duck season, we would rise at 6:00 a.m., head for the pond, put out decoys, and be hunting in 30 minutes. This went on for several years, until the boys grew up and left the roost. Marilyn and I were fortunate to have raised three great kids, and I have to give some credit to duck hunting. When you sit with a young boy, just you and he, in a 3' x 5' foot duck blind for four or five hours, you are going to get to know each other. Those conversations were so important in raising our kids, and for straightening me out on occasion. You cannot be a good parent without being a good listener.

George Brichetto would invite the *Gallo Bunch* to his ranch at Bentley and Patterson Roads every year for pheasant hunting. Bob Gallo provided a wonderful spread and barbecue along with a few Gallo wines, yet to be released. The Gallo kids and our kids all hunted together, along with some Gallo employees and little John Brichetto. There were about 20 people in the hunting party, and everyone usually got their limit of two pheasants. Again, when the circle was completed hundreds of birds got up so shooting a couple was little problem. One of the hunters from Gallo was Jack Fields who was the vice president of production. He could be a jerk on occasion, and on a trip to San Francisco with Greg and me to see a 49 Niner's game, he accused Greg of taking something from his car. Poor little Greg, who was about 12 years old, was in total denial and cried most of the way home from San Francisco. When we got to Jack's house, we found the missing object in his drive way. He never even apologized to Greg. Later that year when we were pheasant hunting, Greg and John Brichetto peppered Mr. Fields with bird shot while shooting at a low flying bird. An accident, of course, or was it? Anyway, Mr. Fields left, never to be seen hunting with us again. As crop patterns changed, and more and more farmers went to crops other than clover, the habitat disappeared along with the birds.

Our family's hunters were never much into hunting big game like deer, elk, antelope or bear. My very first deer was killed on the Brunker Ranch about 10 miles east of Oakdale near Knights Ferry. I was 19 years old and working at Cookie's gas station when the ranch manager, Fred Valenzuela, invited me to go hunting at the ranch. I showed up one Sunday morning about 6:00 a.m., and Fred and I drove east of the ranch toward Table Top Mountain. I had no deer rifle, so borrowed my brother Dode's .308 caliber Savage. When we came around the corner near the top of the canyon, low and behold there was a beautiful five-point buck just standing there. I shot from inside the pickup but the deer just stood there, so I shot again, and the deer bolted and ran. "For Christ's sake! How could anyone miss a deer from 100 feet?!" exclaimed Fred. I had never been so embarrassed. Fred got out of the truck and walked over to where the deer had been standing, got down on his knees, and found blood. He walked another 50 feet or so and yelled for me to move the pickup. There on the ground was my deer, dead as could be, with two bullet holes in him. What a relief! Back to ranch headquarters where Fred dressed it out, keeping the liver and heart for his own consumption. We threw it into the trunk, and

I headed for the meat locker in Oakdale. It weighed in at 158 lbs. Not a bad deer for this area.

That was kind of my last deer hunt until about 1977 when I decided to go elk hunting with Greg in Idaho. I had a high school buddy, Joe Schuler, who owned a little place right on the river at Clark's Fork, Idaho. He was in Oakdale at the time, but told me that Greg and I could stay there, so he had made arrangements for us to hunt on some property not too far away. Greg and I arrived there late in the afternoon, so for supper we wandered into the little town and had dinner. It was still early in the evening, and there was a bar and pool hall adjacent to the restaurant, so Greg and I decided to entertain ourselves for a couple of hours. In the pool hall shooting pool were three or four kind of rough looking guys that had more than enough to drink. I had always been a better than average pool player, so could hold my own against almost anyone (except my brother Jim). One of the guys ordered a beer for Greg and I which we accepted with thanks. Then he asked if we wanted to play a little eight ball, he and his buddy against Greg and I.

During the ensuing conversation, they found out we were from California, and that was not good. There was a sign as we came into town that read "Californians must be dipped before entering Idaho." Should have been a clue. Well, after beating them four straight games and winning $20.00 this guy all of the sudden grabs Greg and puts him in a head lock. I choked up on the pool cue and just before I was going to I let him have it he starts laughing and says there is no way we are from California. I buy a round of beer, we laugh and joke, and all ends well. The next day Greg and I were out near a large meadow to do our elk hunting. I place Greg near a fence just inside the tree line and tell him to just sit there and be patient, and an Elk just might come by. A couple of hours went by and here came Greg to my location about 200 yards from where I had placed him. I thought he was bored but he just said, "Dad, there are no elk here." The next thing, we heard a couple of shots from the direction Greg came from, so we wander over there, and low and behold some local had this huge elk down. Patience has its virtues, right Greg?

A couple of years later, it was off to Wyoming for deer and elk hunting. No kids this time. It was Joe Schuler, Jim Lamatis, Mike Russell, and three or four other people whose names I cannot recall. We camped out in tents somewhere around Rock Springs, near the Flaming Gorge, in the middle of a big snow storm. We all sat in a big tent, eating, and of course, drinking. When the Greek Metaxa was gone, Joe thought he would be gone also. He staggered out of our tent and headed for his camp trailer that he had dragged along and parked about 50 feet away. We all went to bed and looked forward to a good night's sleep before leaving at daylight for our hunting area. When I came out of the tent in the morning, it was still snowing lightly, and I noticed a large lump in the snow that was not there when I went to bed. I approached the lump, and it was snoring. There lay Joe, clad only in pants and a tee shirt, sleeping away. I tell you that guy was one tough SOB.

It was just breaking dawn, and we headed out in three pickups for our hunting grounds, and as we came around a hair pin turn, this huge deer was just standing in the road. Of course, no one had a loaded gun, and it was chaos as everyone scattered, trying to load. The deer bolted and headed for high country. We got off maybe ten shots, but the deer was not scratched. I had not shot, and the deer was a good 300 yards away by now. I lead him by about three feet and fired. Boom, he goes down, shot right through the head. Everyone was amazed, but not me; it was just like shooting the head of a match! The next day, I was staked out on top of this mountain in a little enclosure of large rocks, ferns, and moss covered trees, just enjoying the solace, pristine, and sheer beauty of nature, when behind me, I heard an ever so slight noise. I turned slowly and right there, not thirty feet away, was the most majestic seven-point bull elk you ever saw. I raised the gun ever so slowly, so as not to frighten him. He was in my scope, a sure kill. He just stood there, staring at me. I held this position for a good twenty seconds, and then as mysteriously as he appeared he slowly moved off into the trees. I never went big game hunting again.

* * *

## Fishing

I always liked fishing better than hunting, simply because it was something the whole family could participate in, was relatively inexpensive, and did not require much equipment. Of course, you have to forget the $ 20,000 boat, $ 200.00 fishing rod and reels, and airline tickets, but putting that aside, it was cheap.

As a six-year old, my favorite fishing hole was just below the bridge on the south bank of the Stanislaus River. The fish and crawdads just seemed to love this spot, perch, catfish, black bass, and once in a while, a striped bass to be caught. There was a large 10-inch metal pipe that discharged water and some solids into the river at this point, and it was only years later that I became aware that this was where the City of Oakdale sewage was discharged. In those days, there was no sewage treatment plant, just raw sewage into the river, but the fishing was good, and the fish always had a very distinct taste all their own that was difficult to describe.

Just upstream from this location was the local swimming hole. A small point of land jutted out into the river with a tree on it that the kids who could swim would jump and dive off of. I could not swim at that time. The water was over ten feet deep just off the point, and I frequently fished there. I had no fishing pole, so usually broke off a willow branch and attached a line and hook to it, casting it and a worm out into the water. Early one morning while sitting there fishing and bored to death, something grabbed the bait and literally yanked the pole right out of my hand and swam off with it. It must have been a large carp, or perhaps a sturgeon. I hot footed it into town and went right to the Western Auto and spun my tale to Mr. Pollard. I told him I wanted the biggest and strongest line he had and the biggest fishing hook, as well. The line he showed me was, in my opinion, much too small for the giant fish lurking in that hole. I settled on a piece of clothes line, about a quarter inch in thickness, and a hook that was made for something other than fishing but as big as a ping pong ball. With a big smile, Mr. Pollard said no charge, just bring that big fish in here so I can see it. Back to the fishing hole, and after two days of sitting there 12 hours a day, I gave up.

Further up the river, about a mile, was the Oakdale City dump. There was a fairly steep embankment along the river all the way from the bridge to the dump. You could follow a narrow trail along the cliff all the way there. One day while traversing the trail, I came upon a hole in the embankment that had been made by some critter, so out of curiosity, I stuck a long stick in there to see if I could flush anything out. Out came this huge owl right into my face. I went tumbling about 50 feet down the cliff and right into the river. Luckily, there was an old tree in the river that I grabbed and pulled myself out; otherwise, I might have drowned.

The city dump was something else. Anyone could dump anything there anytime they wanted. You just backed your truck or trailer up the edge of the embankment and unloaded. The debris and or garbage just went tumbling down and into the river if it got that far. It was a wonderful place to scavenge, which I often did. This is where the local garbage company dumbed the garbage they picked up in Oakdale, on a daily basis. Oakdale's water supply was pumped from the ground at this location and stored in a humongous wooden storage tank nearby. From an environmental perspective, you have to wonder how we survived.

* * *

The boys and I did an awful lot of back packing in the Sierras, a hobby I picked up when I was at Camp Jack Hazard in my early years. Once as an eleven-year old, I hiked into Relief Reservoir to fish and stumbled onto what I thought was an old gold mine. Actually, it was the remnants left over by PG & E when they built the dam. I discover back in this cave, where PG & E had stored dynamite, what I thought were gold flakes. I very carefully took off my tennis shoes and filled them with this newfound treasure. I hiked three miles back to Kennedy Meadows barefooted. I had blisters on my blisters, and it is a wonder I did not lose both feet. When I got back to Oakdale and showed my friends my newfound wealth, they laughed their heads off. Pyrite: FOOLS GOLD! Another lesson learned.

\* \* \*

One of my very earliest hiking/fishing trips, was with my ex-father-in-law, Al Berg. When you go over Sonora Pass on Highway 108, you drive about 10 miles or so, and you come to Leavitt Meadow. Now, if you have never been there, you need to go. As you drop down east of Sonora Pass, you come to Leavitt Falls. A beautiful overlook, restrooms, picnic tables and of course, the falls. Take a lunch, a bottle of wine, and I guarantee it will be a day you will never forget. Leaving the falls, you drop down into Leavitt Meadow and a pack station and trail head. Hiking south on the trail, you go about two miles, and then turn east and hike over the ridge to Poore Lake, elevation 9,000 feet. No trees, just barren ground. Al Berg took me there in about 1954 or so, and I want to tell you, the fishing was unbelievable. Brook trout up to 16 inches, and you caught one on almost every cast. The next weekend, I drove all the way back there, almost 100 miles, hiked over the ridge, and tossed my line into the water. Not a single bite all day, but that's fishing.

In 1964, I returned to Leavitt Meadow with my son Ron, who was 10 years old, and a policeman friend, Gary Wiens. Our goal was to backpack to Fremont Lake, about 10 miles south of the meadow. Off we went, and after a few miles, we came to a marsh full of aspen trees, water, and tall grass. Gary and I decided to hike around this obstacle, but not Ron; he was going to take a short cut and go right through the meadow. After about ten minutes, we heard Ron screaming and running through the trees, no backpack, and no hat, just a wet frightened kid. Off to his right, we saw a very large black bear running just as hard to get away from Ron. He never got more five feet away from us after that.

\* \* \*

One of our very favorite fishing spots was an area called French Canyon, located off highway 395, just north of Bishop, California. Take Pine Creek Road by vehicle for five miles, then hike up a private road to the tungsten mine, on another 10 miles to Pine Creek Pass, elevation 12,000 feet. Then, it's downhill to French Lake and golden trout. On one particular trip, along with the boys and my nephew, Jamie Dufour, we decided to rent horses and pack in rather than hike.

Pack trip to French Canyon

After about 6 miles on the trail my horse started acting up and wanted to run and even gave a couple of bucks. I was getting a little nervous and basically was afraid of horses anyway. I called the wrangler back and told him to get me off of this animal. Greg, who was walking, took my place. The wrangler said he could not understand it, as this horse had been with him for over 20 years and never acted up before. "Yep," he says, "I sure cannot understand what got into old Apache." We got to our camp site and immediately had a couple of beers to relax a bit. No beer for Greg, as he was only 16 years old. Well, later that night, we all got sick, throwing up, headaches, and just generally miserable, all except Greg, and he was just fine. By pure deduction, it was obvious that the beer was bad, as Greg was okay, and he didn't drink any beer. So, Greg, have a couple of beers, and see if you get sick. Well, as a sixteen-year old, he loved that idea, and all he got was happy. We later concluded that it was altitude sickness, but for some reason, it did not bother Greg.

Testing the beer at French Canyon

Frank, Greg, and Kurt years later on the way to Secret Lake

Frank with a beauty

\* \* \*

My son Kurt and I had a little lake we loved that was just north of Yosemite Park, out of White Wolf campground. In about mid-May, the ground was usually covered with snow when we set out for *Secret Lake*, fishing for brookies. It was only about a four-mile hike, but in May you had to go through a lot of snow, so sinking up to your crotch makes for a pretty rough hike. Secret Lake is one of the most serene spots on earth. About 5 acres in size and usually almost entirely covered by ice and snow, that time of the year makes it ideal for fishing. No bugs or mosquitoes, water is safe to drink, lots of firewood, and the fish are hungry.

Kurt could put more stuff in his back pack than anyone I ever saw. This one particular trip, we got there and set up camp, built a fire, and got ready for dinner. The lake was frozen, except for about a 40x40 yard spot, right in front of our camp. We decided to wait until morning to start fishing. I pulled out some dry food packages and said I would fix some dried vegetables and beef. No way, says Kurt, and out of his backpack came two beautiful rib eyes. "Dad, do you want coffee or just water with your dinner?" he asked. "Well, I have a surprise, also," and I pulled out a bottle of Gallo's first varietal, a 1978 Cabernet. We had the steaks and the wine and were really just mellowing out, wishing we had another bottle of vino. Out of Kurt's pack came a bottle, 1964 Charles Krug Reserve Cabernet. That kid never seems to stop amazing me.

It was a full moon, and as we sat around the fire looking at the beautiful hillside, all covered with snow, sipping our wine, we heard a coyote howling. Moments later, a lone adult coyote crossed the moon-lit hillside with three little cubs in tow. What a sight, what a remembrance. The next morning, the fishing began. I made 12 casts and caught 12 fish, all over 14 inches. Kurt did equally well. We packed six of the fish in snow and delivered them to Julio later that afternoon. He was most appreciative. Kurt and I made several trips back to Secret Lake along with Greg, but there was never a night like that one.

* * *

I think about all those fishing trips I had made to Canada over the years, and setting aside trips to our vacation home on Stuart Island, British Columbia, three trips really stand out. In 1967, my optometrist, Dr. Richard Weinberg, asked if

I would like to fly to British Columbia and do some fishing. He had heard of this resort located just north of Kamloops that had the best fishing ever. Dick had a nice little Cessna 150 that seated three people and only went about 115 miles an hour, but he assured me it was safe and reliable. So early one June morning, he and I and a friend of his, named Wes Hall, left Modesto for the Bonaparte Plateau in British Columbia. I had not flown much in my life at this point, especially in such a small plane, so I was just a little nervous. We flew past Redding and began to climb, and there just ahead was snow covered Mt. Shasta. I had never seen it before, and it was spectacular. Higher and higher, as we flew over the Siskiyou Mountains, suddenly at about 7,500 feet altitude, the engine began to sputter, then quit altogether. "Holy shit! This is it," I told myself. Dick tried to restart the engine, but no luck. He turned the airplane around and began to glide back toward Red Bluff.

The plane was light and small, so it held its altitude pretty well. We glided along, gradually losing altitude, but hoping we could glide to a landing spot. Suddenly, just as we reached about 2,500 feet, the engine restarted itself and ran fine. We landed at a little airport near Redding and taxied to a hangar that looked like it might have a mechanic around. Well, sure enough, there was a guy there that was qualified to check out the engine. He tinkered around and finally decided we must have bad gas. Dick thought about that and agreed with the mechanic. The gas tank was drained, the gas discarded, and the plane was refueled. It ran fine, so we made the decision to continue on our trip. We got over the mountains and were doing fine, but as we approached Portland International Airport at 5,000 feet, the damned engine quit again. We began to look for a place to land, in case we could not get to the airport in Portland. Bingo! 2,500 feet and the engine started up again. We landed at Portland and taxied to a large maintenance building. A mechanic was found, and he told us he could check it out, but it might take a day or two before he could get to it. We decided to leave the plane and continue our trip in a rented car.

We drove to Kamloops BC, chartered a float plane, and in an hour or so, we were at Bonaparte Lake. The fishing was beyond belief. We were using Monte spinners, and at the end of the day, there would be absolutely no paint on the lure. We had a great time, and before you knew it, we were back in Portland. The mechanic had fixed the problem. Seemed that when the carburetor was cast by the manufacture, there was a small pin hole left in the casing, and when you reached a certain altitude, the carburetor sucked air, diluting the fuel mixture. That was fixed, and our trip home was uneventful.

\* \* \*

My neighbor here in Oakdale was Roger Schrimp, probably the best, safest, most conscientious pilot you could ever expect to meet. Roger passed away this year, and we will all miss him. Roger loved to fish, and as you might have guessed, owned his own airplane. In 1976, we decided to take a little trip to Saskatchewan, Canada to fish for pike and pickerel. My coworker and vice president of the Fresno and Livingston wineries, Bob Slayton, had a former employee who had started a winery in Alberta Canada and had been trying to get Bob up there for some fishing.

To make a long story short, Bob approached me with the idea of somehow getting to Calgary and meeting up with his Chinese buddy. I knew that Roger had a neat little Beech A-36 Bonanza 6 passenger airplane, so I approached him with the idea. He was more than enthusiastic, so we set a date and five of us, including my son Kurt, met at the Oakdale airport and departed for Canada. First stop, Seattle for fuel, and then on to Calgary where we met the *China man* as Bob Slayton referred to him. His given name was Calvin. We were met by Customs right on the tarmac and received clearance with no trouble. While we loaded Calvin's gear into the airplane, Roger wandered over to the flight center and filed his flight plan. All aboard as we headed down the runway for LaRonge, Saskatchewan and four days of what we hoped would be great fishing.

The runway at Calgary was a little over 13,000 feet, and we used every bit of. Actually, Roger almost aborted the takeoff; it seemed Calvin plus his baggage put the plane over its maximum load limit. Roger was pissed, but at himself for not being there when we loaded. We could land at LaRonge, but Roger said there was no way we could take off, especially after we took on a couple hundred pounds of fish. We filed a new flight plan over the radio and headed for the town of Prince Albert. We landed, rented a pickup, and drove the hundred miles to our destination, Lake Besnard. Our accommodations were fantastic, the weather perfect, and we had the whole lake to ourselves, as we are the only ones there. The next morning, we headed out fishing, two of us to a boat, along with an Indian guide.

Pike have the most god awful looking mouths you ever saw. A million teeth and razor sharp. You use wire leader and attach a large spinner or plug to the end. You cruise around near the shore line, trolling, and on occasion, you will see a pike as long as five or six feet. It is incredible. We caught fish after fish until it almost became boring, but not quite. Our Indian guides thought we were crazy, but they saw this all the time; to us it was fishermen's heaven. Everyone limits out each day with both pike and pickerel, some of the pike up to 15-20 lbs. We came home with some of the best fish you could ever eat.

After a couple of years, it was time to take Greg on a big fishing trip, so I contacted Roger and proposed that we fly to Lake Bonaparte and do a little fishing. So about a month later, Roger, Greg, me, Bob Slayton, and his friend Ken headed for Canada again. Roger then owned a twin-engine Cessna, I believe a King Air, and so there was lots of room and a better cruising speed. As we flew by Mount St. Helens, it actually erupted as we went past. We were maybe 50 miles west of the mountain, but the sight was spectacular and never to be viewed again. That being said, the event was horrific, leaving in its wake several hundred square miles of destruction, 57 people and thousands of animals dead (Wikipedia, 2016). The damage caused by the eruption cost the US over a billion dollars; it was the largest eruption in the contiguous US since the Lassen Peak eruption of 1915 (Wikipedia, 2016). A once in a life time event. We had a little different arrangement at the lodge this trip. We made plans to fish out of canoes without a guide. There were several lakes connected by small streams to Lake Bonaparte, so we paddled from lake to lake, and seldom saw each other. The fishing was good but nothing like it was with Dr. Weinberg. Our trip home was uneventful, except when we refueled in Portland when the guy started to put diesel into the tank instead of gas. Roger never missed anything (except baggage loading).

# RETIREMENT

I had fallen in love with Stuart Island having been there while fishing along with Julio on several occasions. You could get there from Campbell River by float plane in 20 minutes or by boat in about an hour and a half if you launched your own boat at Browns Bay north of Campbell River. It was 30 miles as the crow flies to the resort. A friend of ours who owned a cabin on the island and lived in Washington called us one evening in Oakdale and said there was a cabin for sale at a very reasonable price if we were interested. The next week end I flew to Stuart Island to have a look. This was in October and the fishing season had closed for the year. I spent the night in the cabin and had dinner with Bob, the caretaker who spent the winter on the island. The cabin was pretty neat, actually it was a duplex with full accommodations in each unit. While it needed a little tidying up I loved it. I flew home the next day, discussed it with Marilyn and decided to buy the cabin.

Frank Browning Clark

Marilyn at Stuart Island

Our vacation home on Stuart Island

Lisa and Greg Clark on a visit to Stuart Island

Marilyn, fisherwoman extraordinaire

Frank and Daryl Boddicker with a 68 lb salmon at Sitka, Alaska

We also went boat shopping on the premise that I could only buy a boat that could not be sunk. We settled on a nice little 17 foot Boston Whaler. The next year and the following eight years we took two weeks of vacation, hooked up the Whaler and headed for Stuart Island. We had all of the kids up there, as well as Alleene and Alvie, my aunt and uncle and several close friends over the next several years. It was some of the best times of our lives.

But all good things must come to an end and they did. A very wealthy individual owned the norther portion of the island. He had built a 10,000-square foot house, tennis courts, and yes, a nine-hole golf course on his property. But he would not be satisfied until he owned the whole damned island. He gradually bought everyone out until he got down to us and we would not sell. His lawyer contacted us and very nicely reminded us that his client now owned not only the water rights but the docks and the power producing generators for the entire island. He jacked his offer up a little bit and being between a rock and a hard place we decided to sell. Our little 17 foot Boston Whaler turned out to be a great asset when we built our house at Tulloch Lake 20 miles east of Oakdale and brought three grand kids to live with us. It became a tow boat for tubes, boards, and just running around on the lake.

During our time at Stuart Island we met and became very best friends with Don and Hilda Duncan. Don eventually became half owner of the resort which he helped to manage and use until it was sold to money bags in the mid-nineties. Don and Hilda had a beautiful spacious home near Port Angeles in Washington that was situated just below Hurricane Ridge in the Olympic Mountain range. We visited them numerous times and I just fell in love with the area.

I was determined to move there when I retired from Gallo and began to look around for property. I found 40 beautiful acres with a fantastic view of the mountains to the south/east and the Straights of Juan de Fuca to the north. There was a two-story rock house build in about 1880 on the property. I imagined a little work and moderate expense and it could be a wonderful home. I was excited. Had I given much thought to Marilyn's input on this issue? Not really. That night we headed home and were staying in a motel in Ashland, Oregon. Laying there in bed the light came on (Hello, Challis, Idaho!), and I asked myself, can you leave your family, friends, community where you have lived most of your life and relocate to a place you are absolutely unfamiliar with? Ever been on or near Hurricane Ridge in the winter? How do you think that place got its name dummy?

A couple of weeks after we arrived back home Marilyn suggested we take a drive to Tulloch Lake about 20 miles east of Oakdale and look at some 10 acre parcels in a gated community that was being developed. Such a location might provide whatever I thought I wanted in Washington and it did. We purchased a ten-acre parcel with a spectacular view of the lake and adjoining Table Top Mountain. We spend a lot of enjoyable time together planning what was to be our retirement and final home in our life. We began construction that spring and by fall 1990 we moved in. A fantastic 3500 square foot home with all the amenities, the view, the spaciousness, everything you could ask for in a home. We had never been so happy.

A couple of years pass and my mother, who was 88 years old, is in the hospital. The doctors say she only has a few days left so Marilyn and I decide to bring her to Tulloch and make her as comfortable as possible. Another miracle! Marilyn gathers up mom's medicine, and there was a lot of it, and throws it away. She begins to give her tender and loving care feeding her nutritional food and spending hours just talking with her. In just one week, mom was up and walking around and then my sister Terry takes mom in at her home in Escalon.

In a few weeks, she was a completely healed woman and went on to live another nine years. God bless you Marilyn and Terry!

Come 1997 we find our son Ron and his wife have lost their home, job etc. And gone their separate ways. She became just a street person, and when she was around, she was with her mother in Oakdale. Ron was not without his problems. There were three children involved, Sabrina 12, Sherri 11, Ronnie 8, and they were staying with the grandmother in Oakdale, also. That household was not conducive to a healthy environment for these kids. One day out of the clear blue sky Marilyn and I made a decision that would forever affect all of our lives. We drove to Oakdale, went to the schools, picked up the kids and headed for Tulloch. We told them that from now on they would be living with us. We didn't ask for anyone's permission we just did it! It was pretty rough at first, but we had gotten them out of a very alarming situation, and someone would be looking after their best interests. Sherri proclaimed to hate me (but we soon loved each other from the bottoms of our hearts) Sabrina was always a good kid, and well, Ron was not easy to deal with as he got older.

After a couple of years driving to Oakdale twice a day Marilyn and I got real tired of the situation all of us were in. We made what I call the ultimate sacrifice and sold our dream home and moved back to Oakdale, so that all of us would have a calmer day to day life. In retrospect, it was worth the choice a thousand times over.

# DAD

Dad, where was dad? Always a mystery. He made an unannounced departure when we lived in Richmond in 1949. With the exception of a post card to his brother, Hershel, in 1950, which was kept confidential until only recently, neither I, nor my siblings had any knowledge concerning his whereabouts. One of grandma's friends or distant relatives ran into Dad in Brownfield, Texas, in 1959. The friend or relative disclosed this to grandma in a phone call. Grandma was taken back and learned that dad was working on the Smith Ranch near Tokyo, Texas. With that information, Grandma tracked him down, and began to communicate with Dad, but kept it to herself for a few weeks, eventually breaking the news to mom, who told the rest of us.

Dad, United States Navy, 1918

My brother Marvin contacted Dad, and in 1959 he came by train to Richmond, California and was picked up by my brothers, Dode and Marvin and taken to Concord, to Marvin's home. Everyone in the family, including mom, made it up to Marvin's from Oakdale for a grand reunion. My recollection was that Dad reacted as he had never been away, and all was copacetic with the entire family. Boy, was he in for a surprise. He returned to Texas shortly thereafter, and I think, with every intention of returning to Oakdale and beginning life where he left off in 1949.

My dad started corresponding with me by mail in 1960 and continued to write letters for a couple of years, never mentioning that he was intending on returning "home". Well, one day he showed up on Fourth Street at my mom's house driving an old Ford pickup, pulling a trailer with all of his worldly possessions. Came there like nothing had ever happened and expected to get an open arms welcome from everyone. By then I was on the police department in Modesto, married to Marilyn, and expecting our first child, Greg. My younger brothers and sisters really had no idea who this guy was that moved in, started giving orders, trying to run the show. I have heard that he even tried to get mom to sell the house and move out into the country somewhere and rent a place. By now mom was having none of that, thank God. With such a cool reception, and deservedly so, after a few months, dad packed everything up and headed back to the Smith Ranch in Texas.

He began to write to me every couple of months and was very hostile to the whole family. He could not understand why, when he wanted to love everyone and be with us, no one reciprocated in a similar fashion. He just never got it or understood or accepted the ramifications of his actions over the past 10 years. It was just a "poor me" mentality. I next saw Dad in the summer of 1963 when as a detective, I went to Texas to extradite a prisoner from the state prison in Huntsville. I flew to Lubbock, Texas where Dad and one of the Smith boys met me and took me to Dad's house for a visit over the following few days. Dad lived in an old, run down house with sand piled up around it three feet deep and almost as much inside. We had some long conversations, but the subject of his running away or being rejected when he came back to Oakdale never came up.

The last night I was there, we went to Mr. Smith's house for a wonderful old fashion Texas dinner. Fried chicken, gravy, yams, apple pie. It was delicious. We had a few drinks, and as I suspected, but hoped it would not happen, the Devil popped up. Dad got stinking drunk and could not drive, nor could he give me directions to get to his house. It was like 11:00 p.m., and I was driving down this dirt country road with no idea where in the hell I was. I could not get anything out of dad; he was passed out and totally unresponsive. I saw headlights coming my way, so started flashing my lights and stopped in the middle of the road. A pickup pulled up next to me, and I explained I was lost. Before I could say much more, the man driving the pickup inquires, "Is that old Dave Clark in there with you?" I said, "Yes," and I followed him to Dad's place. Thank god for that Texas hospitality. The next morning, I was off to Huntsville.

A few years later, Dad had a very serious heart attack, and Marilyn and I flew back to visit him in the hospital for two or three days. Luckily, he made a full recovery. I went back alone a few years later to visit. Dad was living in an old, run down, dilapidated one bedroom trailer. It was full of old tools, clothing, miscellanies junk and enough packaged groceries to get him through two or three years. You could hardly turn around inside. Had you attempted to move the trailer, it would have come apart. He made room for me to sleep on a cot, which was adequate. While I was there, it was like 105 degrees and I was beginning to stink. I asked Dad what he did for bathing, and he replied he never bathed, just washed down with a rag, but if I wanted to take a bath, there was a bathtub in the trailer. He volunteered to take all the food items and other crap out of the tub, so I could use it. I filled it with hot water and had the best bath ever. When I finished, I reached over to pull the drain plug, and luckily was not in the water. I got the worst electric shock, ever. It actually brought me to my knees. Another miracle that I was not electrocuted while I was in the tub.

\* \* \*

In 1975, Marilyn and I decided to fly Dad out to Oakdale for a couple of weeks visit and stay at our home on the golf course. We had a great time. Dad rode around in the golf cart, we ate at the country club, we had a tour of the winery, and Bob Gallo even agreed for Dad to go up in the Gallo helicopter, have a tour of the valley, and a view of the winery and Oakdale from the air. It was topped off with Frank's Famous Frog Fry at our house with the Gallo's in attendance. Dad was in his glory, and I would like to have heard the stories he told when he got back to Texas. Julio in particular really enjoyed my dad. Dad told some of the craziest stories, but hey, it made Julio laugh, so I guess they were okay.

Dad commented one day, when I came home from work, just how friendly the people playing golf were. He told me he was standing out in the middle of the fairway that ran next to the house, and "You know where they stand to hit the ball (tee)? All those ladies started yelling and waving at me. They did not stop until I wandered back to the house. Sweet ladies indeed. I was a little suspicious that Dad was sneaking into my liquor cabinet, so I marked the level of liquids on three bottles and sure enough, they had gone down, but before I could talk to Dad about it, low and behold, the levels came back up. Pretty smart old codger; he simply put water in the bottles until they were at the level he thought they should have been. We had a nice discussion, and I told him if he wanted a drink then just wait until I get home, and we could have one or two together in the evening. He was embarrassed, and the next day said maybe it was time for him to return to Texas. After three weeks, both Marilyn and I were ready to get him on the airplane. When he got home, he had an interview with the local newspaper reporter and she wrote a story that he sent me about Dad's exploits in California and meeting the Gallo family. What a story!

In 1981, my brother Marvin and his wife drove to Texas and picked up Dad and all his belongings and returned him to Oakdale. He was now 81 years old, and while mentally alert, physically it was hard for him to take care of himself, and my mom certainly did not want, nor deserve that burden. Marilyn and I were left with the responsibility of making sure Dad was looked after. We made arrangements for him to be in a care facility here in Oakdale, but after a few weeks, we were contacted by the manager and asked to remove Dad, as he was disruptive.

We found a place in Salida, (15 miles from Oakdale) that could take Dad in, but after only a few weeks, we were once again asked to come and get him. We were told that there was a home owner over by the high school that had a care facility in their home and only five patients. We check that out, and they accepted Dad. He remained there until his death in 1982, just short of his 82nd birthday. When Dad died, he owned not one single thing of value, nor had one red cent. Someone even stole his wrist watch the day he passed away. I once asked him, if he could live his life over, what changes would he make. He looked me in the eye and said, "Not one damned thing." And you know, I think he meant it.

Dad was never an abusive person, and I can never remember him even spanking one of us kids. He always seemed happy, jovial, and friendly to everyone. Unfortunately, he was just not very responsible. To my knowledge, Dad never showed any remorse for abandoning mom and us kids, nor did he ever apologize to mom, or ask her forgiveness. In actuality, his leaving the family in 1949 was a blessing in disguise. Although very rough initially, because of mom's tenacity and hard work, our family survived, and for the most part, we became good responsible citizens. Mom was indeed an angel from heaven.

# CONCLUSION

With three grandkids in tow, Marilyn and I moved into a nice little two-bedroom house at 2304 Belsera Drive in Oakdale, next to the golf course, almost where we were 25 years ago. Where the past 16 years have gone, and with the speed of light, I have no idea. We moved in here with the three grandkids. When Ronnie turned 15, he moved in with his other grand-mother in Oakdale. The two girls, Sabrina and Sherri stayed here until they went out into the world to make their own way. The two sweetest, nicest grandkids you could ever want. Our other grand kids, Kristen, Frankie, Cody, and Bryan are the best. And then there are the great grandkids, Olivia, Jacob, Dylan, Davin, Ronin, and Sevrin, all of them the joy of our lives. I am winding down my activities and concentrating on just growing old with dignity and a couple of glasses of good wine (there is no bad wine) each evening. I lost my best friend this past year, Charlie, my black lab. I really miss that guy. He was a sweetheart, and I know I could never replace him, won't even try. During the past several years, I have tried my best to give back to the community for all Oakdale has done for me and my family. You truly could never live anywhere better in the whole world. While never expecting any recognition for my involvement in the community, I took extreme pride and with a great deal of humility in being named Citizen of the Year in 2005 and then The Life Time Achievement Award in 2012.

I have been so very blessed in my life time, having the most wonderful and caring mother possible, a loving devoted wife and mother of our children who is beyond compare, our children of which we could not be prouder, a long list of faithful and loyal friends who have always been there for us, and last but not least, my home town of Oakdale. God bless all of you.

* * *

Suddenly you realize you are nearer the end than the beginning.

Charlie 2001-2015

# REFERENCES

Wikipedia (2016). 1980 Eruption of Mount St. Helens, Retrieved from https://en.wikipedia.org/wiki/1980_eruption_of_Mount_St._Helens

CPSIA information can be obtained
at www.ICGtesting.com
Printed in the USA
FSOW02n1013030317
31381FS